The Ancient Egyptian Mysteries of the Kybalion

A Hermetic Mystic Psychology Primer

SEMA INSTITUTE

P.O.Box 570459
Miami, Florida, 33257
(305) 378-6253 Fax: (305) 378-6253

First U.S. edition © 2014 By Reginald Muata Ashby

All rights reserved. No part of this book may be used or reproduced in any manner whatsoever without written permission (address above) except in the case of brief quotations embodied in critical articles and reviews. All inquiries may be addressed to the address above.

The author is available for group lectures and individual counseling. For further information contact the publisher.

Ashby, Reginald Muata
ANCIENT EGYPTIAN MYSTERIES OF THE KYBALION: A Hermetic Mystic Psychology Primer
 ISBN: 1884564860

Library of Congress Cataloging in Publication Data

The Kybalion: Ancient Egyptian Mysteries

Contents

MAXIMS OF THE KYBALION TEACHING 5
  FOREWORD 5
PART 1: A Brief History of the Kybalion 6
  INTRODUCTION 6
    About The Kybalion: Hermetic Philosophy 6
    About The Hermetica.. 8
    About The Term *Trismegistus* or "thrice great". 8
    Hermetic Texts found in Egypt... 12
    Ancient Egyptian Anunian Tradition and the Position of Djehuty.................... 16
The God Djehuty and the Company of Gods and Goddesses of Khemenu 20
    Djehuty And the Hermetic Philosophy 26
    Khemenu Theurgy and The Ogdoad of Djehuty.. 28
    The Book of Djehuty 32
    The Ancient Egyptian Djehuty as preceptor and prototype of the Greek
    Hermes 33
PART 2: MAXIMS OF THE KYBALION 35
  Principle of Mind 35
  Principle of Correspondence 37
  Principle of Vibration 37
  Principle of Correspondence 37
  Principle of Rhythm 38
  Principle of Cause and Effect 38
  Principle of Gender 39
PART 3: GLOSSES ON THE MYSTICISM OF THE KYBALION TEACHING 40
  CHAPTER 1 THE TEACHINGS OF THE KYBALION PRINCIPLE OF
  MIND... 40
  Mind, Illusion, Reality and Enlightenment.. 46
  Commentary by Seba Dja 64
  Chapter 1 Principle of Mind Part 2: Q & A 66
  MEDITATION ON PRINCIPLE #1 76
  PRINCIPLE OF MIND   Q & A... 83
  Commentary by Seba Dja 83
Chapter 2: The Principle of Correspondence 85
  The Principle of Correspondence Part 2 96
Chapter 3: Principle of Vibration – From The Kybalion 112
  The Ancient Egyptian Concept of Vibration 113
    The Principle of Vibration Pt. 1 115
    The Principle of Vibration Pt. 1A Q&A 124
The Principle of Vibration Pt. 1B Q&A 127
  Q and A Continued 127

Chapter 4: The Principle of Polarity Pt. 1 137
   The Principle of Polarity Pt. 2 145
Chapter 5: The Principle of Rhythm Part 1 B 158
   Commentary by Seba Dja 167
   The Principle of Rhythm Pt. 2 Q & A 169
      Commentary by Seba Dja continued 169
Chapter 6: The Principle of Cause and Effect Pt. 1A 174
   The Principle of Cause & Effect Pt. 1B 182
   Commentary by Seba Dja 195
   PRINCIPLE OF GENDER PART 2 210
   Commentary by Seba Dja 227
Other Books From C M Books 229
54. Maat Philosophy Versus Fascism and the Police State: Understanding why Modern Society does not Experience the Peace and Prosperity of Ancient Egypt ... Law and Order, and Spiritual Enlightenment 262
Music Based on the Prt M Hru and other Kemetic Texts 263
MAIN VIDEOS 266

MAXIMS OF THE KYBALION TEACHING

FOREWORD

This Volume is divided into three sections. Part 1 INTRODUCTION presents a brief history of Hermeticism, its origins in the Ancient Egyptian Mysteries (Neterianism) the Kybalion and the origins of the personality known as *Hermes Trismegistus*. Part 2 presents the essential teachings of the Kybalion text, a set of MAXIMS, without interpretation. Part 3 presents glosses (commentary and explanation) on the essential teachings of the Kybalion based on the philosophy of the Ancient Egyptian Mysteries as determined by Sebai Dr. Muata Ashby based on studies and translations of original Ancient Egyptian Hieroglyphic texts; the source from which the Kybalion teaching is derived. The Glosses are an edited and expanded version of Lessons given by Sebai Dr. Muata Ashby in the form of lectures on the teachings of the Kybalion.

PART 1: A Brief History of the Kybalion

INTRODUCTION

"The principles of truth are seven, he who knows these, understandingly, possesses the Magic Key before whose touch all the Doors of the Temple fly open."

About The Kybalion: Hermetic Philosophy

The Kybalion: Hermetic Philosophy is a 1908 book, published by the Yogi Publication Society, purporting to be the essential teachings of Hermes Trismegistus. It was published anonymously by either a group or a person under the pseudonym of "the Three Initiates".

Separate from the "Tree Initiates," Hermes Trismegistus (Ancient Greek: Ἑρμῆς ὁ Τρισμέγιστος, "thrice-greatest Hermes"; Latin: *Mercurius ter Maximus*) is the purported author of the Hermetic Corpus, (Corpus Hermeticum) which are a series of sacred texts that form the basis of Hermeticism. In Islam, during the first centuries after the creation of Islam, the Hermetic "cult" was accepted as being the Sabians mentioned in the Qu'ran in 830 CE. (Churton pp. 26-7).

The Kybalion: Ancient Egyptian Mysteries

Image HermesTrismegistus from the middle ages or renaissance

Image: Hermes Trismegistus, floor mosaic in the Cathedral of Siena (c. 1480s)

TEXT:
Take the letters and the laws of the Egyptians, right on the stove, which kept a sphinx // God, the creator of all things, with God himself created the visible and created the first and only person who was glad, and very loved his own son, who is called the Holy Word

About The Hermetica

The ***Hermetica*** (or Hermetic literature) are Egyptian-Greek wisdom texts that date back to the 2nd and 3rd centuries CE. These texts are most often presented in the form of dialogues in which a teacher, who is generally identified as Hermes Trismegistus, enlightens a disciple through the Hermetic wisdom teaching. The texts form the basis of Hermeticism. They discuss the cosmos, the divine, nature and mind so as to lead the listener, the disciple, to attain higher consciousness, to discover the higher order of being which is a mystic self-realization, the coveted goal of all mysteries systems and mystical philosophies of the world, transcendental enlightened consciousness.

About The Term *Trismegistus* or "thrice great".

A view of the Temple of Esna in 2004.

Copenhaver reports that this name is first found in the minutes of a meeting of the council of the Ibis cult, held in 172 BCE near Memphis in Egypt.[1] Another explanation is that the name is derived from an epithet of Thoth found at the

---

[1] Copenhaver, B. P., "Hermetica", Cambridge University Press, Cambridge, 1992, p xiv.

Temple of Esna,[2] "Thoth the great, the great, the great."[3] Muata Ashby identified the Ancient Egyptian hieroglyphic text from which the term is derived and is presented below.

"Djehuty aah-u" is an ancient Egyptian hieroglyphic title of the god Djehuty. It means "Thoth three times great." This same title in the Ancient Egyptian language makes use of the glyph which means "great." The use of three glyphs can be taken to mean three or plural. The same term appears in the Hermetic period of Greek culture in association with Ancient Egypt in the term Hermes Thrice Greatest. Hermes is the Greek name for the Ancient Egyptian god Djehuty. Therefore, the ancient tradition in the form of the title was transferred into Greek philosophy during the late period of Ancient Egyptian history and the post-classical period of Greek history.

---

[2] known to the ancient Egyptians as Egyptian: **Iunyt** or **Ta-senet**
[3] Hart, G., *The Routledge Dictionary of Egyptian Gods and Goddesses*, 2005, Routledge, second edition, Oxon, p 158

The Kybalion: Ancient Egyptian Mysteries

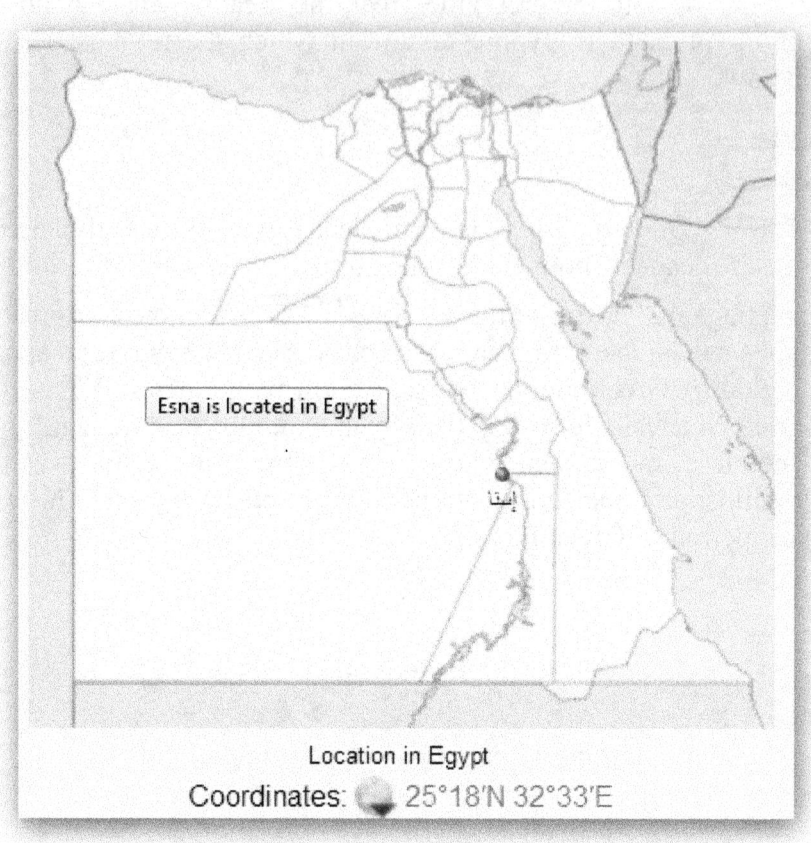

The Ancient Egyptian God Djehuty

Below: Image of the god Djehuty fulfilling one of his main roles as the recorder of the result of the balance of the human heart against the feather of Maat. [from the Papyrus of Ani]

Hermetic Texts found in Egypt

Sir W. Flinders Petrie places the Hermetic texts between 200 and 500 BCE. (Abel and Hare p. 7) Plutarch's mention of Hermes Trismegistus dates back to the first century CE (1-100 CE). In 1945 CE, Hermetic writings were among those found near Nag Hammadi, Egypt in the form of one of the conversations between Hermes and *Asclepius* from the Corpus Hermeticum, and a text about the Hermetic mystery schools, *On the Ogdoad and Ennead*, which was written in the Coptic language. Coptic is the last form in which the Egyptian language was written (Way of Hermes, pp. 9-10). The concepts discussed within the Corpus Hermeticum are distinctly ancient Egyptian. This includes the concept, "All is one, all is from the One" (Way of Hermes, pp. 10). Additionally, the concept of an "ogdoad" is also directly derived from Ancient Egyptian cosmology.

The Kybalion: Ancient Egyptian Mysteries

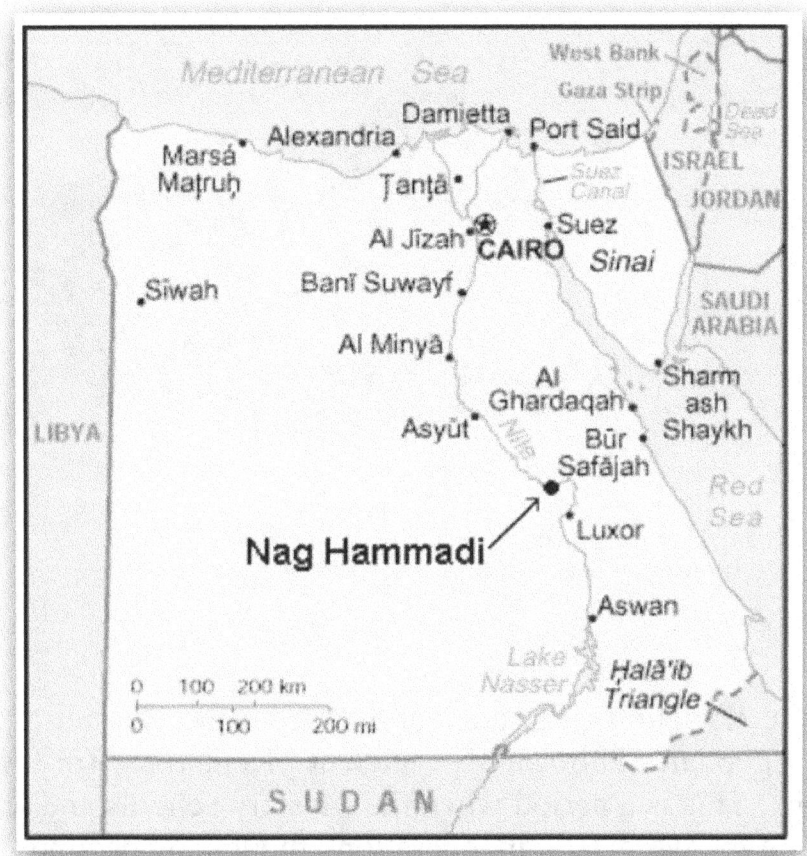

The following excerpt comes from the Hermetic Gnostic Ancient Egyptian text known as *Asclepius* from the group of texts known as the Nag Hammadi Library that was found in Nag Hammadi Egypt.

> Do you not know, Asclepius, that Egypt is the image of heaven? Moreover, it is the dwelling place of heaven and all the forces that are in heaven. If it is proper for us to speak the truth, our land is the temple of the world. But you should know that a time will come when Egyptians will seem to have served the divinity in vain, and all their activity in their religion will be despised. For all divinity will leave Egypt and flee upward to heaven. And Egypt will be widowed; it will be abandoned by the gods. For foreigners will come into Egypt, and they will rule it.
>
> —Asclepius, Nag Hammadi Library

The Kybalion: Ancient Egyptian Mysteries

Nag Hammadi texts

Finally, the Kybalion is an ancient text from the Hermetic period of ancient Egyptian Philosophy, ancient Kemetian (or Kemetan) Philosophy. This is a period when the Mystery schools and temples of Ancient Egypt were still in operation, though in decline. It is the period where, the ancient Greek students of the great temples of Kemet, such as Plutarch, had adopted the teaching, that was given to them by the Ancient Egyptian priests and priestesses and they were associated with the ancient Egyptian temples; these are not the students or the people who later took the Ancient Egyptian principles and changed them; rather these are the ancient Greek people who received them from the source and studied them and tried to promote the original teaching. Therefore, whether we are looking at texts that were written during the Hermetic period (c. 600 BCE-300ACE) or by subsequent writers who are following the teaching of those texts, we are ultimately studying Ancient Egyptian philosophy which came to be called Hermetic Philosophy even as it might have had some elements of Greek religion or philosophy added to it. This issue was confronted by the sage Iamblichus (Greek name) also known as Ab Amun (Egyptian name) in his monumental work called *On the*

Mysteries, where he identifies such elements and sets the correct parameters for understanding Ancient Egyptian Philosophy apart from the extraneous and or misconceived notions from other traditions that all existed at the same time especially in Greek culture.

This philosophy is also called Hermeticism, but the term Hermeticism or Hermetics is derived from the name Hermes and as you well know, as we have already noted, the personality Hermes, the God Hermes, is the name that the ancient Greeks gave to the ancient Egyptian God Djehuty. So the Greeks and the Romans adopted these teachings. This is before Christianity. During the late period of ancient Egyptian history, Hermeticism began to develop after the first Greek philosophers, such as Pythagoras, Socrates, Plato, Thales, Eudocius and others, began to study in the temples and bring the teaching back to Greece.

So we are talking about a period in history between the years 600 B.C.E and 100 B.C.E. It is a late period considering that the teachings had already been in place in Kemet since 5000 B.C.E or earlier. They began to be intellectually espoused, by the Greek students and the seven Hermetic principles, are the distillation of those. Throughout this volume we will discuss the principles. But before we discuss the first principle of the Kybalion, first we should know a little about the God Djehuty. Djehuty is a son of Ra, part of the Anunian tradition of Neterianism, Shetaut Neter religion, the religion of ancient Egypt. And as you know, all of the Gods and Goddesses of Kemet, they have a special teaching related to them, they represent principles; and some were accorded so much respect and honor, that they became the divinity of a particular city and particular scriptures were developed around them. So Hermeticism is a particular scripture related to the God which the Greeks called Hermes (also known as Thoth) which was also the name they gave to the Ancient Egyptian God Djehuty (or Djehuty). But the important point here is that they were speaking about the ancient Djehuty, from which Hermes is derived.

The Kybalion: Ancient Egyptian Mysteries

Ancient Egyptian Anunian Tradition and the Position of Djehuty

One more item is important to be understood in order to comprehend the deep background of Hermeticism originating in Ancient Egypt. Where does Djehuty fit into Ancient Egyptian religion? Ancient Egyptian religion or what is also referred to as the Ancient Egyptian mysteries, is actually a collection of related traditions (mythic, ritual and philosophical) that had the same origin, Anunian Theurgy, and which coexisted in the same country; sometimes in operation at the same time and at others, over a time span of more than 5,000 years, some operating more prominently than others. Yet none was repudiated or in competition with the others since all were understood to be manifestations of the same teaching as rendered by the priest/esshood of the particular tradition at a particular time in history. Therefore, they were complementary.

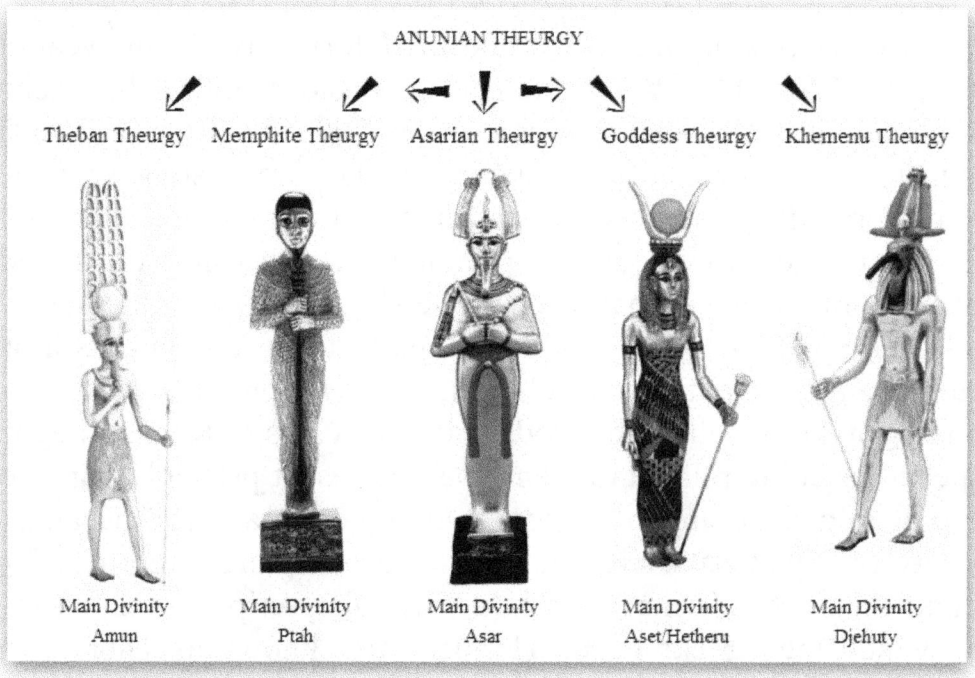

Ra may be seen as the Soul of Creation and Djehuty may be seen as the Cosmic Mind of Creation. Additionally, Djehuty is the wielder of the Caduceus and master of the Serpent Power, the discipline referred to as *Kundalini Yoga* in India; Djehuty is the Creator of the Hieroglyphic writing [Medtu Neter]; Djehuty is the recorder of the teaching (the Sebait, the Ancient Egyptian mystery philosophy) he received directly from God Khepri, the Creator (a form of Ra). Khemenu Theurgy, which relates to the wisdom and teaching of the God Djehuty, later gave rise to Hermeticism.

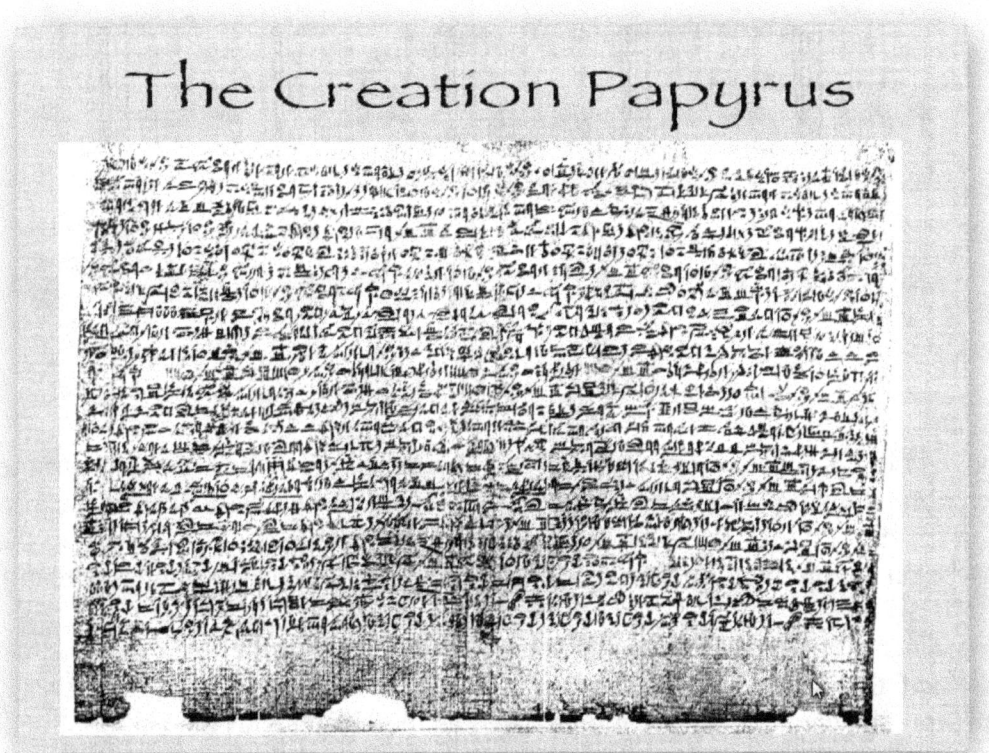

In the Ancient Egyptian Creation tradition, Djehuty acted as the scribe of the Creator, Khepri. In his capacity he codified the wisdom that was told to him about the nature of Creation and the wisdom of existence.

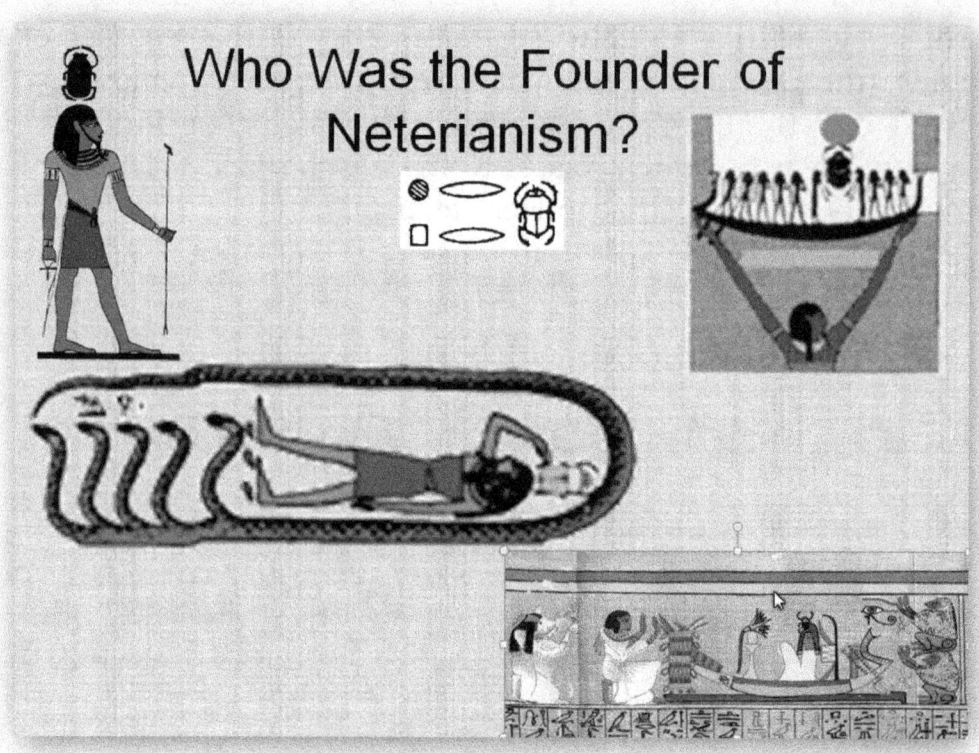

Above: Lord Khepri brings creation into being by lying down on the primeval ocean and causing the great primeval serpent, *ashra hrau* to churn the ocean. Then the divinity of the primeval ocean, Nun, raises the boat of Khepri so that it may begin a journey of millions and millions of years so as to maintain Creation.

After Khepri brought Creation into being then Khepri in the form of Ra Hrakhty sustained that Creation and then brought forth nine gods and goddesses that constitute the elements of Creation as well as the elements of the personality. The image below illustrates the main divinities of Anunian Theurgy as well as their relationships.

The Kybalion: Ancient Egyptian Mysteries

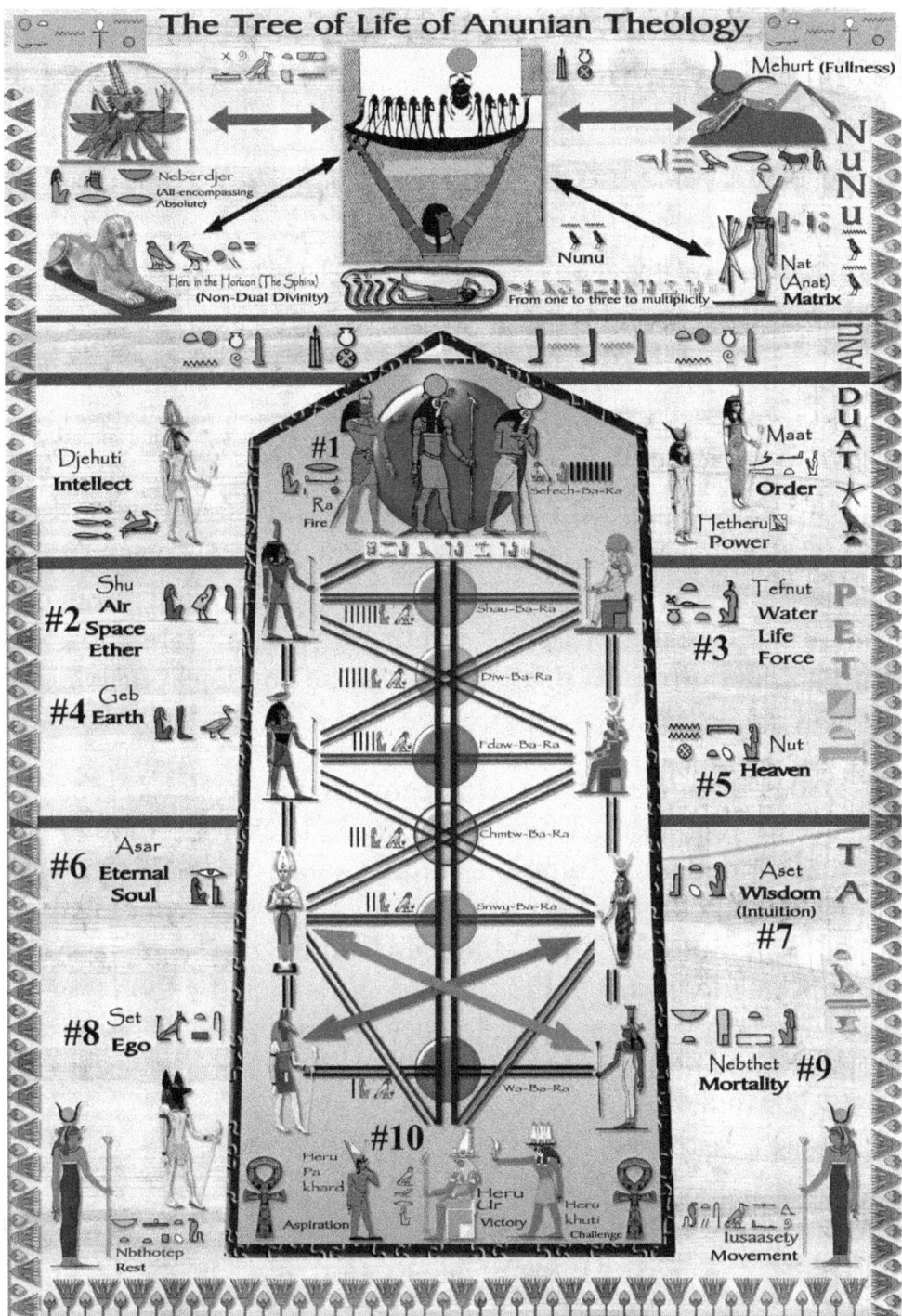

The image above shows the main gods and goddesses of the Anunian Tradition of Ancient Egypt. Djehuty represents purified intellect and the reflection of god consciousness (Ra's mind). For more see the book African Religion Vol. 1 Anunian Theology.

The God Djehuty and the Company of Gods and Goddesses of Khemenu

Pauti Khmn Anu
"Company of Eight Gods and Goddesses of Anu"

The term Khemenu, or city of the eight, relates to the city where the worship, reverence and teaching of Djehuty was recognized as primary. The Ancient Egyptian Greeks called this same city *Hermopolis* **(Greek: Ἑρμοῦ πόλις μεγάλη[4]) [Hermo (about Hermes) and Polis (city)]** after their name for Djehuty which was *Hermes.*

The God Djehuty and the Company of Gods and Goddesses of Khemenu are related to Anunian Theurgy. Therefore, they are to be viewed as an adjunct tradition in the same way as the Asarian Tradition although the Khemenu[5] Tradition was not as popular as the Asarian Tradition or the Anunian until the late period of Kamitan/Kemetic history. Firstly, the god Djehuty along with the goddess Maat deserve a special place of prominence because they emerged along with Ra in his Divine Boat of Creation the first time he surfaced out of the Primeval Waters.

 Eye of Djehuty (left eye, lunar)

---

[4] Steph. B. *s.v.*; Ptol. IV 5. § 60
[5] Hermopolis of the Greeks

Secondly, Djehuty is referred to as the *"heart and tongue of Ra."* This means that he was the mind (intellect) and mouthpiece (performer of actions) of Ra, so he was Ra's viceroy and minister. He transmitted to the world of time and space, the desires of Ra and carried out his bidding on earth. He is therefore regarded as the *Lord of Words* and the *Wheigher of Words* in the great Hall of Maati where the heart of the deceased is weighed against the standard, the feather of Maat (right and truth).

The city Khmnu (city of the eight) became the seat of the worship of Djehuty and the Company of Eight Gods and Goddesses of Anu became the Company of Djehuty. Djehuty had a Divine Boat wherein he sat, a man with the head of an *Ibis* bird, with a Crescent Moon headdress, along with his second popular form of manifestation, the baboon. (see below) The Baboon form is often seen offering the left eye of Heru, (which is the same left eye of Ra). He is also known as the "Healer of the Eye" and the "Pacifier" of the combatants, i.e. Heru and Set. One more important quality of Djehuty is that he is the controller of the caduceus, the staff with two serpents which is the *"Staff of Life"* or wand that promotes spiritual awakening.

Below: The Ancient Egyptian god Djehuty holds the caduceus (from the Temple of Seti I, Abdu, Egypt).

The two aforementioned forms of *Djehuty* are composite (ibis headed man), or zoomorphic (baboon). Djehuty has an anthropomorphic form, *Yaah-Djehuty*. In this form he is the god of the moon, i.e. the mind. In this form he appears as a mummy bearing the crescent moon (increasing intellect) on his head, and holds the symbols, *nekaku* -flail (discipline and command), *heka*-shepherd's crook (royalty-leadership), *djed* (Asarian higher consciousness), *ankh* (life force), *uas* -capacity to allow the living higher consciousness to flow), *hensekti*, side lock (youth), *menat* (female creative power).

The Kybalion: Ancient Egyptian Mysteries

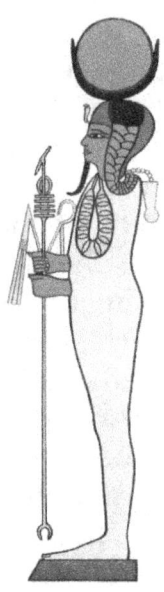

Yaah-Djehuty

Forms of Djehuty

Djehuty is the symbol of right reason, the link to the Higher Self. When the determination to pursue the Divine arises, the struggle becomes a holy war against ignorance and illusion within one's consciousness. If this process is not understood as a struggle to overcome anger, hatred, greed, bigotry, jealousy, etc., within one's self, the energy of the struggle becomes directed to the world outside of oneself in the form of political, religious, social, ethnic, gender, etc., conflicts.

In the Ancient Egyptian myth of the Asarian Resurrection, Lord Djehuty plays a pivotal role in the survival and facilitating of the upbringing of Heru and his ultimate victory against the unrighteous Set. The struggle between Heru (higher self) and Set (lower self) does not end with either destroying the other. Heru pursues the path of reason seeking counsel with the wisdom of Djehuty. Wisdom follows the exercise of reasoning in peace, and reason follows the practice of studying, questioning, reflecting and inquiring into the nature of truth. In Neterian myth Set, the lower self, refuses to abide by the decree of wisdom but he is eventually sublimated through his own humiliation and ignorance. In the end, when the aspirant is aligned with all the divine forces, the lower self can no longer struggle. The overwhelming force of the Divine pushes the lower self into a position of service rather than of mastership; this is its rightful place.

Two of Djehuty's most important titles are ⟨hieroglyphs⟩, **Djehuty aahu** *"Djehuty Thrice Great,"* and ⟨hieroglyphs⟩, **Neb Neter Medtu** *"Lord of the words of power."* The Greek-Hermetic philosophers of the time period between 300 B.C.E. and 500 A.C.E. adopted the title *"Hermes Thrice Greatest"* as the name for the originator of the Hermetic teachings, thus openly acknowledging their Kamitan (African) origins.

Above: from papyrus Nebseni, the oldest known rendition of Djehuty depicted as a baboon watching the balance of the heart.

The God Djehuty has two principal forms of manifestation, the Ibis and the Baboon. Both of these animals symbolize intelligence and perseverance. The Ibis with its long beak can feel deep into the muddy waters to discover tasty morsels-symbolizing acute intellectual capacity to see through the mucky and murky waters of life and time and space in order to grasp fragments of truth that brighten the intelligence.

The baboon is intelligent but also meek. In the myth of Hetheru and Djehuty, He acted as her spiritual preceptor and came to her in the form of a baboon to teach her the wisdom that leads to spiritual freedom and awakening. Baboons are known to have been well trained in Ancient Egypt. They performed many tasks like harvesting fruits for farmers and even clearing off tables at restaurants. In the form of a baboon, Djehuty fixes the eye of Ra, i.e. Hetheru (Hetheru and the right eye of Ra are identical). Thereby she became enlightened and freed from all sorrows and ignorance.[6]

Djehuty And the Hermetic Philosophy

Djehuty, as Lord of Words of Power was also known by the Ancient Egyptians as *"Djehuty Lord of Divine Words"* and was known as the creator of Medtu Neter (Ancient Egyptian hieroglyphic writing). As such he is the supreme exponent of the philosophy of the Shetaut Neter and thus he is said to have written the books of the Pertmheru [Ancient Egyptian Book of the Dead] himself with his fingers and his beak (as his pen). According to Clement Alexandrinus[7] in his *Stromata* VI, Hermes (Djehuty) was also the author of 42 books dealing with laws, gods and goddesses, education of the priests and priestesses, worship and services of the gods and goddesses (sacrifices, offerings, etc.), history, geography and hieroglyphs, astronomy and astrology, religious compositions and medical science.

---

[6] See the book *The Glorious Light Meditation* and *Temple Ritual* by Muata Ashby
[7] Clement of Alexandria (150?-?220), Greek church father. His full name was Titus Flavius Clemens. He studied in Alexandria, Egypt, where he founded a school that became a center of learning. Several writings have survived, including his Hortatory Address to the Greeks, the Paedagogue, the treatise Who Is the Rich Man That Shall Be Saved?, and the Hypotyposes. Christian truth is joined to Greek philosophy for Clement, but his work paves the way for specifically Christian doctrine. Random House Encyclopedia

In the very late period of Ancient Kamitan history, when the Greeks conquered Egypt, the Greek philosophers began to study and translate the Ancient Egyptian texts and a new genre of literature that was ascribed to Hermes, whom they equated with Djehuty, was commenced. The ancient Egyptian term *Djehuty aahu-* literally *"Djehuty three times great"* became *"Thrice Greatest Hermes"* to the Greeks of the Hermetic period. Though a compilation, authored by Djehuty, labeled as 42, besides the 42 precepts of Maat in the Pert M Heru (Ancient Egyptian Book of the Dead [Book of Enlightenment]) has not been discovered, the writings of the "Hermetic Texts" coupled with the earlier hieroglyphic medtu neter texts certainly cover the range of subjects mentioned by Clement.

Above: Divine boat of Djehuty.

As all other major divinities Djehuty has a Divine Boat. In this boat he moves through Creation establishing the teachings he codified in the Medtu Neter.

Above: mask of Djehuty.

As a character in the mysteries, the priests who reenacted the part of Djehuty in the practice of the Temple rituals (Divine Plays) used a mask in order to enhance the experience of adopting the character, feeling and wisdom of Djehuty.

Khemenu Theurgy and The Ogdoad of Djehuty

In Theban Theurgy, in the form of Kamutf, the God Amun brought the Creation into existence along with and through eight divinities, each symbolizing one of eight complementary (male-female) cosmic principles of Creation, i.e. the opposites of Creation. These divinities were later regarded as the Ogdoad. This scheme or matrix for Creation (cosmology) also was used in the city known as "Khemnu" or "City of the eight." The gods and goddesses of the ogdoad were:

Cosmic force represented	Goddess	God
Primordial waters	Nunet	Nun
Infinity	Hehet	Heh
Darkness	Keket	Kek
Hidden Essence	Amunet	Amun

Above: image of the Ogdoad

In later times the position as the head of the Ogdoad was given to the god Djehuty due to his popularity in the city of Khemenu. Note here that the gods and goddesses that form the companies of gods and goddesses of varied traditions are sometimes interchangeable and fulfill expanded or contracted roles depending on their function in the given tradition or myth they are being used in. Ogdoad of Amun is a reworking of the Ogdoad of Ptah. So this same teaching is carried forth through the main Ancient Egyptian traditions. Again, this constitutes another *Correlative Theological Statement*, which links the Neterian traditions, once again showing that behind the apparent multiplicity and variation there is a calculated pantheism underlying the mythic systems that reflects the fundamental teachings and principles in seemingly different divinities.

The Kybalion: Ancient Egyptian Mysteries

Below: the God Djehuty (far right) gives life-breath to Asar (far left).

Temple of Asar, Lord Djehuty holds the Caduceus in is left hand and gives life to Asar with the Ankh in his right hand

Below-left: the Greek God Hermes holding the Caduceus-compared to the image of Djehuty

Below: Aesculapius, the Greek god of medicine. Right- Caduceus of Aesculapius.

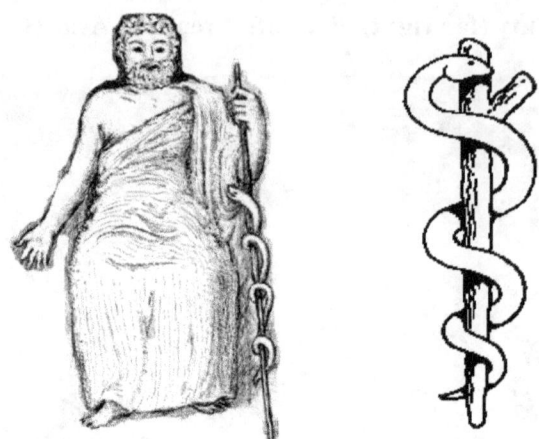

The Book of Djehuty

One of the most important texts of Khemenu Theurgy is the Book of Djehuty. This text covers the wisdom of the Serpent Power and the nature of Creation that is attained when Higher transcendental consciousness is achieved. Many allusions have been made to a special book of Hermes, in later Hermetic history. One such book is referred to the "Emerald Tablet" However, the Ancient Egyptian Book of Djehuty fulfils all of the mystic expectations of a high mystic tradition and it is accessible for the avid follower of the mysteries. This teaching is covered in the book *The Serpent Power*.[8]

From the book of Djehuty:

Setna Reads the Book of Djehuty

---

[8] see the book Serpent Power, by Muata Ashby

15. *And he went to the deathless snake, and fought with him, and killed him; but he came to life again, and took a new form. He then fought again with him a second time; but he came to life again, and took a third form. He then cut him in two parts, and put sand between the parts, that he should not appear again.*

The Ancient Egyptian Djehuty as preceptor and prototype of the Greek Hermes

Above: - Djehuty restoring to Hetheru the Udjat (Uatchit) Eye, 𓂀, (right eye) which had become blinded by ignorance.

Above: -Djehuty restoring to Heru the Udjat (Uatchit) Eye, 𓂀, which Set (egoism) had blinded.

In Ancient Egyptian mythology, Djehuty is the divinity that most perfectly fills the role of spiritual preceptor in the form that is later present in the Greek Mysteries and in Hermeticism. He is a mystic physician as he heals the eyes of intuitional vision, i.e. through his teaching he cleanses ignorance and enables a disciple to attain higher consciousness and spiritual enlightenment.

Djehuty is the spiritual preceptor of two important Kamitan Divinities, Hetheru and Heru. He fixes their faulty vision, i.e., he enlightens their intellect in the myth of the Divine Cow (also known as the Story {Myth} of Hetheru and Djehuty) and the myth of the Asarian Resurrection. The picture above-left is from the latter myth, where Djehuty repairs the higher vision of Heru, that was damaged by Set, the ego consciousness. In this manner, the aspirant should allow {himself/herself} to be enlightened by the teaching. In this manner the Serpent Power becomes effective and powerful.

The following section (Part 2) has a listing of the Principles of the Kybalion and the wisdom statements related to each principle.

Part 3 will present the wisdom expositions by Sebai Dr. Muata Ashby expounding on the teaching of each principle.

PART 2: MAXIMS OF THE KYBALION

Principle of Mind

"The all is mind; The Universe is Mental."

●

"Mind, as matter, may be transmuted, from state to state, degree to degree, condition to condition, pole to pole, vibration to vibration. True transmutation is a Mental Art."

●

"Under, and back of, the Universe of Time and Space and Change, is ever to be found The Substantial Reality: the Fundamental Truth."

●

"That which is the Fundamental Truth, the Substantial Reality, is beyond true naming, but the Wise men call it The All."

●

"In its essence, The ALL is Unknowable."

●

"But the report of Reason must be hospitably received, and treated with respect."

●

"The Universe is Mental, held in the mind of The ALL. The ALL is SPIRIT"

●

"The infinite mind of The ALL is the womb of Universes"

"The ALL creates in its Infinite Mind, countless Universes, which exist for eons of time, to The All, the creation, development and death of a million Universes is as the time of the twinkling of an eye."

"Within the Father-Mother mind of The ALL, mortal children are at home."

"While ALL is in THE ALL, it is also true that THE ALL is in ALL. To him who truly understands this truth hath come great knowledge."

"There is not one who is Fatherless nor Motherless in the Universe."

"The half-wise, recognizing the comparative unreality of the Universe, imagine that they may defy its Laws-such are vain and presumptuous fools, and they are broken against the rocks and torn asunder by the elements by reason of their folly. The truly wise, knowing the nature of the Universe, use Law against laws; the higher against the lower; and by the Art of Alchemy transmute that which is undesirable into that which is worthy, and thus triumph. Mastery consists not in abnormal dreams, visions and fantastic imaginings or living, but in using the higher forces against the lower, escaping the pains of the lower planes by vibrating on the higher. Transmutation, not presumptuous denial, is the weapon of the Master."

"The wise ones serve the higher planes and rule the lower, in this way one operates the laws instead of being a slave to them."

The Kybalion: Ancient Egyptian Mysteries

Principle of Correspondence

"As above, so below; as below, so above."

Principle of Vibration

"Nothing rests, everything moves; everything vibrates."

"To change your mood or mental state, change your vibration."

"To destroy an undesirable rate of mental vibration, concentrate on the opposite vibration to the one to be suppressed."

Principle of Correspondence

"Everything is dual; everything has poles; everything has its pair of opposites; like and unlike are the same; opposites are identical in nature, but different in degree; extremes meet; all truths are but half-truths; all paradoxes may be reconciled."

Principle of Rhythm

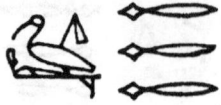

"Everything flows out and in; everything has its tides; all things rise and fall; the pendulum-swing manifests in everything; the measure of the swing to the right is the measure to the left; rhythm compensates."

●

"Rhythm may be neutralized by an application of the art of polarization."

Principle of Cause and Effect

"Every cause has its Effect; every Effect has its Cause; everything happens according to Law; Chance is a name for Law unrecognized; there are many planes of causation, but nothing escapes the Law."

Principle of Gender

"Gender is in everything; everything has its Masculine and Feminine Principles; Gender manifests on all planes."

●

"The wise ones serve on the higher, but rule on the lower. They obey the laws coming from above them, but on their own plane, and those below them, they rule and give orders. And, yet, in so doing, they form a part of the Principle, instead of opposing it. The wise man falls in with the Law, and by understanding its movements he operates it instead of being its blind slave. Just as does the skilled swimmer turn this way and that way, going and coming as he will, instead of being as the log which is carried here and there-so is the wise man as compared to the ordinary man-and yet both swimmer and log; wise man and fool, are subject to Law. He who understands this is well on the road to Mastery."

-The Kybalion.

PART 3: GLOSSES ON THE MYSTICISM OF THE KYBALION TEACHING

CHAPTER 1 THE TEACHINGS OF THE KYBALION PRINCIPLE OF MIND

THE TEACHINGS OF THE KYBALION

PRINCIPLE OF MIND

We spoke earlier of the origins of the Kybalion text as being from the Hermetic period but deriving its teaching from the Ancient Egyptian Mysteries system and in particular from the wisdom surrounding the Ancient Egyptian god Djehuty. Djehuty is a reflection of the High god, Ra. Ra is the sun and Djehuty is his reflection so Djehuty is associated with the moon, which shines due to the reflected sunlight. It is said in the Anunian Theology, the Theology of the city of Anu, that Djehuty was one of the sons of Ra and Djehuty actually represents the reflection of Ra in time and space. It's like when you see a reflection of yourself in a mirror or more precisely, the reflection of the light of the sun on the moon.

We are currently here on the East Coast of the United States, we are in the middle of the day and the sun is shining, in twelve hours from now, the moon will have risen and we are approaching the full moon period, which will be in a few more days, but even now you can see the reflection of the sun in a very dynamic way, but it is a cool way, it is not in a hot way. The sun shining is hot and the moon shining is cool. And the moon therefore represents the subdued aspect of the spirit, what I mean by that is Ra represents the fire and the moon represents the coolness of that fire.

If the sun was to blaze on the earth constantly, just realize that the earth would not be able to survive, to sustain life, there has to be a hot and cool period, and the balance between those two. If the earth gets too cool, or the earth gets too hot, there will be an insufferable condition. And so it also operates in the human being also. You have spirit and then you have soul, Ra is the spirit and Djehuty is the soul, as it were. The reflection of the spirit in time and space, so specifically reflecting in the mind.

Your thoughts, your mental apparatus, your mental capacity is actually a reflection of your deeper consciousness. And again, if there is an imbalance of either one of those two, there is going to be an (again) insufferable condition, an unworkable condition. If you are always conscious of your spirit self and never conscious of your mental self, your time and space self, what will happen? You would be existing in spiritual realms exclusively, and if anyone were to come to talk to you, you would not be able to answer them, because in that state you would not be aware of them since you are only aware of the spirit realm, of all-encompassingness. If people are only aware of time and space, then you can easily see what happens; people become egoistic, only aware of the world and nothing beyond the world, nothing beyond what the senses can bring; nothing beyond time and space. Spirituality then becomes what people consider a myth in the pejorative sense, what most people think of as something unreal, something that is illusory, something that is a lie or at most a legend without any basis that stupid or ignorant people believe in. You are to know that myths are not meant to be literally true but are true in the sense of the principles they relate in the form of a Creation story with characters that represent aspects of Creation and the human experience that lead us to understand a spiritual origin and reality that transcends the physical Creation. Without balance, the knowledge of that teaching of myth and or the knowledge of time and space, are distorted, perverted and human beings become twisted shadows of their higher self, manifesting as animals in human form.

So there must be a balance, between those two. And if the teaching of Djehuty is learned, one can transcend time and space, while not needing to destroy or leave behind time and space but rather, discovering its illusoriness and thereby becoming free from it. This is also the teaching of the Kybalion, as we are going to see. Learning how to develop dual consciousness, this is the task of every aspirant; developing consciousness of the world and consciousness of the spirit.

And so Djehuty had a particular city, the city of Khemenu in Kemet. Khemenu or chemenu means eight, the number eight; so he is the God of the city of the eight. And it is also said, he is the manager of eight Gods and Goddesses, the eight gods and goddesses are essentially the same as the eight Gods and Goddesses of Memphite Theology, they are the Gods and Goddesses of the eight opposites of creation;. which is one of the principles of the Kybalion, which we will get to at a future class, but for now, we are staying with the wisdom aspect.

The first Principle which Djehuty talks about in the Kybalion is mind. Djehuty being the God of the mind, and particularly, intellect, is always seen in Kamitan/Kemetic or Neterian iconographies or reliefs at the balance of the judgment of the soul. He carries a scribe's pallet and he is writing down the results of the balance. What is being weighed is your righteousness, your conscience is what is being weighed. Your level of awareness of virtue, and his hands are Shai and Rennenet, fortune and destiny. The person who is actually handling the balance is Anpu, and Anpu represents lower mind; Djehuty represents intellect, in this particular mythic iconography. And he is associated with the Goddesses in the balance scene. This is one of his main functions. He is associated with the Goddesses' Meskhenet, who is the Goddess of the birth, specifically the future birth, i.e. the next incarnation [reincarnation]. Djehuty is recording, writing down the result of the judgment, based on your own fortune and destiny. The judgment is based on your own actions and then bearing the fruits of your own fortune and your own destiny; that is going to come to you in your future astral life; in your reincarnated life, or your transcendental life. There are three possible results in the balance, and this is what Djehuty records on his scribal pallet.

The first possible judgment is that your heart is heavier than the feather of Maat and this means that you are an unrighteous person, your mind is heavy, your conscience is heavy with worry, with doubt, with ignorance, with vice, greed, lust, jealousy and so on and so forth, all of which makes your heart heavy; heavier than the feather of Maat, which symbolizes a state of mind that is in balance or devoid of such mental thoughts and feelings that weigh on the mind and cause worldly worry, anxiety, fear desire, etc. which all amount to egoism. If your heart is judged to be heavier than the feather then you are going to experience hellish conditions after death and then you reincarnate, to try it all over again.

If your heart is equal in the balance with the feather of Maat, then you are judged to be worthy to come into the presence of Asar, and to be his servant; and being a servant of Asar, a shemsu Asar means that you… or really a Hem, Hem is really the term for servant, almost like a slave and as you know, that is the same term, for priests and priestesses. As you do that service you become purified thereby, you become worthy one day, to do what the people whose heart is lighter than the feather of Maat do, you will go to the judgment balance and if the heart is found to be lighter than the feather of Maat, they go directly to join with Asar, who in this context, is the Supreme Being, they become one with God essentially.

The Kybalion: Ancient Egyptian Mysteries

Above: from the Papyrus of Ani, the soul of Ani (far left) observes the balance of his heart.

The term "unrighteousness" in the context of its usage here in relation to the results of the judgment of the balance, does not necessarily mean, you are a bad person. It can mean that but more often it means that you are ignorant and that you don't know, the true meaning of life, you don't know the spirit, you have not learned what is beyond time and space, that you are more than a body, a mortal and finite being. It also means suffering and reincarnation because you have pursued goals in life, based on illusory notions that have led you to sorrow, pain and unfulfilled desires. If you fall into the other two categories, you don't come back to the world. It means you are sufficiently spiritually evolved (gained in the knowledge of self) so as to merit not suffering and returning to the world of time and space physical reality. You move on to the astral plane and you transcend eventually from there either gradually or immediately. And Djehuty presides over all of this; meaning your own intellect presides over all of this, and your soul is a witness just as the soul of Ani (human head with hawk body watching the judgment-see image above-on left side) witnesses the results of the judgment. And your higher self is also a witness, Asar is watching over all of this; but the higher mystical and philosophical key to understand this is that, your own mind (which is Djehuty) presides over all of this so reality is perceived and experienced in and through the mind and therefore, you yourself control your own fate. So, the first principle of the Hermitic teaching is the All is Mind, the universe is mental.

Mind, Illusion, Reality and Enlightenment

Think about it, the high philosophy of this teaching, the universe is mental, what does that really mean. When you are aware of your mental body, when you are asleep, when you are imagining things, when you are hallucinating, when you are having thoughts that carry you into your fanciful notions, fanaticizing about the future, reminiscing about the past, your desires and so on and so forth, that is when you are aware of your mental body. Think about it, during that period you are not aware of your physical body, for a few seconds, or minutes, things happen in the physical world but you are, as if, removed from that awareness even as your body continues to operate in it. You may even be walking down the street and you start fantasizing. It's as if your body takes an automatic kind of mechanical function, and your mind is thinking elsewhere, all of a sudden you come back to your conscious awareness of time and space, the physical reality, and you realize you walked the whole block, you didn't even know what happened. That is when you are aware of your mental body. You're living in your mind; you are perceiving a reality that's in your mind and not at that time aware consciously of the world of physical time and space.

All experience is in and through the mind. When you touch something you are experiencing sensations but you are not in direct contact with any object, even your body. So what is the nature of that mental experience? When you are in the waking state, you are perceiving a "physical" reality that you believe is and recognize as the "world of time and space". When you are dreaming you perceive a different reality, a different world that you believe is correct time and space but all the while none of these experiences are real, none of these experiences are absolute or abiding, either in the physical or the dream world. What is happening is that you are perceiving with your senses. Your senses are impressing your mind and your mind is ascribing reality to those perceptions and this process is called "experiences". Those perceptions that you are becoming aware of in your mind, are being given value by your concept of reality which is based on your unconscious mind's awareness of self and knowledge about the nature of being and existence itself which is based on your past experiences, feelings and actions, which is termed aryu in Ancient Egyptian religious philosophy. So if your awareness is limited to the physical then your ascribed values to the experiences are relegated to the context of physicality, etc. Since we know by the ancient philosophy and now also by quantum physics, that physical reality is actually not abiding, not real, except to the gross senses, then we also can conclude that physical reality is illusory and therefore the perceptions and feeling of reality of the experiences in time and space is relative to the perceiver, based on the contents of their unconscious mind, their aryu, that ascribed to the experiences the judgment of being "real". In other words, what is real to some people is not real to others; this goes for objects as well as concepts and ideas. Therefore, some people may believe in certain things or fear certain things while others will not. If a person is ignorant of the higher philosophy, the higher understanding, the higher awareness of reality, that is beyond those illusory perceptions of an illusory physical relative reality, that perception that that person has assigned a reality to, that becomes their truth, their "reality" and they cannot escape that reality, as long as they have given it that value of being "real" and as long as their capacity for perception, based on ignorance of higher understanding and experience, is limited.

The cause of this way of perceiving is due to a misconception of the three aspects of your consciousness. You have three aspects to your experience; the first aspect is the witnessing aspect, there is something in you that is aware of things, that is called Amun; and then there are objects that you become aware of, that Amun becomes aware of, and those are called Ptah. The means of Amun interacting with Ptah is called Ra, your senses, your mind, your instruments of your senses. So there is a triad that constitutes the capacity to have "experiences", and that triad allows the personality to engage in the capability of perception. This is the triad of mental experience. Without any element of the triad the "experience is not possible. There is, however, a fourth element of being, a fourth aspect of existence, which is Neberdjer. Neberdjer is the "ALL", it is the same ALL talked about in the Kybalion. "The All is Mind, the universe is mental."

Neberdjer is "All Encompassing Consciousness", undivided by the trinity of human experience. If a person were to fully understand the illusoriness of the triad and discover the unitary experience, that is Neberdjer, then that person would achieve the goal of the Mysteries and this is the purpose of the teaching of the Kybalion and all mystery or mystical texts. The problem occurs when a person, who's spirit is intrinsically Neberdjer, uses the triad to have experiences. This is when a person changes perception from all-encompassingness to perception as an individual, finite, mortal human being. The Amun, or witnessing aspect of the mental triad, has come to believe it is the true I Am, the ultimate I Am, forgetting the Neberdjer deeper self, and that's how every individual comes to think; this condition may be termed "egoism". Forgetting the ultimate deeper identity of the ALL, the Neberdjer, the individual perceiving person adopts <u>given name</u>, "my name is John," "my name is Larry" or "Jean," whatever the name is and they believe that is their ultimate reality, their only reality. The egoistic person perceives the world with the senses and thinks that the world is "real" and yet the senses are incapable of perceiving reality because they are limited. It is not possible for a person who uses the physical senses and the idea of egoism, to perceive reality with the senses, it's impossible because the senses cannot perceive the totality of existence, in and through a limited mind, a mind limited by the individual concept of self. It is like when you look at the wheel on a car, there are people who like to spend a lot of money on their cars, they put on these expensive wheels on them that have elaborate designs, the chrome wheels or the gold spokes, the racing wheels or this or that, and there can even be empty spaces. When they are standing still, they look very cool, very nice and very "snazzy", whatever term you want to use... the bomb, etc. However, when they are in motion you really can't see the design, what you see is a blur, so you can't see those designs anymore. All you see is one blur. And it looks like there is a solid piece there. Another example is when you look at a fan, the fan is spinning fast, you can't see the spaces between the blades of the fan and this motion the Kybalion calls vibration. When the ignorant perceiving mind confronts that illusory perception that is in motion, it is easily fooled by the illusion of the experience. Such a mind is referred to as "ignorant", "deluded", etc. The physical universe is not real in an abiding since but it is a mental experience that has been mistaken for abiding reality; it has been mistaken due to incorrect, ignorant, deluded mental processes, for the sages have discovered that if that delusion were to be dispelled then a higher perception of reality and deeper insight into the nature of self, beyond egoism, would be revealed. This delusion is dispelled through study and correct understanding of the wisdom teaching, reflection on the wisdom teaching, practice of the wisdom teaching and meditation.

So then why is it that we cannot perceive that the universe is mental; the reason is because we are so caught up in the mundane reality, the time and space reality and we have not learned how to separate ourselves from that. And the Kybalion goes on explaining, mind as matter may be transmuted from state to state, degree to degree, condition to condition, pole to pole, vibration to vibration. True transmutation is a mental art. Transmutation is something that every initiate, every aspirant must learn to do.

You are to realize that physical matter is condensed subtle matter. It's composed of, the same matter that you see in time and space in the physical world and in outer space. This is what people refer to as matter, the air water, fire and earth; If you want to be more scientific about it, then add the whole table of elements. Now when we look closer we realize that there is a subtle aspect of those elements and they disintegrate into pure energy. In other words, you are also composed of gross elements and can potentially move yourself towards purity and subtlety, towards a state where you can perceive a subtler reality of existence. If you want to be more esoteric about it add ether and these subtler aspects of the elements compose the thoughts that occur in the mind; so mind is composed of subtle elements and energy and the world is composed of gross elements and energies.

Think about it, when you are moving thoughts around in your mind, you are actually moving subtle bits of matter. Like the computer, when you are moving documents from one folder to another, or from one folder archive (memory) to the screen (conscious awareness), you are moving little bits of information which are little bits, pieces, of subtle matter, and that is what we refer to as mind and the awareness aspect of the personality, the Amun, is what is referred to as consciousness or awareness. And if your consciousness engages with and intensifies the worldly thoughts then those thoughts become more coagulated and less subtle and the mind becomes clouded (because the now grosser thoughts begin to make the mind more opaque to awareness of subtler realities of existence, to the higher reality. This means that that mind will not be able to understand that the universe is mental and discover the illusoriness of the world of time and space and the subtle higher nature of self beyond time and space; again, this is called ignorance, the opposite of enlightenment.

Consider that if you had an electron microscope and were to look at a piece of paper, you would be able to see beyond the piece of paper. You would see a universe of atoms, protons, electrons and neutrons and if you were able to go deeper, beyond where the electron microscope can go, you would perceive energy and beyond that there is pure essence of all-encompassing divinity (Neberdjer, the ALL). An example that is used to point out the illusoriness of the senses is the sense perception of animals. Animals perceive differently from human beings because they have order of senses. A bloodhound can smell something two miles away; can a human being smell something two miles away? The bloodhound is living in a different world, his senses have a different capacity, he is aware of something that you are not aware of.

Cats can hear from fantastic distances; they can hear very fine sounds. You ever notice how cats are, when they walk around; you learn a lot from cats, we have two cats here, they are walking around nicely, cat like, softly and all of a sudden they will turn around, look up and down look to the side, they are like, "what's going on?", "what's that noise?"; have you ever noticed that, you look at them and think they are crazy but they are perceiving sounds and vibrations and perceptions that human beings cannot. They are hearing things that you can't hear. Dogs have an interesting perception also. They can know you are coming home, even when you are blocks away, driving home. How do they know that? Way before you come they start barking at the door, sitting by the door, what is that all about? They have a different capacity for perception, than what ordinary human beings have, and we go on down the line, there are animals that have such wondrous forms of senses that lead them to perceive a totally different reality from each other and from humans. This means that perception with mind and senses is relative and based on the perception instruments and capacities. Therefore, perception with mind and senses is not abiding and hence illusory. This is an important key to understanding the overall Kybalion and ancient Egyptian Mystery teaching. And what is to say that their reality is worse or better than ours? The idea is that the human senses are very limited but before you start thinking that it would be nice to have the olfactory glands of a dog and the hearing capacity, poise and relaxation of a cat reflect that while animals with expanded sense perception may have greater awareness they too cannot perceive the totality of abiding reality.

Thinking about cats, seems like all they seem to do is sleep and they run around chasing things and they eat whatever they want, and they come to you so you can pet them; when you examine the situation it seems that you are actually their pet. So wouldn't you like to be a cat and have all that great luxury? They seem to live a life better than human beings; they get fed and they don't give anything to you, they take everything. Before you start thinking that, you better start realizing that, all the animals and all their fantastic senses put together, cannot equal the glory of the human being, meaning the potential glory of a human being which has the capacity to transcend the illusoriness of the senses and time and space. As I said before, human beings can have a special capacity that animals don't have and that is mind and the capacity to understand this teaching. Animals cannot understand this teaching about the universe being mental. They can exist in it using their rudimentary, instinctual mind, they can be affected by it and be controlled by, susceptible to the world of time and space, but they cannot have more than a rudimentary, instinctual understanding about the world and their instinctual mind does not rise to the level of the intellectual capacity of an adult. Human beings have a special capacity, that of potentially being capable of understanding what is going on and thereby transcend it. Animals do not have that capacity; but they are some drawbacks being a human being too; I don't think you have ever seen the birds in the morning, when they are singing, when they are waking up to the sun, I don't think you have ever seen them get up and say ohhh I've had a bad dream last night, I hate to sleep in this mess, and my life is a misery because my little chicks would not get out of the nest and they are hanging out here and they wouldn't go to work and find their own life; you never heard a bird say that. The lizards, you never hear them talk about how they can't find a little ant to go and eat, or you don't hear a lizard say that he is worried about a bird that might come down from a tree and grab him…, they don't worry, they just live from minute to minute; all the animals are like that, unless there is some kind of danger at the moment, but apart from that, they don't worry or perceive concepts about the past or the future. If you have a pet such as a dog, he is happy to see you when you come home because the last time he saw you he did not know where you disappeared to or when you might exist again but now that you are here in the present he knows you and is happy to see you, now, in the present moment.

    Human beings are constantly worried about not getting what they want, constantly worried about losing what they have, constantly worried about how the world is going to blow up; or their lover is not going to come; or they are not going to get to go to a party; or this, or that, not enough money in the bank, or whatever it is. Your parents want to kick you out of the house, you can't get a house because it is too expensive; why did they bring me into the world, etc. All these things that people think and worry about, animals don't think or worry about. They go living from day to day, but also they have no aspiration, they have no capacity to dream, or to...aspire, from the standpoint of envisioning the higher reality. So therefore, human beings have a higher potential, a higher capacity, but they also have a lower capacity, human beings can actually become very degraded, to become lower than animals. They can descend to a level of consciousness that is worse than that of animals. People can worry themselves to death, literally. They can lead themselves to ulcers, to disease by their mental condition, but also, they can lead themselves to Sagehood, and that is why the choice is always best to be a human being, to have the chance to make that attainment. While in human embodiment, it is always best to try to learn the teaching, to try to become virtuous, to try to transcend the balance (of Maat between the opposites of Creation) and not to come back to human embodiment, because you never have a guarantee of what you are going to come back as. It is your aryu, your karmic basis, your past previous actions, thoughts and feelings and the concept of who you are that those past actions, thoughts and feelings come together to form your conscious awareness of who and what you are that is being weighed by Djehuty, that is to say, your own unconscious. Depending on that, that is what leads you to your *Shai and Rennenet,* your fortune and destiny. Therefore, it is wise to be virtuous, wise to learn the teaching, wise to purify your mind, to develop purity of heart.

You may come back as an ant and somebody may step on you, without even knowing it. Then you may come back as a lizard; then you may come back as a rat; then you may go and come back down, you may go and come back as an amoeba. That's why it is wise to apply yourself to the teaching now, not just so that you wouldn't come back and that is something else, even after death, but also right now we are talking about even while you are alive, you can have the best kind of life possible, by being able to control your mind, if you learn to understand that the universe is mental. Your experiences, everything you desire, occurs in your mind. When you touch something, you are not actually touching it with your true self, only your finger is touching it. Whatever your finger is, remember we do not perceive what the fingertip is; you are touching a piece of wood, we do not even know what the wood is, we are not perceiving it properly with our mind and senses. Whatever it is that is going on, that message is transmitted, as if by radio, to your brain. Your brain impresses upon your senses, upon your higher senses, your mental senses. Your intellect puts a value on that perception in relation to your idea of yourself as an individual human being who possesses consciousness of self-existence. In other words, animals do not have a notion of being an individual that exists with a past, present, future and with relationships and they have no idea about death, though they have an idea of instinctual experiences such as pleasure, pain, fear, etc. That is where the experience occurs for a human being, in the mind, and with the conceptions of past, present, future and relationships to the world, other people, etc., and not in the world of time and space. In the state of ignorance, human beings can believe their existence is tied to the senses and that the perceptions of the senses are THE experience itself. However, that idea is discounted when we reflect on the fact that dreams seem "absolutely and abidingly" "real" when they are happening and when one wakes up it is realized that the perceptions were not realities but only transitory mental experiences. The experiences in the waking physical world are actually the same though they are a little more abiding than the dream world, yet the physical world and the dream world are both made up of the same elements though the physical world is more coagulated, more dense but yet both are equally illusory and the perception of both occurs in the mind. So whatever the physical world or the dream world may be, it is not being perceived by the mind directly but rather through the limited and imperfect senses and the process is thus inherently illusory. When a human being develops their spiritual awareness he or she can find that they can wake up in the middle of a dream to the fact that they are dreaming and then also control the events of the dream. When a spiritual aspirant wakes up to the philosophy of the illusoriness of the physical world, he or she can control their experience in the world of time and space and thereby change their destiny from being controlled by the world to being the architect of their own destiny. Therefore, just as a human being can learn to control the events of their dream they can also direct the course of their life in the waking state.

"Whatever" is going on in time and space that's whatever "it" is. What I mean is that we cannot perceive "it" the way "it" is due to the limited senses, as we discussed. The universe is a projection, your reality is a projection of the spirit in time and space, your mind becomes aware of that perception. So you yourself, the higher self is projecting whatever "it" (limited perceptions) is that you are perceiving that is going on in time and space in your limited mind and your mind is becoming aware of "it" to the limited extent that it can. You are the creator and you are the awareness of your own creation. What this comes down to is that, you can transmute, that's what the teaching says, you can change that reality, if you so desire. Really what we are talking about is shifting, changing, from the perception of reality that is limited to one that is based on a higher perception that provides a higher reality, an abiding reality of what is absolutely real and true as opposed to what is limited, ephemeral, mortal and transient.

So what is the procedure in changing this reality, first to understand that the universe is mental, as we have been explaining. So if this universe is mental, it is also virtually infinite in its capacity. If you were to be able to be alive for a million years, do you realize that every time you go to sleep, you will be able to have a different dream, you will be able to create a different world. Sometimes you have more than one dream a night, and this can go on indefinitely. And when you are asleep, when you are musing, when you are aware of your astral body, that is your abiding reality for that period, meaning that when you asleep, you don't think of your waking reality, it has no meaning; it doesn't have anything to do with you. Think about that, that personality that who that you think that you are, at that time, what you learned how to be through your limited senses and limited education and upbringing, whatever your name that your parents gave you, etc., it appears so real; but when you go to sleep, that goes right out the window, you throw that personality and it's possessions, relationships, worries and concerns out, and you take on another personality and concerns. What does that say about your waking personality, if your waking personality is so real, how come you don't take it in with you to your dream world? What I'm getting at is, you don't even treat it and experience it as your abiding reality. Reflect on that profoundly before reading on.

When you wake up in the morning, the waking reality seems more abiding; things change more slowly, and seem to be real, don't they. Take this classroom we are meeting in again, for example. You see the same pictures on the wall that you saw last week, don't you, the same tiles on the floor, etc., but yet if you examine them with higher scientific instruments, you will see that nothing is exactly the same as it was last week. The tiles on the floor seem so hard, but if you examine them, there is a little bit of change in their molecules, they are disintegrating, falling apart. For example, consider our new African Origins book, the huge book that we have now, a six hundred and eighty pages, hard cover book, that we can put out here on the table. If we were to leave it here and then if we could come back in a hundred years we won't find the book, it will be disintegrated, it will be gone. However, the mind is fooled because if you come back tomorrow, it will still be there, you come back next week, it will still be there, but if you look closely even over a period of weeks you could notice small amounts of deterioration from week to week, a little bit of deterioration, a little bit of fading, etc. This process of dissolution is called *apep*. The reason for this is that this world takes longer to dissolve all your creations as opposed to the quick changes in a dream world and for the reason you have come to believe that this physical world, that you experience in your waking state of mind, is solid, abiding and real; yet, everything in it eventually breaks down, just as in the dream world. So, the physical plane (waking world) of existence is just a slightly more coagulated version of the Astral plane (dream world) of existence. That is called the teaching of entropy or chaos and in ancient times the divinity Apep (Apophis) presided over entropy and as such he is the enemy of the god Ra-Horakty, the one who sustains Creation. They are in constant struggle to maintain Creation or dissolve it back into it's constituent parts known as Nun or undifferentiated consciousness. Order (Maat) in the universe, that allows the sun to shine, planets to stay in their orbits, gravity and the other laws of physics is a temporary and artificial creation of the cosmic mind (Neberdjer, through the creative agency form of the God Khepera). It is a conditioning process of the mind, you have conditioned yourself to believe in certain ways and therefore you are caught in and limited by that conditioning, you are circumscribed by what you have created. If you learn how to uncondition your mind, you will realize that the reality you have created, is really one of several possibilities, and that you are the master of all those possibilities, whatever you have decided to create.

Nothing stays the same, everything changes. That change is what you are perceiving as time. Time actually does not exist either. Time is a misconception. The idea that we are going to start this lecture at 12:15 pm and we are going to finish at 1:15 pm or an hour later, this is an illusion; this is a convention, something we are agreeing upon to bring order to our activities. In the morning the sun is at the horizon and at the middle of the day it is at the top of the sky, this is a change of movement of objects in space, but you are creating some kind of philosophy that says from the movement of the morning to the noon, that is a passage of time… essentially time does not exist. The change of your childhood to adulthood and to your death, is a change of matter not a change of time or a change of life to death. Nothing has happened in time, shall we illustrate further. There were some people who were trapped in a cave once, only one person had a watch and he knew what time it was, according to his watch, but the other people didn't know and they kept asking what time it is ,when are they coming to save us and he gave them the time, reduced by a factor of let's say ten. So ten hours passed, he told them one hour had passed; a day pass… oh two, three hours had passed. So people had this idea they could survive, they had a long way to go before they die, right, because they are mentally conditioned, that they could only survive a certain amount of time. Couple days later, miners came and dug them out and they were in good condition, but the guy who had the watch he died. Yea, consider when you are having a good time; time passes fast; when you are having a miserable time, time passes slow. When the activity is tedious or distasteful the time is perceived as tedious or distasteful, miserable or even terrible…People may say things like "this job that I hate, all day long, the grind." But when you love your job or something else you are doing that you like to do, "oh boy, I just came this morning and it's time to punch out, what happened, where did the time go? That's the illusion of time and the relativity of human perception through limited senses and the impact of those perceptions on a conditioned mind.

When you go to bed at night and you have your dream, you can dream a whole lifetime over one evening. What time frame did it happen in? A person that falls out of a plane without a parachute, their life flashes before them, what time frame did that happen in? There is no such thing as time. The universe is mental, you are projecting a concept and that projection that you believe in is controlling your life. If it is a negative projection, then you can have a miserable existence. You have a positive projection, and then there is no limit to what you can experience, including higher consciousness.

Are you hearing what this means, do you see the grandeur of it? About this wisdom, the Kybalion says: *the lips of wisdom are closed except to the ears of understanding,* are you understanding? Are you listening to this? You won't get this in your regular school. *The Principles of Truth are seven, he who knows these understandingly, possesses the magic key before whose touch, all the doors of the temple fly open. When the ears of the student are ready, then comes the lips to fill them with wisdom. Where falleth the footsteps of the masters, the ears of those ready for the teaching open wide.* This is like that joke I use to give; those of you remember the old *EF Hutton* commercial? They used to say: "When EF Hutton talks, people listen!". Are you like, as a spiritual aspirant, that attentive with the teachings? Do you stop and drop whatever it is that you are doing and open your ears wide and lean in to listen carefully at what has been said? All this really means is paying attention and stopping your mind, stopping your egoistic conditioning about worldly desires and that also includes desires about what you think the teaching is or should be. You have conditioned the teaching also, in accordance with your expectations and opinions. One of the biggest dangers for an initiate of the mysteries is imposing your opinions onto the teaching and thereby only listening to things that agree with your egoistic and ignorant conditioned mental thoughts. Then you don't want to listen to whatever the teacher is saying the teaching is, so therefore you have created a reality for yourself of what the teaching is, and that leads to failure as you are following a path led by an ignorant person, yourself! Even if you do not impose this egoistic notion on the teaching and the spiritual path, if you are not led by an authentic spiritual preceptor you can fall into the trap of falling in with groups of ignorant people that follow teachings based on faith instead of science (mysticism and the Egyptian Mysteries is a science, not a faith-based religion) and an initiatic tradition managed by a qualified spiritual preceptor. So, unless you are on an authentic path you can delude yourself or you can be deluded by the world. Even if you do not create an illusion about reality, the illusory reality conditions you and controls you, and leads you down a path of worldly experiences of alternating happiness and sorrow but ending in ultimate disappointment and death without having discovered the meaning of life and the glory of self-mastery and enlightenment. Therefore, a life in ignorance is like a life of slavery and a life of wisdom is the life of self-mastery.

"Salvation is the freeing of the soul from its bodily fetters; becoming a God through knowledge and wisdom; controlling the forces of the cosmos instead of being a slave to them; subduing the lower nature and through awakening the higher self, ending the cycle of rebirth and dwelling with the Neters who direct and control the Great Plan."

-Ancient Egyptian Proverb

Let's say that you are a religious fanatic, you think everything is to be taken in a literal or fanatical way; you go and create a fanatical life for yourself, and if you are not a fanatic, but you are ignorant, the fanatics around you are going to control you and lead you to have a fanatical life since you do not know any better. All this capacity to become fanatical or a follower of the fanatics, is due to the ignorant perceptions throughout life and ignorant conclusions about the meaning of those perceptions. This is referred to as a soul that is fettered to bodily ignorance and desires.

So unless you have this wisdom teaching and fully understand it, however you get it, either through Neterianism or some other authentic religion, your life is doomed, you are doomed to have a miserable existence. Therefore, the teaching, the wisdom teaching is the best. It is the glorious way of life; it is that which aspirants throughout history have striven for. Do you understand the grandeur of what we are talking about here? This is the means by which you can truly begin to control your life. The means by which you can truly begin to discover what life is all about, and not be caught up by the illusions of other people, or your own illusions. For that there must be humility, there must be a willingness to listen. You can discover the magic key that makes the temple doors fly open. And Djehuty opens those doors; Djehuty is your own intellect. Not the intellect of intellectuals or intellectualism, but the enlightened intellect that has learned to discern the illusoriness of the world, from the absolute abiding reality.

"The principles of truth are seven, he who knows these, understandingly, possesses the Magic Key before whose touch all the Doors of the Temple fly open."
-Ancient Egyptian Proverb

That abiding reality is the underlying essence of who you are, beyond all of those transient experiences of consciousness that we have discussed today; what is the reality behind your waking state right now, you are awake right now, hopefully you are all awake and you are not dreaming somewhere, or fantasizing, you are listening to me. All of you on the internet, everybody, wherever you are, even if you are reading this book in the future, you might have become temporarily lost in thought or been fantasizing a few minutes ago, your attention might have wandered, but I'm calling your attention right now, "hey wake up! Listen now".

That can happen. The mind that is unaware of the deeper underlying reality and caught up in the reaction to the senses which is based on the aryu can be constantly dragged around to pay attention to things that are not abiding, not real, while treating and experiencing tem as if they were real. Since they are not real or abiding, they change constantly, offering no consistency for the mind to hold on to. This is why the Ancient Egyptian proverb says, **"there is no happiness for the soul in the external worlds."** This happens because that's the nature of the ignorant and weak mind, to wander and be distracted by the perceptions. This teaching is about the discovery of the internal worlds. It is the duty of the aspirant to reign in the mind whenever it wanders during spiritual studies or practices. I've been talking all this time, you have probably faded a dozen times since I started and you brought yourself back to awareness, back to the talk. This weakness of the mind, the struggle to concentrate on the teaching, this is one of your worst enemies as an aspirant. Not being able to concentrate your thought process, your attention, on the teaching. Remember what we talked about, how to be a successful student, one of the critical things is to be able to concentrate, when you are listening to the teaching, so that it can be impressed on your mind, in a powerful way. That is when the student is ready.

The Kybalion: Ancient Egyptian Mysteries

"There is no happiness for the soul in the external worlds since these are perishable, true happiness lies in that which is eternal, within us."
-Ancient Egyptian Proverb

If you are one of those students who listen to the teachings and says "this sounds great, I get it", "I have heard this before", but they do not reflect deeply and practice what they have heard but only think about it when in class, then go home and live life doing worldly things, not applying the teaching to those worldly activities, you may come back for the next teaching, and the next, but taking it in superficially and not profoundly but to the extent that is comfortable or palatable, then you may fall back into the world, that is not being ready for the teaching. That will not allow you to have a successful spiritual evolution. That will only allow for a partial movement, sometimes forward and sometimes backward. By the time you are ready to have the great judgment, you will be one of those people who will fail the judgment, and will be one of those who will come back to earth to do it all over again. Your heart will not be measured equally with the feather, or it will not surpass or be lighter than the feather, because your mind is too heavy with desires, delusions, fears, insecurities and worldly feelings from the past. You believe too much in the world and initiates, followers of the hermetic teaching, do not believe in the world and that's what this first principle is all about, they believe in their mind.

People who are worldly, if something happens to their body, they are all broken up and distraught. People who have the mental concept, they realize that they can do powerful things with their minds, even though their bodies may be broken up; think about Steven Hawking, his body is virtually useless and yet his intellect is shining bright. He can still come up with fantastic theories of quantum physics. He has learn to control his senses and his body, when you have transcended the body hold on you, you have controlled it, you have transcended it. When your body does not get in the way of the intellect discerning truth that is when you have transcended it, you may continue to have a body and yet it is no obstruction, it has nothing to condition you, to hold you back. At that point it cannot fool you anymore, the senses cannot fool you. So this teaching needs to be meditated upon, it needs to be reflected upon, you need to repeat it, as many times as the inputs you are bringing into your mind through your senses; you need to impress that mind with the words and sounds of this teaching. Reading the teaching, studying it, repeating it and reconditioning, this is the path of the transmutation of the mind.

HTP
END OF CHAPTER 1

Commentary by Seba Dja

Just to comment on a few things that were discussed by Sebai MAA. I wanted to start off by reading a proverb from the Kemetic proverbs book that is in harmony with the message today, which I've related before and it is in the section of the illusion, born from the human senses. It says *"It is very hard, to leave the things we have grown used to, which meet our gaze on every side. Appearances delight us, whereas things which appear not, make their believing hard. Evils are the more apparent things, whereas the Good can never show itself unto the eyes, for It hath neither form nor figure."*

So what is the good referring to that can never show itself unto the eyes, what is the proverb referring to. Everybody agrees, your true essence is the good that can never show itself unto the eyes, because it does not have a form or figure. So it's talking about the higher self, the Asar, the Amun, whatever name you want to call it, because look around, where is Asar?, where is Amun?, where is Aset?, where is Heru?, where is Djehuty? You might point to a picture on the wall, but I am saying, no I want to see them as I drive down the street, where can I go see them and yet the self is everywhere and in all things and that is the only reality that there is.

The evil are the more apparent things, and here the term Sebai MAA referred to earlier, evil not in the term of hellish conditions, not in the term, you might think in the terms of Christianity, but in the terms of ignorance, in terms of the mind being caught up in the trap, in the illusion, in the veil of Aset. So the evils are the more apparent things, the ignorance in the world. How many times do you turn on the television and see that they are reinforcing the good, the truth, the higher self, the spiritual nature, how many times do you see the T.V. saying; you are the Self, you are everywhere, how often do you hear that being reinforced... pretty much not at all . So the proverbs also says *"their appearances delight us"* whereas the things that don't appear make their believing hard and you know they are many atheists, they don't believe in God, because where is God… show me, show me, show me. Yet they believe in gravity and they can't see it, they believe in air and they can't see it and they believe in all of these different types of ideas. They believe in the pilot driving the plane, he/she is okay and competent and they are going to get them to where they are going, safely and soundly. So they buy the ticket, they believe that, they don't know it, that's not apparent necessarily, they didn't check the pilot out, do a drug test and see if they are okay, but no, all of these things are taken for granted. But yet, what is really true and real cab be easily dismissed and cannot delight us.

How many times is your mind captivated or captured by someone's beauty? Especially in this western culture, where everything is about looks and how beautiful that person is, their buns and their thighs and their abs, you know. Even nature, we become captivated by it, they are appearances that delight us don't they, am I lying. When was the last time you were captivated by, oh it is beautiful, it is really wonderful, it is really cute. But what about the Divine, what is the relativity in this world that you see, in this world of time and space, relative to what you may not have experienced, but what the scriptures tell you about the Divine. What is the relativity, seeing beauty out of something, whatever beauty you see in the world of time and space, how much more beautiful is the Divine supposed to be… if you were able to capture that. Why is it that you don't capture that, perhaps your mind is not on that. How can you capture something, if you are not thinking about it?

HTP

Chapter 1 Principle of Mind Part 2: Q & A

Commentary by Seba Dja cont:

A human being is often beset with inordinate distractions, concerns and manufactured obligations. There are all of those pressing engagements and all those things to do, think about and run after, that you have to do and you can't stop. If someone says, "hey stop, think for a moment, take a half hour to go meditate. Set all your problems aside, go relax, go meditate. It is good for you." many people reply: "I can't, I have to go do this and if I don't get it done, this is going to happen" and then all of a sudden, it comes to about nine, ten, eleven o' clock at night, and the mind is still occupied, still concerned, still preoccupied and anxious… "I have to keep going, I have to go do this." But what happens when it gets to that point, you know that point; That point where there is that poke in your side that says, "hey get up and go to bed" and regardless of what you want to do, you will fall asleep wherever you are, because that's where you are and there is nothing more comfortable than where you are, because you are asleep. At that particular time, what happens to all your worries? What happens to everything you previously could not let go of? Nature pushes you to let go and you leave it behind and it seems like you are doing okay, because here you are, in your sleep state, devoid of those concerns and yet you are alright. You thus exist in a non-troubled state because the trouble and concerns are not pressing on the mind. So if there is a state where they cannot press on the mind that means that they are not abiding and that you have invited them to press on your mind. You have allowed them to cause you discomfort. If you were to discover how to exist in the space where the troubles and concerns of the mind are kept at bay then you would discover and experiencing peace even in the midst of worldly troubles and concerns. This is control of mind and the discovery that you are separate from the mind. The mind is your possession, your instrument, your tool, and not who you are.

So what is the process of holding onto these worries, why must they be held on to? Well, people say I have to plan, but planning is different from worrying. Planning is okay, if you are scheduling things. Worrying is that state of mind, where you are burdened by the plans, where it is a problem. Instead of it being a challenge it's a problem for you and along with that problem comes a whole set of physiological types of manifestations, it clogs the intellect, so forget about these wisdom teachings, forget about everything you heard today, all this leaves your mind. At that time you can't think about "mind is all" and "I can transmute my mind." You can, though, at a stage before it really, really starts to come down and before you become very constricted, accosted by the thoughts and feelings of worry and anxiety. You can catch it before it gets really, really constricted, you can control it; but if you don't, it will keep constricting you… closing in and closing on you.

So you get that migraine, you get that headache, you can't breathe, so you have to yell at somebody to let it all out. The aspect of understanding the illusoriness of the world, they always make the comment right, the three first letters in illusory are what? What do the three first letters spell, our language tells us very well, what these things are, you believe in an illusion, you will get *ill*.

It is an ill-usion and it will lead to disease, a lack of ease. You will become tense, you will become stressed. All of this is egoism, the conditioned mind. This is the power of the mind, as Sebai MAA told you. Here is another example. There was also a study done of some students in Japan, thirteen students were taken, who were allergic to poison ivy. They told the students that we are going to rub one arm with poison ivy, and one arm with a regular leaf, a non-poisonous leaf, and what they did was that they switched it on them. So when they were rubbing the arm with the poison ivy, they told the students we are rubbing the arm with a regular leaf. When they were supposed to be rubbing with a regular leaf, they said they were rubbing with poison ivy.

Guess what happened? When they rubbed the arms of all thirteen students, with the regular leaf, but they told them it was poison ivy, they all reacted. When they took the poison ivy and they rubbed it on them and told them it was a regular leaf, guess what happened, eleven out of the thirteen didn't react. That's the power of the mind.

So what are you telling your mind, what are you doing with your mind. Do you really believe that you are infinite, or unconditioned, or that whatever you want to do in life, that you can do it? That you have the capacity to be anything you want to, or are you reacting to every little harmless leaf? The world of time and space is filled with the Divine Self but you are reacting to things as if it was poison ivy. Every time something happens, you break out. You break out in anger, you break out in passion, you break out in tears, you break out in fear, you break out in anxiety, you break out in worries.

So as Sebai Maa says, this issue should really be reflected upon. Are you using the power of the mind, relative to these teachings with respect to the aspect of past present and future and the illusoriness of the time? Sebai MAA went into how time doesn't exist and how we experience time differently, according to our actions in what we are doing. He also talked about how you come back to this lecture hall every week and from week to week you're going to think that this is the same place and nothing has changed, as if it is the same because from week to week it doesn't seem as if its changed but yet it has.

Time is illusory; we have this idea that the past exists because we can remember it to some degree, but where is our past? It's in our memory and not in existence; only the present exists. If you are driving a car and you stop right there, you look behind, and there is no past, because in the past, you were not where you were in that moment, you were back there and when you are to look back there, you are remembering you were back there, but you are not back there now. So the whole thing has changed up already, it's not the same, your memory is not the same, or what you are saying is the past, it's gone.

And the same you do with your future, you are definitely not there as yet, even with this relative term of speaking, but you can create it, you can bring all of the subtle elements out of the *"akash"*, (ether) to bring it in, to make it whatever it is that you want, because at this level you believe in appearances, you believe in the concreteness of the world, you believe in what you see, in what your eyes tell you, what is subtle, what does not appear, it is harder to believe in, you forget it a lot more easily. This is why it is said: *'amma su en pa neter, sauu – k su emment en pa neter au tuanu ma qeti pa haru'*; give thyself to the Divine, keep thyself daily for the Divine and let tomorrow be as today.

The teaching is written this way because its practice has to be done every day. This is because the world is as if hammering away at you, again, and again, moment to moment. So how are you counteracting this hammering effect… one, two hours on Sunday ain't gonna do it and your Shedy disciplines a little haphazard here and there, ain't gonna do it. Twenty-four hours a day it's there, turn the TV anytime there it is again, and again. The commercials, the programs, people going here, there, doing this or that… again, and again, are persistent. Do this, buy this, get this, to be happy, etc.

And this is the beauty of the Kemetic spiritual discipline; this is the beauty of Sema. Sema means Yoga, Union of the two ends, union of the higher self and the lower self. This is the beauty of it and the integral path, because it allows you to be whatever you are, whatever you are doing at any moment, to be able to, at the same time, have this awareness of that which is good, which is beautiful. To use that power of your mind, if you don't use it, it is going to abuse you.

It is difficult, it is hard, how can I remember, I keep forgetting. Well every time you forget, do you realize you are remembering? Every time you remember you forget, you are remembering, so that is what you have to do, you have to keep more and more, oh I forgot again, oh I'm not doing, every time you say that you are doing. So if you can have more moments of realizing you are not there, each of those moments are times when you become present in the present moment, which is the only place where you can find yourself and come into harmony with your true essence.

So it is a process of training the mind, through the devotional practices, through the divine singing, through the drumming. That's important, because you have an emotional capacity. Don't tell me 'oh it is so hard to love God or the Goddess', because when you can go home and I'm sure I can ask you to write a list of things that you love in life, the things which appear wonderful to you, the things which are beautiful to you. Do you love what you do, your family, friends, pets, home, city, etc? You can turn those loving emotions into the Divine. You have an intellect, so listen to the teachings, and study the teachings.

So, you are going through the world, your mind is working, maybe it is just the repetition of the hekau, whatever your hekau is that you meditate on. Om maati maakheru, if your mind is on Om maati maakheru, it can't be like… oh that's so beautiful over there. Because you going to think O Maati maakheru is the most beautiful thing and she is everywhere.

So you have your wisdom teachings, you have your meditations, meditations to give you that experience of what it means to put everything aside; and what happens when you put everything aside and you get that stillness, so you get that sense of discovery, that beauty, and which one am I leaving out. The one that is probably most significant for most people, the one that really steals them away. Which one, which discipline did I not mention… I said wisdom. I know the Answer, I'm asking though. Go through them, use that mind, the power of the mind, use it, what did I just say, what did I just go through, what things did I relate them to. What did I talk about, I talked about meditation, what did I talk about? I talked about studying, what else did I talk about? What was the first one I mentioned?

So emotions we talked about and then your actions. This is where people get caught and trapped; because this world of time and space is about what?

Everything changes, everything is moving. So how can we become steady and still, even while you are moving? How can we become the action less actor? This is what gets people trapped and then they start doing something, but who is doing it…

I'm doing it. Who did this? I did it.

Whether it is good or bad, right; I did it. And in that "I", who is the doer, the actor? Is it the Divine Self acting through me, flowing through me, doing whatever it is that is being done? Is my mind on the fact that all of this is an illusion? Okay so if this is an illusion, then… "I kind of am the Self", I don't really exist. So what I'm doing, doesn't really exist; so the objects I'm doing this to doesn't exist. So is anything really being done here. Kind of takes the fun out of it doesn't it? Takes that little ego, pulls the plug in that little ego, and deflates it. It's like you are feeling so wonderful, because you did this, you are doing such a thing, it's like oh, I don't exist. Oh I'm not doing it anyway. Oh nothing is being done anyway. And yet so many wonderful things are being done in spiritual personalities.

At the same time it is all, in a way, nothing relative to the world of time and space. But it is a nothing that must occur, that must happen. So self-less service is a very important discipline to practice, feeling yourself as the Divine, flowing through you. And a way to do that is also by actually setting aside time to volunteer. To go somewhere, because every action in your life is supposed to be self-less service, but one of the requirements to success in that is training. You need to go someplace, where you are really doing it. Where you do not need anything, you are not wanting anything, asking for anything; you are just giving yourself to it. That allows you to start to cultivate, what it feels like, how it is.

To really give yourself to something without asking for anything in return, is the deeper issue. As you continue to practice it, as you continue to apply it, in every aspect of your life, even though you get a paycheck at the end of the week, it becomes kind of meaningless to you. The tree does what it does. It gets whatever nourishment it gets from the earth to sustain it.

It just does what it does, it gets what it needs. So you take your paycheck, that's fine, but you didn't work for the paycheck. You work for what is called "purity of heart"; you work for becoming aware of your true essence, becoming one with that true essence. You work for dispelling the illusion. The illusory mind that constantly says, "I'm the one who is doing this", "I'm the one who is doing this job". I'm so tired now. My boss wants me to stay later and I'm tired.

I'm the one that is tired.

So the teachings must be applied; and if they are applied as yoga, as Sema, as a spiritual philosophy science, with a formula, if it's applied, in the way that the teachings are given, the results will be had. And the results are that peace and that oneness and that bliss that is your true essence. And that is being able to walk around and see the Divine everywhere, in all things and be absorbed in that beauty all the time and not be distracted or disturbed, by the…, even though you are existing in the world of time and space and you are recognizing objects. You are not becoming mesmerized by them. You are not lost by them, lost into them; absorbed into them.

And one last comment, that Sebai MAA made and I saw the note takers didn't actually note on this. Hmmm, so I just wanted to repeat it again, because I thought it was pretty profound. (*Laughter*)It just sounds like one of those things to be meditated upon. When your body does not get in the way of your intellect of observing the truth, then you have transcended your body, then you have transcended it. So when your body does not get in the way of observing truth, you have transcended it.

So there you are, say you are meditating and observing truth that way. Then there is a sensation in the face, a little pain in the back.

Is it getting in the way of you observing truth? Do you have to stop the process of what you are doing with your mind, to try to observe truth, to correct it, to go to it, to deal with it? You have a little cold, a little sneezing, can you not study the teaching, can you not be a wonderful, gentle, sweet personality? Do you have to yell at somebody, do you have to be grouchy and grumpy? Because you have a cold, because you don't feel well, cause the body is not doing well? Are you complaining, or can you be your blissful self?

Your car is your vehicle, your car is here, and say your car is broken down. Are you going to be complaining, oh my engine is bad, my transmission is bad, my fluids are not pumping through. No you walk away from the car and you don't feel bogged down, because of the car on a personal level. You feel bogged down because you don't have transportation, but not on a personal level. Your body is not absorbed with it. So likewise as you said like Steven Hawking, your mind can fly free of the body and that is something to be cultivated. So when the body starts its little complaints, you have to be kind of like your childhood. You want your child to grow up strong.

If you have a little child and the child is complaining about every little thing that bothers them. Every little thing bothers them, are you going to encourage that in your child? Everything his friend does or says "oh he hit me, oh he said he didn't like me, oh he said my toys are not good". What are you going to tell your child? 'Oh he is terrible, oh yes your toys are not good, he shouldn't say that. Its okay don't worry about it, that's how it is, don't worry about it, and go on, it doesn't matter. So when your body starts to tell you all these little things, what will you tell it. Oh yes, that feels very bad, oh yes. You can be aware of it, but you have to have this whole conversation with it and bring it down to a reality, so that it shifts you. And if it brings you there, does it have to shift you away from yourself? Sure you can be aware that your car is broken, but you don't have to identify with the car, I'm broken.

So you can be aware that there is a stomach ache going on and it hurts, but you don't have to identify, I am hurt. I have a stomach ache, or if you say I, you better know who that I is. So when your body does not get in the way of your intellect observing the truth, you have transcended it. So I think that is a good practice, a good awareness to spend a week, just being aware of how many times your body does get in the way of observing the truth.

Another example is, you walk by a Burger King or McDonalds fast food joint or whatever it is, still maybe you have a little something in there left. You smell that and you are tempted; those of you who are trying to become vegetarian know, because you go through a phase after becoming vegetarian, when you stop eating meat. You know those smells that still come to you. It takes a while before they are not even noticeable by you anymore or at least not troubling, not enticing, where your mind is not focused on it. It is like that picture, where you are not tuning into it anymore, because you have shifted your awareness, to something more profound than that. You have shifted your awareness to a deeper understanding of health. So that it doesn't bother you anymore.

Hetep. - *End of Seba Djas' Comments*.

MEDITATION ON PRINCIPLE #1

Sebai MAA: Hetep. (four times) Response from attendees (four times)

We will have a brief meditation on the first teaching of the Kybalion. The universe is mental. All is mind.

A brief meditation: Closing your eyes, sitting with your back straight, allowing your abdomen to expand as you breathe in, allowing it to contract towards your spine as you breathe out. Right now we are going to concentrate on being aware of the present.

This will be a guided meditation. Wisdom meditations are always guided meditations; Reflections on the wisdom teachings, leading to a one pointed reflection on a single thought. Breathing in …., one, two, three, four. Breathing out …., One, two, three, four. Being aware of the breath as it comes in and out of the body. Be aware of the posture, the position in which you are sitting, being aware of the room that you are in and the sounds that you can hear. Be aware of your body the way it feels. Are you tired? Are you energetic? Are you excited?

These are forms of thought; this is your mind perceiving this limited reality of the universe. Coming to a little bit deeper awareness, let us be aware now of that which in you which is aware of those sense perceptions, the "I am" in you.

That is the higher reality, the deeper reality. Consider that when your body is experiencing or when it is not experiencing. Both those times you are still experiencing, you are aware of not experiencing. So therefore awareness is the higher principle, the higher reality within you and you are aware in your mind. So therefore you are more mind than body, you are not the body, and you are not the senses, not the physical world. Not things you derive pleasure for, from, or things that you hate. You are none of those things.

Most people think their mind and body are one and the same, that their mind-body is their personality. If you learn the reality of this teaching, you can begin to have an existence that transcends time and space, meaning that you live in your higher self, the higher self that experiences through your mind. You cease to externalize yourself and lose yourself to the world of time and space, which leads to all the miseries of life. In your mind nothing can touch you, nothing can hurt you, and nothing can take anything away. You can have everything and since the world is a reflection of everything that you are, you can have everything in the world of time and space also. If you only realize that all is Mind, the universe is Mental. In this sense the universe is a mental projection of the mind of God, the All Mind, which if you can discover, becomes your reality also and thus you become one with the source of that projection.

Think of the thoughts that are coursing through your mind, the voice, the sound that you are hearing acts like an anchor to guide you through this meditation. But if I was to cease talking for a minute, where would your thoughts lead you?

Attempt now for the next minute to reflect on the teaching you have just heard. As you continue breathing, allow your abdomen to expand, as you breathe in, contract in towards your spine now as you breathe out. Continue now that awareness, I am Mind and all is Mind.

If the Mind strays it is because you have not understood fully that you are the awareness in the mind, the controller of the Mind, you have lost yourself in the world of time and space. And you can think great philosophy, but thinking is not reality, awareness is the higher reality, awareness that all is Mind. So therefore reflect that all the thoughts that pass through your mind, all of these are projections, projections that you have created, but who is the Creator. Don't attempt to stop the thoughts, allow them to just go on, but just become aware of them; aware that you are the one who is aware of them. And practice in this way, allowing yourself to strengthen that awareness, not holding on to any thoughts, dreams or fantasies; Concentrating on the fact that you are the witnessing consciousness. Om hetep, hetep, hetep.

(Response) Hetep.

For those of you who want to follow the path of wisdom, this is a wisdom meditation, such as we would practice in the Temple of Aset and in the Temple of Djehuty also. For those of you, who want to follow this practice, you should continue in this way, as we will continue with the teaching of the Kybalion next time, and expand on this first principle. Hetep.

QUESTION. The Question is, one of the things that I said that order is an artificial construction of the mind. It is a concept created by the mind and if that is so, why is it so important to become orderly or to study the order of nature, in order to discover the meaning of the universe, or the higher reality behind the nature of the universe.

Sebai MAA: One of the answers to this Question comes from the creation myth itself. In the Anunian creation myth but actually all of the creation myths contains this. The Anunian creation myth, the Menefer creation myth, and other Kemetic/Neterian (Ancient Egyptian) creation myths tell about how, in the beginning there was undifferentiated consciousness and then that undifferentiated consciousness became differentiated into the forms of Creation. The analogy is of water; the primordial consciousness that brought existence into being through cosmic mind is likened to water.

Undifferentiated consciousness is like water in the sense that if you put water in your freezer and you put it in the ice tray you can make little ice cubes; now you are conditioning the water; the water is taking on a particular form it will hold as long as the temperature stays cold enough. You are bringing order to the water. If you let the water warm up it will go back to its original state, it goes back to its undifferentiated state, the amorphous state. Anything and everything that can perceive with mind in the world of time and space has been conditioned into a form but in reality it is composed of coagulated consciousness. Your thoughts are the same, composed of undifferentiated consciousness but given form by your desires, opinions, feelings, etc. However, as soon as you condition your thoughts, they start to revert to the unconditioned state, that's what we are talking about so you have to hold them with your will, with your feelings, thoughts, desires, etc. In the world also, no matter how solid thoughts, desires or worldly objects may appear to be, no matter how abiding they may appear to be, they eventually go back to the undifferentiated state. And that is the original state; that is the underlying state. But the objects of nature can persist for a long time just as the perception of worldly objects by the human mind can persist but that persistence in the human mind is due to ignorance and desire. So once ignorance and desire subside then too the persistence of the perception of the objects of time and space as real and abiding also subsides and thereby a human being can discover a reality that transcends the apparent, though illusory solid appearance of time and space reality. Therefore, time and space is a relative reality and not an abiding reality because it is relative to a different time and space, the mental time and space. But the mental time and space is also relative to something that transcends time and space altogether and that is the ultimate and abiding goal.

Now nature has been conditioned in such a way, that it can become a teacher for human beings and that is one of the functions of nature, is to be a teacher of this philosophy, of this understanding. Nature also gives a venue for human life to exist. Think about it, if the sun did not consistently keep on shining, if the sun was not continually turning and you get a period of darkness, a period of light. If the moon was not in its position, to keep the world steady, the world would be wobbling all over the place. If there was no order to these things, there would be no capacity to have coherent existence, no ability to learn the wisdom of the underlying essence of nature.

What I'm saying may sound a little bit paradoxical. What I'm getting at is…, let's say that I'm telling you to study a book, find any subject, study a book on history, but I tell you, while you are studying the book, turn around in a circle.

How can you turn around while you are trying to read the book? No you have to stop, you have to sit down, you have to take it in an orderly way and read calmly while keeping your head steady and then you can start to understand if you are in harmony. In chaos, if you are in the undifferentiated state.

What are you going to be able to understand about anything if you are distracted, disturbed, agitated? What are you going to understand about yourself if you are diffused with everything else? There has to be a certain order, you have to have a demarcation line, you have to put this next to this and then see how this relates to that. If everything is undifferentiated, everything is related, everything is homogenous.

And even though that is the original state, actually it is the continuing underlying state even now though it is not perceived with the gross and ignorant mind; nevertheless, you have to come to some kind of basic order before you can come to understand that, as a human being using a human mind. You can't understand the undifferentiated state, which is amorphous, unconditioned, disorganized, etc. without coming to an order, in other words, in the mind, in the way of thinking and understanding. Once there is proper understanding, then it is possible to reflect back and then to be able to see what that undifferentiated state is. So it is necessary for an aspirant to gain an appreciation for the whole philosophy and step away from individual objects just as an artist painting a picture, if she stands two inches from the picture, can't see the picture; She has to separate, to detach, to put some distance between herself and the picture in order to gain some perspective and discern the order of how things fit with other things on the canvas and see the order that she wants to discover in the artwork. Separation is order in this sense because the separation causes the opposites to come into being. When she is close to the canvas she is as if one with it and cannot see the whole because when is on top of it and one with it. When she steps away from the canvas, then she is separating from the object and thereby causing opposites to come into existence, herself and the object, the canvas.

If you are together with the object, then you can't discern it, because you are one with it. Without a mirror, how can you see yourself? You can see yourself because you are contained within yourself. Nobody can see their own face, have you ever seen your own face, really, except for a mirror. Nobody can see their own face, because it is all you. You can see other people's faces. But think about it ..., if you had your face right in front of somebody else's face, can you see their face, no you can't, you are going to see a part of it if anything. So there has to be that order that separation and with the understanding that, that order and that separation, that duality, is illusory, it is temporal and transient, it is limited.

All that appears to be going on, at the end of another billion or two years, the sun will stop shining, all of this will dissolve and go back to its state where it came from before the sun came into being. So what does that mean? And speaking from a cosmic point of view, the order of the universe, is created and sustained by God. And to God all of this is as if not really happening. It is happening like say in an instant. All of these billions of years that we experience, they occur for God in an instant. So actually, the closer you raise your consciousness to God consciousness, the more you realize that this is actually not even happening now, as we speak. It appears to be happening but if you realize that something is not real and therefore, not happening in its beginning or in its end, then it is also to be realized that it never happened in the middle of when it appeared to be happening, just as upon waking up you realize that a dream you had during the night was not real and never happened, even though it seemed real and compelling while it was being experienced during the night.

What I'm getting at is that, you come from a standpoint of ignorance as an aspirant and you begin to learn this teaching, that the world is an illusion and time doesn't exist, doesn't really happen and all of this kind of thing. You can't follow it right now, because you're just coming into it, you are just trying to get over the conditioning that you have in you, the illusory reality you are caught up in. Let's say in another year or two or ten, you do realize it fully. That's like waking up and seeing your dream, your life, this world of time and space, the politics, the history, your family, your desires, your personality, etc. didn't exist because they were merely forms changing in time and space, forms composed of transcendental and immortal consciousness that coagulated into those forms temporarily and you held those forms together based on your ignorance and desires. Your dream is an illusion, it is something that appear to be happening but didn't really. It appeared to be real while it was happening and if you realized that at the end of your dream, that means that the periods during your dream and before your dream were/are also illusory.

So think about the dimensions, implications, the ramifications of these teachings. And you have to train yourself, through the disciplines that have been discussed in order to have that realization. You have to live the life of virtue, you have to study and apply yourself and so on and so forth. And part of that is bringing a certain degree of order to your life. The people who want to be free and happy go-lucky and you know, don't want to go to work, just want to hang out at the beach, that's not being …, discovering the undifferentiated state of the spirit. That's loafing in the world of time and space; that is just hanging out.

So a differentiation has to be made and only enlightened people are able to be free and happy go-lucky so as to have this truly relaxed awareness of life. Otherwise you are always going to be *in tension* to some degree. Remember that we said, in a few lectures before, faith is the first step that allows you to start relinquishing some of that anguish, worry and anxiety and so on and so forth. But that will not free you fully; faith alone cannot free you fully, only understanding can do that, only enlightenment can do that.
 Hetep.
End of lecture on Principle of Mind.

PRINCIPLE OF MIND   Q & A

Commentary by Seba Dja

About the use of drugs, the drugs damage the nervous system and therefore the wiring now is damaged, therefore the Life Force energy, is trying to flow through the wiring, but the wiring is damaged.

So, sometimes, there are going to be limitations on how much healing can take place, even though you can apply the principle.

Sometimes it's irreversible, but to whatever degree you can apply the principle, there can be some benefits for each personality. But ultimately, it may involve them dying to come back to a new body, to have that chance to try again.

Some of the impressions though, the intense impressions will carry over into their lifetimes, so they still have to deal with those impressions, those *"seed"* impressions, those egoistic impressions. Life will put them into another situation, a different situation where perhaps the impressions of the egoistic tendencies are not brought out. Maybe they are put into a family, where a family is very giving, very charitable, very benevolent, that actually allow those impressions to start to dissipate a little bit to open up.

So the whole movement is very positive and very good, but a psychotic state is not the same state as a lucid mind, when we talk about the state where you can commune with yourself, that is the state where the mind is lucid, it's like the sky without any cloud. You can commune with the sun; you can see the sun freely.

Nothing is obstructing it; there is no blockage to that. That free communication, that free experience of your true essence and that is the pure mind. That is where you can communicate with yourself.

The agitated mind is the state between that, where most people find themselves and that is like the sky. You have the beautiful sun, then you have a bunch of clouds, fluffy clouds, clouds come, clouds go, the sun is covered sometimes, it is not covered sometimes and that is where most people are in the agitated state.

End of Seba Djas' Comments.

Chapter 2: The Principle of Correspondence

We welcome those of you who are coming to visit us, to study the practice of our religion: Shetaut Neter. In this lecture we will discuss the principle of the Kybalion that relates to the concept of "Correspondence." Before going forward we should understand that the practice of religion has three main steps and those are myth, ritual and mysticism or metaphysics. The myth talks about the story of a religion. Myth does not necessarily relate to factual events or histories but provides facts about spiritual truths that transcend histories; it gives an idea as to the origins of a people, their spiritual beliefs, the form of the Divinity that they believe in as well as it informs the customs and traditions of a society and more. It gives their culture a character and the rituals related to that myth are the manner in which the people practice certain traditions, certain acts that relate them to the myth, their origins and the divinities and spiritual forces they look to so as to give them purpose in life, to give life meaning.

Chanting and divine singing is a part of the devotional aspect of ritual. Uttering the Divine name, as we have, the words of power that elevate our consciousness takes us to a different vibration. We may be doing many things in the world, but when we come here and we do the divine singing and chanting and hear the vibrations of the drumming and so on and so forth, then we are transported into a different quality of feeling, that allows us to be better in touch with the spiritual planes and the mythic teaching.

There is another important aspect of the teaching, and this is an aspect of ritual practice, it is the study of spiritual scriptures. In the beginning of the process we are studying myth, we are simply telling the story, but when we discuss the teaching related to the myth, then we are doing the ritual of wisdom spiritual practice, the study of the teaching, studying the wisdom teaching, which is what we are about to do now.

Currently we are studying the myth, if you will, the mythic teaching of the Kybalion. The Kybalion is a collection of Hermetic teachings, teachings as we said last time that are related to the ancient Egyptian God Djehuty. We talked about the history of Djehuty, how he emerged, within the whole family of Kamitan gods and goddesses, the Neteru. Let's look again at an image of Djehuty, he is the Divinity on the right who is looking at the balance scales; that is Djehuty.

Above: from the Papyrus of Ani, the soul of Ani (far left) observes the balance of his heart.

You see him with his scribe equipment. He is the one who brought the Medtu Neter, the words of power, to the physical plane and, as we said earlier, he is known as "the thrice-greatest one." He is three times great; and what this relates to is the three worlds in which he operates or in which his wisdom extends. This brings us right into our teaching for today, which is related to the next great principle of the Kybalion. Last time we discussed the mental universe, how the universe is mental; How everything exists, emerges and is perceived in and through the mind, the mind of God, or the Goddess, if you will, and human beings experience a microcosm of that reality through their mind, because they create their own reality based on their capacity for perception which is limited by their aryu which may be pure and enlightened or impure and ignorant.

Remember we discussed that the reality you perceive with your senses is an illusory reality. It is not the absolute reality. We also discussed that there is no time, and that time itself is also illusory, and many of you were taken with that conception. Actually, time is a mental construct, created by the human mental process, to judge the passage or the transformation of energies. You see a car driving on the street and you say the car is over here, and couple seconds later the car is over there. You say time has passed, but actually no such thing as time exist and this was proven by ..., (this teaching comes from thousands of years). But this was proven in the twentieth century by Einstein, with his theory of relativity. You see, anything that is relative, if you can bend something, if you can change something. If something is changeable, it is unreal, it is relative. It is variable. Only that which is abiding, can be said to be real. Therefore that brings the question, what is abiding in you, what is real about you. You are born into this world and you grow older, you go through your adolescent years, then you grow as an adult; you get older, then you get sick, then you die. Did you notice that there is a sequence of events that "happen" or "seem" to happen? In reality nothing is happening but in a sequence things appear to move, interact, change form, etc. but actually the matter that composes the objects in Creation that seem to move and change, from birth to death, etc. actually does not change. The underlying essence of Creation, the energy, the consciousness that composes the apparent objects of Creation, including your body, does not change. Rather, Creation and all the objects in it are a projection of that underlying essence. This means that the world that is perceived by the senses, the world that seems so "solid" and "real", has no more abiding quality than a dream you may have when you sleep at night. So then we need to ask: what is the reality behind you? Did you exist in the beginning? Did you exist when you were an adult? Do you exist when you are an elderly person, when you are on your deathbed, etc.? Did you exist before you were born and do you exist after you die? What is the reality behind all of that?

These are the questions that have intrigued spiritualists and mystics since the beginning of time. These brief teachings are the hallmark of their discoveries since ancient times, when they entered into internal research, research into themselves. The first great discovery and teaching that they came up with was that the universe is mental. Not only is the universe mental, everything is created by mind. Everything exists in and through the mind. There is no physicality and you recall that in the past we discussed that this wisdom predates the discoveries the discoveries of modern quantum physicists of the twentieth century like Fritjof Capra and Stephen Hawking, and their discoveries almost make them sound like the mystics of ancient Egypt. That is because they are also saying that the universe is not physical, that the universe is energy. This is what the Kybalion and other Ancient Egyptian texts have said for thousands of years, long before these concepts were confirmed by modern science including quantum physics.

So, if the physical world is not actually solid, where does that leave us? Why does the universe feel so concrete and real? Why do your life events and experiences seem so real and compelling and so abiding? Remember what we discussed last time; we talked about how, in a dream, when you are in a dream, you are perceiving with your dream senses. When you are on your bed, you are not using your physical senses, to be aware of the physical world. Yet you are aware of the astral world, your dream world. And if someone was to come and say to you, hey this dream world isn't real, this dream world is not solid, it is illusory, what would you say to that person in your dream?

That dream seems compelling, doesn't it, that dream seems solid and real. If you were to find a stone in your dream world, that you can touch, the stone would feel hard but yet it is not real. If there is someone there talking to you or if there is some terrible aggressive thing that is happening, somebody is running after you with a knife, etc. It all seems very compelling, very real, very fearful and you might even feel you will be killed. Or somebody is beating you up, or you have a car crash and you can feel all the tumultuous problems; and yet when you wake up in the morning, what happens to your real, solid, abiding dream? What happens to your compelling dream? You discover that it wasn't so compelling after all.

When you go to sleep at night actually, you are going to sleep to the physical world and you are waking up to the astral world. If someone was to ask you, when you are in the dream world, what do you think about the physical world? What would you say at that point? What would you say then? In the dream state you are so convinced of the reality of the dream world, that you say, "oh that physical world, 'that's not real." Then later, when you wake in the morning to the "physical" world again, you say the dream world is not real. So, which is the real?

What about when you go to sleep and when there are no dreams, what is happening there? What do you say then about the "physical" world and the "dream" world at that point? The idea is that, philosophically speaking, none of these worlds are real, the physical world is not real, and the astral world is not real, and your dreamless sleep world is not real. Yet there must be something that is real, because we are experiencing something, aren't we?

The conception behind those "worlds", the understanding behind that is real; the consciousness that is aware of those worlds is real. Consciousness is like the ocean and your dream world are like waves on top of that ocean. Every once in a while you come out from the depths of your conscious awareness that is beyond dreams, physicality and duality to swim and for some reason you come to think that the swimming is the real and that the underlying essence supporting the swimming, the depths of the ocean, is somehow something illusory. Sometimes you come out so much to swim, that you forget about the depth of the ocean. And therefore, since you have forgotten about the depths, you come believe and say that there is no spirit world, or there is no deepness to me, I'm just who I am, it's my body and my feelings and emotions, that is me. People say those things without realizing that in reality that's their surface, their swimming on the surface and that's all they know about themselves. That becomes their reality and from our perspective that is what we call spiritual ignorance and this is the source of feelings of mortality, limitation, mental frailty as well as all manner of sufferings that a human being can experience in life.

If you ignorant to this metaphysical philosophy, you if you were swimming, say on the coast of Florida, you have a certain myth about your existence; you are a Floridian, and if you should meet somebody who swims on the surface on the coast of Spain, they have a different myth about their reality and existence. And if you two should meet, then you say to each other, well my myth is the reality, because that's what I know, I swim in Florida and I'm a Floridian and you who say that you are from Spain, I don't know about that reality, that's a dream to me so your reality is not real to me and therefore it is also not valid. This is how bigotry, intolerance and animosity between peoples, cultures and societies begin. That is also how people who practice the first level and perhaps the second level of religion, the myth and ritual, feel and talk about those who practice the metaphysical level, which is deeper. Those who are the mythic and or ritual practitioners are swimming on the surface of spirituality and therefore cannot perceive the depth of their own nature nor the depth of the natures of other human beings or of Creation itself and therefore their life is on the surface of perceptions of reality based on the senses and their ego idea of who and what they are. In other words, the higher reality, the spiritual reality, the transcendental reality, is lost to them, beyond their ideas, concepts and ability to fathom.

For people who swim in the shallows of life, the myth aspect of religion is like the surface of the ocean of existence; the myth and the ritual part of religion are like the surface of the perceivable "physical" Creation and of the perceivable "dream" world of the ocean of mind. In this context, mysticism is like the vastness of the ocean of Creation, the depth. As for those people who only swim in the surface of their religion, their always going to be bound to be in conflict with other people, who swim on the surface of their religion too. If people were able to discover the depths of their spirituality, they would discover that their depths are the same depths as the depths of other peoples, regardless of their religion. It's the same essential depth and they all would discover the reality of all of our existence, all existence. Therefore there should be no conflict in religious practice and yet there is in the world, because we are carrying on in an ignorant, limited fashion.

The deeper reality behind you as a new born child is the same reality behind your adolescent years, the same reality behind your adult years, and the same reality behind your elderly years. The same reality behind all that is the same reality behind your dream world when you are asleep and dreaming. It sustains your dreamless sleep world. And it is the same reality behind other people's apparent surface realities as well as the same reality sustaining nature, the planets, stars, galaxies, etc. So, beyond the apparently real but actually illusory solid and physical reality of the waking and the dream states what would you say if someone were to ask you how did you sleep and during your sleep you did not have any dreams? You might say, "I didn't have any dreams, but I knew I was happy, I know I was relaxed, I knew I was feeling full. How did you know you were relaxed, feeling fullness and happiness? That is possible because there is something that is the depth of you beyond the physical, dream and dreamless sleep levels of existence and perception.

Think about it. Think about sometime when someone has come to wake you from a dream, and how you said "leave me alone, I don't want to get up. Leave me, I'm relaxed…" During those times you want to go back to your sleep state, you don't want to come back to this crazy and physical world. What is that that you are enjoying so much in your dream world, that you forsake the physical world for? If the physical world is so compelling and so real, why do you leave it every day? If something is abiding, it should not stop, it should be constantly real. Why do you have to fall asleep, why do you have to leave the physical world; and then why do you wake up from the dream world or from the dreamless sleep states?

Another question is where do you go when you leave the physical world and go to the astral dream world or when you are sleeping but there are no dreams? If a group of people were to fall asleep in the same room they might all start dreaming. Where does the dream world happen? Are all the dream worlds going to start bumping into each other? Before you say that the dream world is not like the physical world, think again. Look to the quantum physicists. Now they are talking about planes that exist in the same space, as the physical universe. Right now there are intersecting worlds in different dimensions or different levels of subtlety that are just as solid and apparently real to those who perceive them. To them this physical reality is the dream. Therefore, this physical reality has no more validity than any other reality and this is what we call "relative reality". Anything that is relative, meaning relative to something else or derivative of something else, or generated by something else, is not the "abiding" reality. If something is not abiding it is relative and therefore illusory, temporary, etc.

The quantum physicists are also talking about forms of energy that permeate, that go through the more dense, the more gross, the more physical world. They sound like mystics to me. But this wisdom was known thousands of years ago. And yet why is it that these hard scientists and their new findings are not studied in school and why have the history, social science, and politics not been adjusted to take these findings into account? Modern society does not deal with their researches, because if we did, we'd have to stop the whole way of thinking that we have about the world and what would happen to the world? You might say well, the world would start crumbling, because everybody would be going crazy, with these crazy theories; I say no, I think the world would be a better place, because people would be living by truth instead of the lies and ignorance that allows a minority to deceive the masses, control society and maintain themselves in power and in wealth while the majority languishes in ignorance, suffering, poverty and locked in a perennial struggle for survival.

The reality behind a tree that is chopped down is made into furniture, and then when the furniture gets old the same wood is broken down again and it is used to make planks for a log cabin is all the same reality. That same wood is chopped into bits and made into particle board for another panel. The termites eat it out and they leave little droppings there. What is the reality behind that wood, behind the same tree, behind that same furniture, behind that same particle board? It is the same reality, but the form changes. And what is real in you, even throughout your form changes (birth, childhood, adulthood, death?

You were there as a child, you remember your childhood; you remember adulthood, your adolescence, etc. What is the reality in all of that? That's what we are talking about here. That reality that existed in the beginning of time and it came into existence so-called, at a particular time and place is the same reality at all times, before birth and during life and after death. You were born at a particular hour and you grew up and you experienced all kinds of activities. Then you die and you supposedly go out of existence. What is the answer to all this changing form and apparent passage of time? What is the reality behind you? The reality behind you is spirit and the way that you are using to "come into reality", that is, to be aware of your reality is mind.

So therefore, the universe is mental, and you, that is, what is abidingly real within you, are aware of the physical reality which is a projection of cosmic consciousness and you are projecting your reality of yourself within that cosmic reality, Creation, as well as your dream world and your dream identity. Just as you project your identity and dream world in a dream, you are sustaining the reality of your waking existence, which is a dream of the ALL MIND. The crux of the matter, from the standpoint of a spiritual aspirant, an initiate, a mystic, is of finding a way to dispel the illusion and discover the abiding reality. If that were possible then at any time you desire you could stop sustaining that illusory reality of Creation or of your dream world relative reality. The process of what we are studying here which is by engaging in three things, myth, ritual and mysticism. If you do not desire to do that, then you will stay away, stray away from those things that awaken you and remain on the surface, forever swimming in the shallows where there are storms and waves crashing into each other, where there is strife, unrest, agitation and distraction that takes one away from the truth. In that case, if you want to stay at the surface then you want to stay asleep to the higher reality. You want to stay on the surface of the ocean and you can remain so, as long as you want, but your deeper reality stays the same regardless of whether or not you are aware of it, even if you stay ignorant for a billion years.

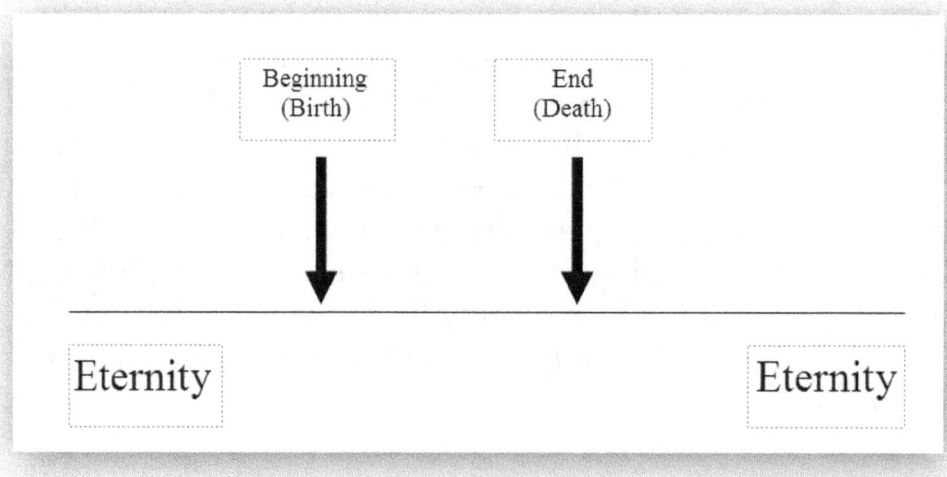

However, if you remain in ignorance, regardless of how you manifest, that period of life that you call existence, as a human being, as a male or female, as an animal, or whatever it is, that is just a segment of eternity that you are calling "time". Time is only a piece of the infinite stream of eternity. Time is the segment or span of a person's lifetime or of a set of events that occur in space but if time and space were recognized as illusory then it is also recognized that the changes and events that seem to occur in time and space are also illusory since behind all that there is eternity. That means, let's say that eternity is a line {though in reality it isn't} but let's use this idea for learning purposes. Then we begin at some point in the distant past and we are going to some point in the distant future and someone is born at a particular point on that line, then they die at this particular point on that line and the ignorant are calling the period between the point of birth and the point of death, time. We must realize that time has no existence, only eternity has existence and what you are calling a span of time is merely a mental construct, so that you can understand some passage of some physical changes that occur in space, which as we saw earlier is also illusory (physical space, dream world space, etc).

If you start to live this way, you start to become free from your physical bonds, from your limitations and your limited ideas of reality, existence and so on and you start to become more aware and more open to the eternal aspect of yourself. If you were to become fully aware of this, you would then be called an enlightened being and when you get to the end of that time span of life, "so-called", of your body's' existence, you continue to be aware of eternity, as you go along. So, having achieved that magnanimous awakening to the higher reality, death of the body does not affect you, does not bother you, and does not hinder your perception of abiding and eternal existence.

As a leaf falls from a tree, that does not bother a tree, and this is recap of what we discussed last week and taking it a few steps further, the mental reality of your perception and that mental reality of the universe is sustained by the All, the all-encompassing Divinity called

Neberdjer. Neberdjer is that essential nature of existence, the consciousness that transcends time and space as well as concepts and definitions, is that which brings forth Amun (witnessing conscience), Ra (interaction medium between witness and projection) and Ptah (projection of reality in time and space) and that brings us to the next Kybalion principle, which is the Principle of Correspondence.

There is a great teaching that is given for this principle and that is, well which I'm sure you have heard it somewhere: "As above, so below and as below, so above." And very succinctly, what this means is that Creation is an expression of the Divine, the underlying essence. When the bible says that God created Man in his image, of course the female gender is left out of that, but in the Kybalion understanding, in the Neterian understanding, the ancient Egyptian religion understanding, this teaching is given as the following definition: the entire universe is a reflection of the Spirit Being, the All Encompassing, which is termed Neberdjer. That means that, not just man, but everything that can be perceived in the universe and things that cannot be perceived in the universe, these are all reflections of the Self, the Spirit. We will develop this mystery in the following section.

The Principle of Correspondence Part 2

And once again, let's study the dream. You see, along with our study we study the microcosm and we get the answers. When we are studying dream, this is mystic psychology we are dealing with. When you have a dream, the objects in your dream are reflections of your consciousness, its expressions. You are projecting them into your dream world, you are projecting the dream world, your own idea of time and space, and you are projecting the objects in that dream world, and that dream world exists because you give it life and it id composed of your consciousness.

What happens in the dream world? When you have a dream, a friend may come up to you and starts talking to you about something that happened that day. And then in that same dream world, you turn around and you see a car driving by. You turn around again and you see there is your house, you turn around again, there is your mother, you turn around again, there is a chair and there are subtler things that happen in your dream, that you don't see happening in the physical world. You can see a tiger and somehow you know that tiger is coming after you, to eat you.

Or there is a snake, and you run away from the snake you close yourself into this hermetically sealed bubble and you say to yourself, "oh the snake can't get in here". But then, all of a sudden, the snake is at your throat. Wild things, unpredictable things, unlikely things and things that defy the rules of the physical world do occur in the dream world. In any case, this is because; you are creating the reality of your dream world. You can create the reality of your physical world too, if you have the strength and the power to do so. But for that you have to dive deep into the depths of the ocean, to get that power. You can't do that by sleeping on the surface.

Try doing that on the surface and the waves are going to push you around. That means that the physical world is going to control you. You won't have control of your existence in the physical world. You will be caught up in worldly situations, confronted with other people and their desires, ignorance and frailties. You will get caught up with theirs and your own frailties, ignorance and flawed nature. It is a mess! You will not be able to stop and reflect, but rather, you will be led and pushed around by nature. The events that may happen, the events of life that you think you are in control of, you will have no control over those, because you are on the surface.

Again, going back to our study of the dream, we said that the objects in your dream, you are projecting them. For example, if you don't look like a car in your dream, you don't look like a tree in your dream, you don't look like a chair in your dream, etc. you can change them, the color, the texture or just get rid of them, make them disappear. But why don't you? Why do those items abide in your dream and cause you to have a nightmare? All those objects, you are projecting them. All of those things and those images are composed of subtle matter given form by your consciousness. In this metaphor, you are above, and your dream is that which is below. You are projecting that dream world and the objects in it and they are a reflection of your thoughts and desires as well as your self-concept, your idea of yourself. This means that they are reflections of part of you, part of your potential, your potentiality.

Imagine all of the things you can imagine, and then think of all the things God can imagine. How many universes have there ever been? How many universes are there in existence on varied planes of existence right now? It's mind boggling to think about. If you can do what you can do with your limited mind imagine what the All Mind can do! So let's not think of, as above so below, as below so above as an exact carbon copy, this is not what we are talking about. A better way to think of it is that whatever is Created, that is, expressed by consciousness through mind and appearing as the objects of Creation, is actually composed of the Creator and therefore are the same as the Creator; therefore, whatever is below (Creation) is the same as what is above (Creator) but not all of Creation is necessarily all of the Creator. When you create a dream world it is part of you but it is not all of you. It is a piece, a fragment, an idea given form temporarily by your mind and held together for as long as your mental power can sustain it. God's power to sustain Creation goes for billions of years and then there is a receding of God's Creation back into the unformed state and then later a new expression emerges and scientists call that a "big bang."

Following up on the concept just introduced, ignorant human beings are so strongly caught up in the ego identity that their potential for expression is limited by that ego. In other worlds, you are so caught in your time and space reality that most of you, when you project yourself in your own dream, you project yourself as you are, in your physical world. If you are a male, you project yourself as a male, if you are a female, you project as a female and may use your physical world name and form.

Why should that be? Think about it. You can be anything you want to be in your dream and yet you choose to be this limited personality of the waking state; why do you that? Some of you might have expanded a little bit and you might feel a little oneness with a bird flying around and then see yourself flying, but mostly you are anchored in your physical reality. You can do anything you want to do and yet you are caught by that; why is that? Then you might say, "Well Muata, if I start going like that, they will start calling me a schizophrenic, psychotic; they will call me a nut." You are only called insane, when you project these things, into the physical world. But if you project them into your imagination, or your dream world, there is no harm done. In any case, the real insanity is the limitation since that is not who you are essentially. The continued forced imposition of the limited personality and the lack of spiritual growth, in other words, expansion of mind and discovery of the higher self, is actually the cause of insanity.

When you start believing in the physical plane, that it is abiding and or all there is, then yes, there is the source of the problem. But this is philosophy; so when you start applying metaphysical rules on the physical, there will also be trouble. You may say "Hey, I'm a bird in the astral plane, the dream plane of mind, so I'm going to fly off the building in the physical world and what happens? …splat!!! That's a problem. And therefore you must understand the teaching and not become exaggerated with it or apply it in the wrong way in the physical plane. There is an application to the physical plane but that is mostly but not exclusively limited to the physical mind. The physical plane is made gross for the purpose of giving spirit an anchor in time and space. That anchor allows human beings to have extended experiences over a period of time; otherwise there would be chaos because the experiences would be too fluid and an orderly thought and reflective process would not be possible. Think about it, how many dreams you can have in one night. If we are living in the physical plane, the way we live in the dream world, there would be no basis for consistency, no basis for you to learn and to understand reality, time to work out the mysteries of life. There needs to be a slow enough pace of time and movement of objects such that it allows sufficient time to reflect and experiment with Creation to discover its secrets. But if the space is too slow hen there will be stagnation; so time and space forces life forms to change and move on in an orderly fashion if they are willing or in a painful way if they are not willing, but all must change nevertheless. One way or another the soul moves on through experiences in time and space, to experience worldly pleasure and pain and if they are wise, to discover the source of pleasure and pain so as to alleviate and even eradicate it by discovering their own essential nature that transcends the time and space experiences altogether.

Think about it; if everything was changing every few seconds and we are sitting here, then we are sitting on the beach in Hawaii. Then we are on the moon and then we fly off to Mars. How can we sit here and have a pleasant and reflective conversation for an hour? That's what the physical plane is for. But remember what we discussed also, if we examine the physical plane, you're going to realize that it is actually changing just like your dream world, only at a slower pace. Everything changes here. Even though it looks to be the same as it did yesterday, in the same place as last week or in the same condition as last year, actually to some degree, everything is changing, little by little.

If you wait long enough, it changes completely, just like the dream world. And in the Wisdom Text of Merikara, the teachings of Merikara it is told that the Gods and Goddesses live on a different plane of time and to them, one of our years is like a day. They have a different time and space reality that they live in and that is because they live on a different plane of existence. Of course this means that our physical time and space is "relative" and also their time and space reality is also "relative" and therefore illusory. Remember, only eternity is abiding and any version of time and space is only a peace of eternity and therefore not abiding.

The teachings of the Kybalion talk about three main planes of existence and in the Ancient Egyptian system they correspond to Amun, Ra and Ptah. Now the Absolute, Neberdjer, is that from which all comes (Amun, Ra, Ptah) and that is the Divine Self, that is Spirit, that is God and that Spirit projects three main planes or levels of conscious existence in time and space. The physical plane, the mental plane and the spirit plane. Each of those planes have seven sub-planes and therefore your reality, your consciousness can be attuned to any of those planes, but mostly people are attuned to the lowest, the physical plane. Since human beings have all levels within themselves they are actually operating on all planes even if they are not aware of it. So with reflection, maturity, introspection and meditation, those other planes can be discovered consciously and this is called "enlightenment". Enlightenment is recognizing intrinsically the transcendental mystery of what Creation is and the transcendental essence of who one is, beyond the mortal, time and space reality.

Most people are so ignorant and weak that even though they use their mind, their mind is not more useful to them than the mind of a dog. But dogs have and use rudimentary mind, instinctual mind. He knows when he is hungry, he knows when he is hot, he knows when to drink water, that is rudimentary mind and not intellect so there is limited intelligence. Now we are talking about intellect. That, which separates human beings from animals, IF the human being develops beyond the animal state of consciousness, is intellect. That intellect allows a human being to become aware of the different planes and that is what makes a human being different from animals. Otherwise, if a human being does not develop, they remain at the level of animal conscious level and are not considered human but only potentially human.

Animals are only aware of their animal physical plane, their egos and their limited personalities in physical time and space. Human beings have the capacity to grow beyond that and transcend, to reach all of the planes, to awaken to a reality beyond the instinctual physical time and space level. If they should transcend and reach higher levels that go into the spirit planes and they are different gradations of spirit beings who reside in those planes. This is where the theory or teachings of angels, archangels and demons in Christianity in western culture and the Gods and Goddesses in Ancient Egyptian African religion and all of these kinds of things come from. In the African culture, the Kamitan (Ancient Egyptian) culture, it is the understanding of Akhus. Akhu is a glorious spirit being, people who have become enlightened, who have become shining stars. They discover the higher planes of existence where the gods and goddesses reside but also even transcending that, to discover the abiding, absolute transcending all levels of time and space.

The Akhu are people who have reached such power and elevation that they are called Gods and Goddesses and they have an effect on the other planes, on the lower planes and therefore it is said that, the wise ones serve the higher planes and rule the lower. In this way, one operates the laws, instead of being a slave to them. The Kybalion teaching, also says that. These people, all these Gods and Goddesses, these Akhus, spirits, Saints, Sages and so on and so forth, who have slipped off their bodies and who live in the spiritual plane, help assist people on the astral level and on the physical level. This follows exactly with the teaching of the Asarian Resurrection teaching of Ancient Egypt.

Let us recall that in the Asarian Resurrection[9] teaching where Asar sends a letter to the court who is judging between Heru and Set. He tells them, "you know, all you Gods and Goddesses, who don't want to judge this situation rightly; your all going to have to die one day, you are all going to have to come to me, the God of the Dead in the Netherworld, to the Supreme Abode and you if you do not do what is righteous you will suffer at that time. You may think you can get away, to escape your fate; you may have existed for millions of years,

---

[9] See the book *African Religion Vol. 4 Asarian Theology* bu Muata Ashby

but at the end you have to end even your astral existence as gods and goddesses." This means that everything other than the Self, the Spirit is relative, it is a projection, it is temporal, it is ephemeral, and consequently, it all will come to an end one day.

If you were to start living your life according to this understanding, how will you live your life? That is the Question. What will you do with your life? How would you reflect on the world and your own existence? How would you develop yourself? Would you walk around like everybody else in the dream world, or would you be walking on air? The Kybalion also says that even though the reality of the world is perceived in such a gross manner and even though it is an unreality, even though it is relative, the Kybalion says, quote 'the court of reason must be hospitably received and treated with respect'.

This is a Kybalion way of saying that, even though we are saying that, even though the world appears to be real to the senses, according to factual scientific evidence and reflection on the mysteries of mind, the wisdom born of those evidences and reflections is higher than the perceptions of the senses and therefore the wisdom must be affirmed over the impressions of the senses. If this is done then one is said to be living by truth; to do otherwise is living in accordance and under the control of the illusion in the mind which believes in the information brought to it by the illusory senses. This is the same thing that the physicists are now saying, that the mysticists have been saying for thousands of years. Even though the practical reality is that matter appears to be solid and abiding, in reality, a car, for instance, is unreal, the car is an illusion; the car is a mental construct. Metal, physical matter, rock, stone, everything you perceive with the senses is illusory. However, from a practical level matter exists in a relative sense and to that extent it is consequential. Even though the physical world is illusory, from a higher level of consciousness, it has practical consequences and therefore is to be respected; a car that is speeding along at 60 miles an hour, you don't get in front of it. Dynamite is not a reality, but don't strap dynamite to yourself and blow yourself up. Don't put a gun to your head. Yes it's unreal, but respect it anyway.

Be hospitable to the world. Live according to the rules of the physical plane. This is what the Kybalion is saying, and explore these things internally, that's what we are really getting at. If you respect the relative reality but do not assign it the status of abidingly real, then you have a chance to dispel its illusion even as you live and interact in the physical world. This is being in the world but not being deluded by it and therefore caught up in the snare of worldly pain, sorrow and disappointments.

Explore these things within yourself, enlighten yourself. As above, so below; as below, so above. Then the great reality behind this teaching is discovered. So, what is experienced in the higher planes corresponds to what is experienced in the lower planes. From the perspective of inner awareness, consciousness that manifests as the world of time and space and physical reality is a reflection of, a projection of and therefore, correspondent with the consciousness that projected it, that expresses as it. The higher you go, all these different gradations of planes of existence, you discover that there is no like gate between them, a specific door, etc… These things are related to level of vibrations, levels of consciousness that you become aware of through your own vibration; and that is the next great teaching of the Kybalion, that we will discuss next time.

(Om htp, htp, htp). End of lecture.

QUESTIONS AND ANSWERS

The Question is when you dream something, you have never seen or heard of before, or a thought or conception comes to you, that you were previously unaware of, where does that come from?

Answer There are a few sources, as we discussed a few minutes ago, an idea can be placed in your mind, by your previous experiences, your aryu of the past in this life or of past lifetimes and your experiences leaves residues in your unconscious and those unconscious residues, when they resonate with a outside stimuli, they are caused to sprout into thoughts and desires, that lead you to certain actions and whereas as we said before, if you are a surface personality, you are not going to be able to control your desires, you are not going to be able to control your acts. You act according to your instinct, with your inner feelings, with your hormones. People like that are called slaves to the world; they are not real human beings, according to the teaching. That is one source, from your previous experiences that impels and or compels you to act in the physical world, to desire, imagine, in the physical or dream realms.

Another source is from your present experiences, your imaginations, your fantasies. If you are a person who is given to fantasy, you learn how to come up with ideas and you aspire to do that and so on and so forth and you are essentially creating illusions. So, another source of imaginations, your fantasies is according to your character, your ethics or lack thereof, which is based on your previous aryu.

Another source is that you can be influenced by higher beings, by gods and goddesses, saints and sages, as well as negative beings and those we call demons. We call them "sebau", which are fiends. Which merely means people or spirits who have negative tendencies, who are unrighteous; these people who lived or live unrighteous lives while alive and then they go on to a certain plane and then they become unrighteous forms of energy for a time. And like seeks like, alike attracts alike. If you are a righteous person, you are going to attract righteous energy to you, good things to you. If you are a negative personality then the opposite occurs.

Have you ever noticed that when you travel to a different country, a different city, whatever it is, isn't it interesting how you attract to yourself the same type of friends, the same type of people, the job you get, etc. You don't get or befriend people who are different personalities from the ones who you were with before. However, sometimes you can break from that pattern set for you by your aryu, if you make it the point to change your life, by following the dictates of the teaching and seeking out khnumt nefer or good association;

association with wise persons, sages, or at least those souls who are seeking to live up to the wisdom of higher philosophy and practice it in practical life. So these are the kinds of places where your experiences can come from. Mostly it's based on aryu from previous lives.

Sometimes you can get premonitions, if you are in touch with the higher planes of existence. That means that you are getting less in touch with physical time and more in touch with eternity. Therefore you can be like the person sitting on the bleachers at the football game. The running back is coming from one end zone, trying to get to the other. You can see the whole field from one end to the next, as opposed to the people who are right down, at game level, they can only see a piece of what's going on. So therefore you get a few little insights into what may happen in the future. But remember that this is, as the Kybalion says, take this hospitably and with respect, but not as an absolute, because what you are seeing is a possibility for the future. Not the possibility of a future that necessarily has to happen.

There is no set fate or destiny for humanity; you make that up as you go along. Whatever it is that happens, you could then say that was your fate that was your destiny to do that, whatever it is. You can't say that about the future, that you are destined to do this, or do that, because they are many variables.

Any other Questions? New York has a Question. New York group you may ask your Question.

Question You mentioned about three planes of consciousness in the form of Amun, Ra, Ptah, that is the causal, astral and physical planes respectively, all of which emanate from the one Supreme Being, Neberdjer. The three planes of consciousness have seven sub-planes as we speak. I wanted to ask what is the significance of the number seven and why is it such a special number in terms of ancient studies, based on not only the Kemetic studies, but essentially universally.

Answer:

Okay, speaking of the Kybalion now, because this is the scripture we are dealing with, although this teaching applies to other scriptures as well and namely the book of Djehuty and other scriptures that you are going to find in the new version of the Serpent Power book, but leaving that aside for now, the Kybalion states that, these seven subplanes, the reason why these are chosen is not arbitrary. The reason for the prominence of the number seven is because this is one of the primary modes in which God has chosen to manifest the world; we, that is to say, Creation, are reflecting that which is. The reflection is related mythically in the concept of the bull Asar and the seven cow goddesses that are serviced by the bull. The myth projects into time and space, the physical reality in the form of the seven colors of the rainbow, the seven notes in music, etc. However, the number seven, though it runs through Creation, is not the only significant number. There are more colors mind you, than those you see in the rainbow so the main seven are only the visible colors. The numbers 1, 3 and 9 as well as 10 and 42 are also instructive. There are other planes, and other levels of consciousness but the main seven are primary in our understanding of Creation through the wisdom of the Kybalion and other texts such as the wisdom of the Serpent Power, which treats the wisdom of the seven psycho-spiritual consciousness centers.

The universe manifests in multiples of seven, but they are other sacred numbers, like the number one, the number one the number of Spirit, the number three, the three planes of existence and Djehuty is the master of those three. He is the thrice greatest one. Then we have the seven planes of manifestation and also there is a teaching of the number nine, which you may know, being that this is a special number that is covered in physics, modern physics, as a primary mode of the manifestation of creation. So it's seven plus the two and you find multiples going into the number twenty-one, forty-two and so on and so forth. By studying the numbers, we are actually making sense of the universe, of how God has manifested the universe and these are numbers chosen by God to manifest the universe.

So in this exercise we are studying what is, through its mathematical essential nature. What I'm getting at is that, this is the basis for the reality of those numbers, it is Gods' choice. God could have chosen the number 50. God could have chosen eleven, chosen twelve, chose whatever *She* wanted to do. And so therefore, this is why we study those numbers, because this is what, how the universe is constructed. When you study music it is the same thing. Music makes sense because it follows set patterns based on how vibrations are set in Creation. So music is embedded in Creation and human beings only discover those patterns and combinations and we call those productions "songs". However, we also are to realize that all music is based on the organization of arbitrary sounds placed in an conjunction or relationship and what one person likes versus another is subjective based on their aryu but it is still based on a pleasing pattern as seen by that person so, though music is based on those patterns it is it's arbitrary in terms of what appeals to one may not appeal to another; some people like classical while others like Hip Hop, so music in terms of human culture is relative and therefore illusory. However, the patterns that reveal the essential nature of Creation, its structure and underlying form, that is enlightening and can be termed "music of the Spheres" and this is a worthy study for it is assistance to the spiritual practice that leads towards enlightenment. In this capacity, the study of the octaves and especially the diatonic scale is instructive.

Think about it, music that appeals to rappers in New York City is not necessarily going to appeal to the Pope in the Vatican. Music that appeals to the Pope in the Vatican is not going to appeal to people who like Arabian Music. People who follow Arabian music are not necessarily going to like the music of China, etc. However, there are certain principles about music that are universal; Western music, Arabian music, Chinese music, etc, all have the same notes and octaves but their combinations and instruments are different but nevertheless, they all use the same notes, musical vibrations even if they use different materials in the instruments that give the vibrations varied sounds (timbre) which seemingly provides virtually infinite variations of the same sounds. In this sense, music is a universal expression but it is based on the underlying numbers; for example, an octave is a set number based on a scale of vibrations whereby the sounds of the follow a certain distinctly progressive tonal quality until they begin to repeat but at a higher or lower level of vibration. Therefore, the scale is set in Creation itself just as the positions of colors in the rainbow are set. What we do with those tones or colors and the way we combine them to make music or art is based on the creative impetus within but it is based on the underlying structure of Creation and it that underlying structure was set in place by God and not by human imagination. Human imagination makes use of it to create derivative art forms but did not create the original matrix from which those creations are derived. So, the structure, the essence, the fundamental vibrations embedded in Creation are the higher reality which gives insights into the nature of Creation but the music itself, that is created by human beings, is relative. To the extent that music created by human beings helps us to discover the underlying essence of Creation, to that extent it is real and reflective of the higher reality, the higher consciousness. To the extent music and art emphasizes the relative reality, the illusion of time and space, to that extent it is a dumbing down process, a process that reinforces spiritual ignorance, a reinforcement of the illusion of Creation. Music and art that emphasize sentimentality, sexuality, egoism and the reality of the world is negative.

So, if you study the architecture of sounds, vibrations and why music that follows the architecture sounds pleasing to the ear while music that is discordant does not sound pleasing to the ear, the theory behind music and why music sounds the way it does, why one octave above the other sounds higher and one below sounds lower and how that relates to the states of matter, solid, gaseous, liquid, etc., you discover what the universe is composed of and why it manifests as it does and then also what underlies Creation itself. The more we study color and art as well as music, which relates us to number; we make sense of the nature of practical reality. Among other things, we come to find that sound and color relate to forms of vibrations and that we are going to discuss next time. About vibrations above, vibrations below; there are basically different forms of vibrations of the same creation, the same matter and it all comes back to the One essence, the ALL. It's all a manifestation of the One transcendental consciousness.

Question In studying the act of waking up in the dream world, is that a way of realizing the unreality of the dream world? Is that a way to study and realize the unreality of the waking world?

Answer: The answer to that question is yes, however, that is a short answer, and it is a lot more involved than that. In order to truly realize the unreality of the physical and the astral world, it is necessary to realize, if you are a true student, a true mystic, a true practitioner, you are going to transcend this physical world, then you are going to go to the astral world, that is going to have its own reality and there are many aspirants who get caught up with that also. They get caught up in the astral plane. The astral plane is the plane you experience when you dream. So we may think of waking up in two dream worlds. Waking up in the dream world that is the physical reality or the dream world that you experience when you are a sleep at night in bed, occurs in the astral plane. Both are illusory but the astral plane is more fluid and changeable so it is more difficult to maintain that awareness of wakefulness, being aware you are dreaming. Yet it is possible and something to be worked towards. This is also referred to as "Lucid Dreaming" but realize we are not seeking to just wake up and realize we are dreaming and thinking we are the waking personality who is dreaming in the astral plane. We are seeking to wake up to both illusory worlds and realize we are the transcendental Self who dreaming that we are an individual personality in the physical or the astral plane. This is going beyond both.

There has to be study of the wisdom teaching, there has to be much reflection and you must be able to impress the mind with the wisdom teaching and there must be continuous impression. The impression of the wisdom teaching must overpower and overcome the impressions of the ignorance, that is, the impressions of the physical or astral world as being abiding realities.

HTP

Question: Ok well going into what you mentioned Correspondence, what would that relate to?

Answer: Understanding correspondence between the creation and that which brings it into being. Creation corresponds to the Divine Self. That is the central aspect of the teaching. God has created the world of her own image.

Chapter 3: Principle of Vibration – From The Kybalion

"Nothing rests, everything moves; everything vibrates."

"To change your mood or mental state, change your vibration."

"To destroy an undesirable rate of mental vibration, concentrate on the opposite vibration to the one to be suppressed."

The Ancient Egyptian Concept of Vibration

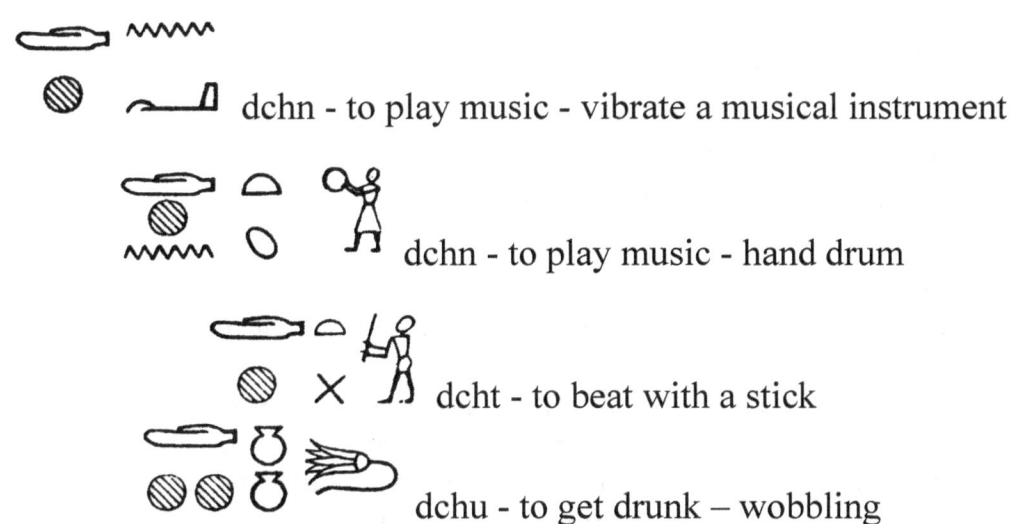

Deck or *vibration* is one of the seven principles of metaphysics presented by Hermes-Djehuty in the Kybalion text. And, as the evidence above shows, the teachings related to Vibration, go back to the hieroglyphic text that Djehuty himself brought into being. All the derivative terms from the original hieroglyphic term "dchn" convey an aspect of vibration related to the shaking or oscillating effect that occurs in nature.

Vibration is the means by which the individual mind (human beings and astral beings) creates thoughts and also the means by which the cosmic mind (God) brings into being and sustains Creation. The faster the vibration the subtler the manifestation of matter will appear as. Conversely, the slower the vibration the more gross the material manifestation will appear as.

In the practice of the Sema Arat Sekhem (Ancient Egyptian Serpent Power Yoga) the practitioner directs attention to the base of the spine and causes the latent energy of the Life Force to concentrate and accumulate there. Then it is cultivated and raised. The Life Force is controlled by the mental meditation on the point that causes it to focus and become dynamic, as opposed to being unfocused and diffused (weak).

The sound "Am" [Om] is used to harness the Life Force energy. Special attention is given to the "m" in Am, which is the universal sound of the original vibration enjoined by the Spirit to bring Creation into being. In this sense the "m" becomes an emphatic "M" that carries the grosser vibration at the beginning of the syllable to a greater level of subtlety as the "M…" is carried into infinity "…" and silence which eventually gives rise to the next chant of "AM…."

> Am is a universal word of power which was used in ancient Kamit (Egypt) and is used extensively in India by yogis. Om or AUM* is related to the word Amun from ancient Egypt and Amun is related to the Amen of Christianity. Therefore, Om is generally useful for spiritual practice. Om* is also not related to a particular deity but is common to all. It is also the hekau-mantra of the 6th energy center at the point between the eyebrows known as the ancient Egyptian *Arat* or Uraeus serpent and the *Third eye of Shiva* in India. You will use hekau for chanting during your worship periods, and at idle times during the day. You will use it from now on to dig deeply into the unconscious regions of your mind as a miner uses a pick to cut into a mountain in search of gold.
>
> *(see *African Origins of Civilization* by Muata Ashby for a more detailed description of AUM and Om)

The movement, "dchn" of objects in Creation causes the illusion in the mind due to the illusory senses, that there exist solid objects and that one is a solid personality. When the vibrations (fluctuations) of the mind are controlled and caused to become subtler, the illusoriness of the physical world becomes evident. Therefore, the chant of Am along with the visualization exercises is to be practiced along with purity of body through righteous diet and job occupation as well as actions in the world based on righteous Maatian principles. Also, the mind is to be purified by studying the righteous principles. Then, with the assistance of the Serpent Power, the mind will open to the higher levels of consciousness. So during the practices of focusing and accumulating the life force the Am chant or chants that incorporate the Am will be used.

Included below are two types of words of power: short, containing one or two syllables, medium length, containing two to three and average, containing six to eight. They are presented as guidelines for practice of hekau-[mantra] repetition practice.

	Number per minute			Number per hour		
	Low	Med	High	Low	Med	High
1. OM	140	250	400	8400	15000	24000
2. Om Amun Ra Ptah	80	120	140	4800	7200	9000
3. Om Asar Aset Heru	80	120	140	4800	7200	9000
4. Om Maati Maakheru	80	120	140	4800	7200	9000

If using the ancient Kamitan music during meditation practice the practitioner will take care to use only those songs that use the appropriate chants and vibrational rate (Steady and processional as opposed to variable and festive).

The Principle of Vibration Pt. 1

Allow yourself to go deeper within because the mental vibration, the mental chant is actually of higher energy than your vocal, audible chant. If I say "Om" [Am] as opposed to doing it mentally and deeper within myself the physical vibration actually has lower power. So at some point you have to stop the audible, gross, physical practice and go deeper within. The deeper you go within, the farther you remove yourself from the physical plane, you go to the Astral (mental) plane, then you go to the causal plane, (higher ethereal plane). It is why the more consolidated your ego is, the more egoistic you are, the more you believe that you are a physical personality, the more you are limiting your power. The more you realize that you are transcendental and all-encompassing and unlimited, the higher is your power.

As you move in this way to elevate your mind to discover these higher rates of vibration by becoming virtuous first of all. That is the first step and then learning how to calm the mind and controlling your mind as was discussed by allowing yourself to vibrate at the level that you choose. Here is the difference between an ordinary person and an initiate. The initiate, the priest/priestess of the mysteries learns how to control the mind to make it vibrate at whatever rate he or she chooses. The mental state can only change when you are at a higher rate of vibration yourself. You are realizing that you are not body, that you are spirit. You can dictate how your mind vibrates. You can dictate whether it manifests a lower energy or a higher energy. You can pick what your moods are. No longer are you controlled by your moods. No longer are you controlled by insanity, your thoughts, by worries, anxieties so on and so forth. You can recognize these negative vibrations and you can repudiate them. You can reject them. This takes years of practice of certain techniques and meditation. This is why the teaching enjoins that you should not be playing music that is agitating, music that is degrading. You should not be living in conditions that are degrading with morose colors and dullness around your life. You should not be living around negative or dull people because people vibrating at certain levels, because if you are a weak personality they are going to have an effect on you. They are radiating vibrations that are going to have an effect on you. You want to be in the company of sages and saints and you want their influence to vibrate on you, to have an effect on you. That is what you want. That is why the teaching of good association has been enjoined. This is why egoism is spoken out against in the teaching. If you are an egoistic personality and you are vibrating at a certain level because of that, your vibration level is going to prevent the influence of the saints, sages and gods and goddesses on you. If you think that way then you are putting out certain vibrations or aura around yourself that will prevent the vibrations from the teacher to penetrate your personality that would have allowed your personality to begin to understand. Understanding allows you to vibrate on the higher level because you are blocking it. Therefore you want to open yourself up to that.

Never mind that some people have higher charisma and they have strong personalities, imposing personalities. They have such control over that aspect of their personality that they can actually control people of lower mind. You see it all the time, politicians with their influences, their advertising, and repetitious power, their vibrating mantra, that's even how commentators on TV refer to it now, as a mantra. Politicians, advertisers, the military, but also individuals try to control others, like singers, parents, peer groups, etc. try to control people on the lower level. They control ordinary people who are ignorant and or weak willed. They are vibrating at a certain lower level of vibration by a song by which they live that has been dictated to them, has been imposed on them. Have you noticed that when people go to a concert or are in the presence of their singing idol, they mouth the words of the songs? Those lyrics are hekau or mantra that inculcate the thoughts and feelings of the song and thereby molds the mind in the dictated fashion. So what music and audiovisual entertainment a person uses is not necessarily harmless. If used properly it can be powerful and beneficial towards achieving worldly worthy goals and worthy spiritual goals or it can serve the purpose of commercialization and or militarization.

Sages and saints have a different melody that they are vibrating at; a different song that they are playing internally. You notice when we do the drumming or we play the music some of you may be off, some of you may be playing a slightly different beat, slightly different vibration. How many of you can stay on track with the main beat, with the main rhythm, and this is the same thing with the physical world and the astral plane. You have a teaching that is at a certain vibration; the teaching itself has a certain vibration. Every book that has given to you has a certain vibration, mental vibration. When you go out into the world and other people are around you with their vibrations and their worldliness and their thoughts and so forth, how are you affected by that? Can you go on and play your music, your song? Or are you thrown off when you hear other people's beats, other people's melodies, when other people's singing off key and this kind of thing? What is that deal? This is your task, to be so strong in the higher vibrations that you cannot be affected by the lower.

Just as music can be reproduced at will and colors, you should learn how to reproduce your vibration at will. Then you can be free of ignorance, free of limitation. At the higher rate that you vibrate, you liberate higher forms of energy. We know that when a certain vibration is matched a resonance occurs which can be destructive or instructive as well as constructive. So one can break glass with sound and one can come into alignment, harmony with the essence of Creation [universal spirit] by rising up to the vibration of spirit and there resonate with it.

As I said before, at that level you can control other people's minds if you choose, these are kinds of psychic powers that develop that you should not use but these develop. The mind is then vibrating at certain levels so you can be in contact with other forms of beings on the mental plane, on the ethereal planes. Now there you just can't see it because you are vibrating at a lower level, ordinary people cannot see them and they are fearful of them. Vibrating at the higher level you have insight into your expanded self. Therefore the Kybalion says finally that, "If all this is done he/she who has grasped the principle of vibration has grasped the scepter of power." Of course that scepter of power is not just the Heka or scepter of power and dominion as if a Queen or King but the Serpent Power; the Serpent of Djehuty; the Serpent of Hermes; the Caduceus. You practice the meditation on each energy center raising its level of vibration, raising the colors and gradually reaching the highest.

This is called mental transmutation. You can transmute, you can transform the color and vibration of your mind. If you were to develop sufficient power you could actually perform upon physical matter and transform its form, change its form. You could turn an apple into an orange. Or you can act upon yourself and make your own body dissolve and then reappear somewhere else in the world if you so choose. These are higher psychic powers that can develop. But these take even more work than just changing your vibration and attaining enlightenment. It can be done, if you want to work twenty, thirty, forty, fifty years practicing meditating on these psychic powers, you can develop them. This is the kind of power that God has. That is what God has done to create all things that are on Earth. This is how Ptah created Creation, by thinking the world into being. Thought vibration acts upon matter which is vibrating at a lower rate and reforms it. This is also why that which is at a higher vibration permeates that which is of lower vibration. The Self, the Spirit is vibrating at a higher vibration deep within every aspect, every particle of creation. Like the sun vibrating at the center of the solar system, the Self is at the center of all matter, all creation. That which you see as the physical aspect of matter, that is on the outskirts, that is on the outer fringe. As I said before the outer fringe is vibrating at the lower level; the inner essence is vibrating at the higher level.

In between these two poles, the higher and the lower, there are millions and millions of individual states of vibration. A human being oscillates between them all of the time. Sometimes you feel up; sometimes you feel down; sometimes you feel good; sometimes you feel sad. These are all levels of vibration and again you must learn how to control yourself to vibrate at the level you want. You must realize that learning how to control your vibratory level also means necessarily learning how to transcend them. Once you control something, you have transcended it. That is the axiom, the law. If you control your emotions, you have transcended them. If you control your anger, you cannot be angry anymore even though you may act angry or express anger so on and so forth. This is why sages and saints are said to have transcended. They are said to be beyond even though their personality, their body continues to exist, and they use those vibrations in order to teach people.

This teaching, this concept of vibration, this is the source of all power that sages and saints use. This is one thing sages and saints must learn how to use. Think about it. A story is given of Aset in the Asarian Resurrection, which is a great epic, a little story, among many in the epic, is told of Aset and Set. Aset is the Goddess of Wisdom and she is of course vibrating at the highest mental level, and she was able to do this by discovering her true nature. That was given in the previous story of Ra and Aset. But in the story of Set and Aset, Set is the ego; remember he is the brother of Asar, who murdered him to take the throne. There was this trial, a tribunal that was convened to see if Set should be allowed to keep the throne or if it should be given to Heru. So Set did not want Aset to be allowed in to the court because he knew that her words are powerful and that she is smart and that she could outwit him as an advocate, or a lawyer for Heru. So he had her barred but Aset found him and she saw him walking down a path and then she cleverly used her power of mental vibration to transmute her body, she changed her body into the body of a beautiful young woman, a beautiful maiden. Set was walking down the path and he saw this beautiful maiden and she acted as if she was crying, as if she was sad. He asked her, "My dear maiden, what is the problem, what is wrong?" She said, "Oh great sir there's this man and he has killed my husband and he's trying to take our land away and the land belonged to my husband and this land that should rightfully belong to my son, he is trying to take that away." "What can I do?" "I'm just a powerless woman." Then Set says, "Have no fear, great and beautiful lady, I will take care of you and your son and know that this is unrighteous and no man should be allowed to kill a man and take his land and then, to his wife and deprive the son from his rightful inheritance". As soon as he said those words Aset transformed herself into a kite, a form of hawk, and flew up into a tree and transformed herself back into her goddess form and started taunting Set. "See now you have decreed your own fate, you who killed my husband, and you tried to take my land away, which is Kemet, from me and my son, Heru, who is the rightful heir. So those who vibrate at higher level of mind can act upon, manipulate, those who vibrate on lower levels of mind and can trick them into certain things, for good or bad.

How can this also work in other situations? There are plenty of myths and parables that illustrate this. There were these muggers who were walking down a street and there was this lady who was walking down the same street and they passed her by. They looked at her and they kept on walking even though she was older and weak physically but looked wealthy. A little further down the road there was this guy and they mugged him. The police caught them and they asked the muggers later, we found this other lady, she is a witness to what you were doing and she saw you there, and she was all defenseless, a little old lady and she had plenty of money on her. Why didn't you attack her? The muggers said, "We weren't going to attack her there was two big guys walking with her." She said, "There were no big guys, I was alone."

What happened in this situation? She was being protected by higher beings, beings of higher vibratory essence, who caused an illusion in the mind of the muggers, the mind of lower vibratory essence. The vision was there because the lady was also of higher vibratory essence which is what elicited the vision. By posing a vision in someone's mind you can change their perception, a simple energy tweaking them in their subtle senses. This can also be done retroactively. The memory of the weak-minded can be manipulated so that they might start believing that the old days were the good old days or that the childhood was miserable even if it was not, etc. Of course, people can delude themselves and distort their own memories based on their current vibratory state, their moods. You make them believe something. Of course, this is also in accordance with your Ari, with your Karmic basis. This cannot happen if you are virtuous and sound of mind. It depends on their level of virtue, metal health including understanding the wisdom teaching. So God, in the form of Maat and Aset, are watching our back in other words. The more virtuous you are the more purer that you are and the less susceptible you are to manipulation by others or your own ignorant or warped egoistic feelings and thoughts and falling for the delusions of life; and if some adversity were to befall you then too you have access to the higher vibratory power of Aset and Heru at your disposal, to confront the situation and successfully make it through. So you don't have to worry what your fate is going to be, you can trust the Divine in other words, and relax.

But turning back to the teaching of vibration, this is the great art that must be learned by aspirants. You should not be like those people who get caught up in and linked into feelings and emotions or ways of thinking that are not based on truth. You should not be a prisoner to your moods. Rather, you should be able to change your mood at will or be devoid of moods if you want to. In this way you can harness the power of moods, the power of emotions to place that power at the service of your ethical conscience, your righteous thinking process. Then you will not go against what you know is right because of feelings or desires and you will be able to handle the situations of the world without being emotionally hurt or crippled by them. When you detect a lower form of vibration in your personality, a feeling of depression, of angst, of hatred, lust or fear, you will be able to act on the mind to oppose that level of vibration with a higher form, with hope, confidence, understanding and peace. This is control of mind, self-mastery that is necessary to succeed on the path of life and spirit. Of course, all this is dependent on your believing that you are worthy and a manifestation of divine agency who has only lost the way but is now on the path of truth and light.

This is learning how to as the text says, "polarize your mind," in whatever vibration level that you want. Of course, as you vibrate at higher levels you are going to eventually dissolve your ego personality; you are going to disintegrate, this is the program of the Serpent Power teaching, Arat Sekhem; the whole object is to dissolve yourself and use the life force energy to do that, to carry you into higher levels of vibration. This is actually a natural process, a reverse of the process that brought your physical personality into being. But here you don't want to disintegrate your physical body. You want to disintegrate your mental body, your causal body, which contain your ego identity and self-concept of individuality and separateness from Creation and the transcendental Absolute. In this process of spiritual transformation your physical body continues until the end of its life. At the time of your death you've already disintegrated your mind so there's no death process to experience and you continue on existing as you were before but in a higher plane of existence; this level we may term gods and goddesses, the Neteru. Of course, if you go to the highest level then you dissolve in the Absolute as a drop of water in the ocean and your existence is universal and of course this level is referred to as Neberdjer, ALL ENCOMPASSING CONSCIOUS EXISTENCE.

So you can see and understand how important the beginner, the neophyte stages of spiritual path are; because in order to reach the successful goal of the spiritual journey it is necessary to prepare the personality for higher vibration and that is done through meditation, acting virtuously, cleansing yourself, your mind and physical body, studying the philosophy, etc. so that when your personality may begin to reach higher levels of vibration, when the higher energy goes through your life force energy centers and your physical body, it will not cause a nervous breakdown (short circuit) or a spontaneous combustion (damage or destruction of the nervous system [including the brain]. The special chants are also part of the discipline. Using the Hekaus, the words of power, the chants you lead your constitution to higher vibration and then to a place of coming to a point when silence and internal elevation is experienced. So when practicing the discipline of chant, you chant them physically, audibly, in the beginning; than mentally and going higher one reaches a point where the chant is inaudible even at a mental level. This is a transcendental level and the chant has carried you, your consciousness there to that transcendental place. That is how the practice is enjoined. This takes several hours of practice per day in the beginning. You must practice two to three hours per day in order to make this happen. Think about it, you have been living and thinking and feeling based on thousands and thousands of hours of worldly egoistic existence so it is not so much to ask for 2-3 hours so as to counteract the worldly vibrations stored in the unconscious mind. Along with that you must act with complete virtue. You must follow every regulation of Maat. You must be faithful; you must sing the Divine song within yourself regardless of wherever the world is leading. Then you will attain the highest rate of vibration.

That is all for this lesson.
Chanting: Om, Hetep, Hetep, Hetep.

The Principle of Vibration Pt. 1A Q&A

Question: Is the Kybalion text related to any particular city or God or Goddess?
Answer: The Kybalion is related to the ancient Egyptian city of Khemenu, that is the city of Djehuty and Djehuty is the God that it is based on. Djehuty is the same one called Hermes by the Greeks.

Question: Can Vibration act as heat energy?

The Answer is yes the higher vibration acts as a form of heat energy, and that heat energy burns up the lower aspects of consciousness, the lower aspects of egoism. It does in this capacity work on the mental level, the mental body as discussed however it can be if it has sufficient power it can be made to act on the physical plane also and you can literally disintegrate. You can burn yourself up and completely dissolve your physical existence also and sages have done that in the past. There are instances of sages who have developed this kind of energy and they have disappeared, they have dissolved themselves physically completely.

Question: is the higher vibrating mind the highest form?

Yes that is correct, everything you said there is correct. The mental principle is the highest principle and it presented first for that reason and within that mental principle what we're talking about is the conscious awareness. What you understand, and if you understand yourself as the highest being that is the highest form of vibration, that is the highest form. So therefore your will, your self-consciousness that is the higher principle, when you believe that you are a degraded personality you are going to vibrate at that level and make things happen in your life that are compatible with that; your vibration is controlled by your belief in other words. So therefore your mental thought processes, your will, your understanding of who you are, that is the highest form of power. Furthermore in order to attain what I've discussed today, you must realize that this is an art that needs to be learned and needs to be practiced and it will take you several years to be able to develop it depending on your Karmic basis, your Ari. If you have done this kind of work which obviously all of you have because you are listening to this now today, you've done some level of work on it. It will take you less. Whatever less time that is, depends on you, how much work, how much you apply yourself in this lifetime to this teaching. But it can take years. Therefore you have no time to waste; you have no time to be dabbling, or to be fooling around as it were. You need to be serious about the teaching; you need to be practicing as I said developing yourself to be meditating 2-3 hours daily in this capacity as it has been enjoined. This really goes for any of the disciplines even though this particular aspect of vibration, the tech and the Serpent Power, this is one of the most powerful paths, the most powerful way. The reason I say that is that if you study the Wisdom path, it requires a lot of willpower, and the Devotion Path doesn't require a lot of willpower, it requires a lot of surrender. The Action Path requires you to understand the teachings of righteousness and requires you to act accordingly. If you meditate, by philosophy alone that requires a lot of energy, a lot of willpower, however the Serpent Power technique is enjoined and allows you to do certain exercises, mental techniques, physical techniques and you can actually develop this energy in a very quick way and you may begin to feel it and it actually begins to help you to discover and to perceive these higher forms of vibration. Especially in this age of agitated mind, the Action Path is a pathway that allows the mental energy to be harnessed very quickly. But again, having said that, one has to be prepared, one has to be virtuous, one has to be physically and mentally cleansed as well as properly initiated into the wisdom, otherwise there can be serious repercussions to the incorrect practice. So the teaching has been given; you have to develop a working understanding of it but the actual practice of it is a different story and this is where most people fail.

Ok the understanding of the practice of using the chants - if you chant slowly, you say, "Ohhhmmm" this is a lower rate of vibration and it is to be used by people who are highly concentrated; when the mind is concentrated you use a high rate of vibration, "Om, Om, Om"; when the mind is very agitated it allows the mental stream of thought to be concentrated to be consolidated. At some point you want to be completely silent and that is where the rate of vibration actually increases. When you are doing the disciplines, physically silent and you're mentally chanting, the subtler the chant, the higher the vibration. The grosser the chant, the lower the vibration will be energetically. The object is to follow the chant to its subtlest level and that leads you to its abode which is the Divine Self and that is the most powerful vibration and those of you who do this practice, if you've ever done so you will discover that there is a transcendental Om that is at the center of the universe that is beyond your mental capacity, beyond your mental Om. The physical Om is just a reflection of the transcendental and that Om is more powerful than a billion atom bombs crashing in your mind, if you can conceive how that would be. It is a totally consuming vibration and that is what everything has emanated from, that is what has reverberated throughout creation in order to cause the forms of matter to take their effect, their aspects, their appearance and their characteristics. But every kind of matter can be transmuted into other kinds of matter in other words because all is made of the same stuff. Hetep.

The Principle of Vibration Pt. 1B Q&A

Q and A Continued

First of all you noticed at Initiation a particular chant is given for a particular personality in relation to their level of spiritual evolution. You notice that when you choose you're a chant or when you are given a chant it is based on the appeal to you. That appeal comes because of the relationship of vibration the chant is vibrating at a certain level that appeals to you because you are internally vibrating at that level. If you practice with that chant, it will actually cleanse, it will vibrate through your body it will cleanse you physically and it will cleanse your mental body also where your thoughts are and if you go deep enough it will cleanse your causal body where your Ari is embedded; your seeds of your Karmic basis. So yes it does have that effect, so the more you chant it, chant it a million times and if you chant it sufficiently it takes on a life of its own because you have infused it with the energy. You have allowed it to become powerful. You must realize that your mind has become powerful thereby, it is really your mind that is radiating that because you have trained it to exist at the higher level, so you have polarized it, and you have used this principle of vibration. You have made yourself vibrate at a certain level, and you are not allowing yourself to be accosted by the world or to be forced by the world to vibrate a certain way or another way. This is the higher practice of the teaching.

Also we've enjoined two or three hours of practice and that is an advanced level of the practice, this is something that you build up to. You start with 5-10 minutes and staying there longer, building it up in accordance with your capacity and developing yourself in that way. Don't think you have to sit there for an hour or two or three and so on; you should also not stay there more than three. More than three hours is not necessary. It will actually counteract what you're trying to do. You need to have a balance in your life between your activities in the world and your activities in your spiritual disciplines; in your spiritual science. Two to three hours is sufficient for that. If you meditate two-three hours and you succeed in this way it will carry you through the next day, actually even further. If you succeed in this practice you can meditate for three hours in this way and you will be vibrating at this higher level for days and perhaps even weeks or months. Just from one single meditation! So you can imagine if you were to do this daily what would happen, without ceasing.

The Question and I know most of you have asked this Question, and many of you are thinking about it is like so if I'm getting some powerful technique here, powerful teaching and yes it is, if you learn how to do it and you practice it and therefore you must be wondering, am I ready for this? Am I really ready to do that? Because otherwise it would be like those ladies who were in the church. Every morning they would come in and sing the song, "Oh God come and take me. I want to go to your Heaven. I want to go with you. Come and take me. I want to be your lover and forever and for eternity. Come, come, come God come." Every morning they would come to the temple. Then the priest used to sleep behind the altar and every morning he would wake up to the sound of these crazy ladies singing there stuff and coming there praising and leaving their offerings. So he said, "Ok, let's see if they're really sincere." So one day the priest heard them, they woke him up and they started doing their chants and their phrases. "Oh God come and take me, we want to go to Heaven right now, come and get us, we love you." So the priest, remaining out of sight, and using a deep sound to his voice, said, "Oh Great Ladies, you have come and I've heard your praises and your calls. Behold I am ready to come and take you with me forthwith. So prepare yourselves. Leave your physical bodies behind. I'm coming to take you up to Heaven." Then the ladies turned to themselves; looked at each other and they said, "Well, I have to go prepare lunch for my husband." The other one said, "I have to go to work now." The other one said, "I have to go to the store and get groceries. I'll see you later, bye." They all ran out of the Temple. So there are many people who say that they are down with the teachings; that this is what they want in their lives. But think carefully. Think carefully of what you really want or where you really are and what you are doing. If you are not ready, then continue studying the teachings; continue your practices but from now on with the outlook of what it really is that we're talking about; what it really is leading to. Have that in the back of your mind as the ultimate goal and prepare yourself and one day you will be ready. Now that you have been initiated into this knowledge about shat the teaching is supposed to be, what your goal is, then you know that this is the destination you must head to someday, when you're ready.

What does it mean to be ready? Another story is given of an aspirant who went to the teacher and he wanted to be given the teachings of enlightenment. He went to the teacher, knocking on his door in an insistent and urgent way. The teacher opened up and said, "Who is this?" He said, "I've heard that you are a great teacher and I want to be your student, I want you to teach me; please initiate me right away; give me enlightenment right away." The teacher said, "Well, it doesn't work that way, you have to come here; serve in the Temple; purify yourself, etc." He said, "Don't give me that. I want to learn the teachings right away. I want to enlighten myself and I don't have time to wait." So the teacher said, "OK come down by the river and I will initiate you. I will baptize you in the morning." So he comes there in the morning and meets the teacher at the bank of the river. The teacher says, "By the power vested in me I initiate you into this teaching." He dumps him into the water and he holds him down under the water. The aspirant is struggling, he can't breathe; the teacher is still holding him down in the water. Finally he lets him up. The aspirant gasps for air. The teacher asks him, "How do you feel, what do you think?" The aspirant says, "What do you mean what did you think during the initiation? I can't think of anything. All I could think of was to try to get some air, a breath of air to survive. That's all I had on my mind!" The teacher says, "That is how you must be if you are really serious to learn the teachings right now, right this very minute." You must desire the teaching like you desire nothing else in the world. Nothing else can be in your way. Nothing else can be on your mind. So the Question is, the statement to you as aspirants is, are you ready for that? Is that all that is on your mind? You have all of these on your mind. When you leave and you are home what are you going to think about? Are you going to stop at the store? Or go visit a friend? Or watch a TV show? Or going to hang out and talk to your family members? What are you going to do? What else is on your mind? If don't only have the teaching on your mind, then you are not ready. I'll tell you straight out. If you love your family and you want to be in the world and you love your job and all of this kind of thing, you must understand that the worldly activities and relations may continue, but those things are neither the ultimate goal of existence nor the truly satisfying path of life because they are changeable and fleeting. So you must strike that balance with the understanding that ultimately everything that you love and desire in this world is an illusion. It should not be desired in that way. You can use it and experience it;

that is fine. You should not want anything more in this world than to be one with the Self and that is the only way. Only at that time will you be ready. But this is not a fanatical practice but rather a balanced increasing intensity.

In the meantime, you should continue the practices to the level of whatever you can and eventually when you are ready you will know. You will take certain final steps that will lead you to that realization. The realization of the highest order of Self. In the meantime you will be discovering little bits and pieces, little glimpses here and there, wonderful things you discover about yourself and expand in consciousness and you vibrate at certain higher levels; you discover certain wonderful things about yourself; certain expanded levels of your mind and that brings you bliss and happiness and joy. But don't make the mistake of thinking that that is The Self. Aspirants make that mistake too. You expand yourself and you feel oneness with everyone in the world; oneness with nature; but something comes in your life that disturbs that oneness and you start cursing it. You were meditating and everything was wonderful and somebody knocks on your door and your spouse or somebody tells you, "Come and take out the garbage." They disturb your wonderful oneness with the world, so you haven't attained it then. If you were truly with oneness in the world when they come and tell you to take out the garbage, or tell you that you're a jerk for meditating all day long or something, you say (internally), "OK fine, I'm a jerk. I'm a fool. I and the garbage are One." That's going to be your response and you're not going to be affected because you are vibrating at such a level that the garbage and the person telling you whatever they're telling you is going to be meaningless since they are speaking out of a lower experience and ignorant egoistic feeling. It is going to be inconsequential. This is what it means to have this kind of power, the one we're talking about. So don't make any illusions for yourself. Realize whether you are ready or not based on what I've said and act accordingly based on what I've said. In the meantime, continue to study the teaching and working on acting with ma'at until your gross impurities are purified and you gain *saa* or understanding, inner feeling and intuition about your path in life, Hetep.

Question: in relation to cleansing and purifying, what progress do we expect with like say meditating 30 minutes or so a day?

Answer: Yes of course, whatever extent you enjoin the practice you benefit. If you meditate 5 minutes; you get 5 minutes worth of benefit. If you do it for 3 hours you get 3 hrs. of benefit. It is cumulative. You can think of it that way. Of course the less your practice, the slower your progress.

Question: So Ptah is the God whose teachings evoke Creation that the universe was mental.

Well, prior to Creation thought, I guess consciousness being the first thing God becoming aware of his consciousness moving on to indicate creation and of these things were manifestations of, well the creation was a manifestation of God. Does the Kybalion teachings flow from that, or come from that point kind of late?

Answer: The teaching of "the universe is mental" is implicit in all of the teachings, all traditions. But it is highlighted in the tradition of Khemenu which is the tradition of Djehuty, which is what this is based on and there is also the Memphite theology which is Ptah, the teaching of Ptah. So those two teachings highlight that teaching but that is not to say that it is not also implicit in the other teachings as well. In Anunian theology as well as the Asarian tradition says that Neberdjer created through Khepri by desire in his heart. That is the mental will, so it is implicit in other words. It is just not highlighted.

Talking about one last thing; I was going to add a few more points to this particular lecture on the practice of the teachings. So we've been discussing what is necessary to implement the teaching and one last thing is that the teaching is that even though sages and saints are people of higher vibration have the capacity to enforce their views on others and their imposing a higher level of vibration on something that is not ready to vibrate at that level is going to damage the object that is at a lower vibration; Especially speaking about living beings. As far as the subtle levels of vibration, like say stories that are given about sages who touch aspirants and they make them vibrate at higher levels so that they make them open their mind and all of this kind of thing, if a person is not ready for that it will not work or it might even push them to go insane. They can very well easily become unhinged psychically and mentally. So that should not be done. It should not be done by teaching and influence, as we are doing now. It should be done by a gradual process of learning. Additionally, there has to be willingness on the part of the aspirant to learn and practice the teaching and without that even the greatest teacher, even Jesus or Krishna, Aset or whoever was to come down, they would have no effect on people who are not ready, not willing to follow the teaching to practice it, and to develop themselves. Forcing them would not fix the problem. It is not possible anyway because if it were the sages would have done it long ago and be done with the insanity of human life, the wars, the destruction of the environment, etc. This is not to say that wars and other situations, like in parenting, that the people cannot impose their will on others, at least for a time. You can control peoples' behaviors but you cannot control their opinions and feelings; you can influence and if people want to they can change themselves. People need to develop ethical conscience and then they will not require coercion to make them do the right thing. This is why you especially see a lot of wars breaking out right now. In the former Soviet controlled countries there were a lot of ethnic differences that were kept in check by the Soviet Army. So the army, the pressure that is keeping the bottle closed is taken away and these things start blowing up, they start boiling over. The only thing that can transform opinions and feelings is influence and righteousness with caring, truth and compassion, forgiveness all of these kinds of virtues. You do that for yourself, you do that for other people, and at the country level, community-wide level and ultimately. At first specifically we're talking about the course of events. What it comes down to is people need to be growing to a certain level at where they recognize the importance of these things. To a certain degree the leadership has to adopt it and that's what she's talking about here. The bottom line is that, is you can see what is happening currently in the situation with the world. Why do you think this last week after months and years of vacillation the United States finally now comes out and says that Israel has to get out of the occupied territories of Palestine? Why do you think that happened last week and not all the weeks and months and years before? Because last week the Arabs were getting up in arms, Ok. What is this up in arms? Not the governments, but the people. Now they are afraid this is going to come to be a serious spreading of a conflict that's going to engulf the whole region. When that region gets engulfed the rest of the world gets engulfed. You must realize that at this point. You think Israel is going to their atomic weapons? I don't think so. Anyway, that's a different aspect. But what I'm getting at is that just as you must become the governor of your lives despite what your leaders say, it doesn't matter what people in positions to obstruct want to do if enough people make their concerns known and make their desires heard. That is the ultimate social power.

However who controls the minds of those people therefore is the person who is in the leadership position. So whoever controls Hollywood, whoever controls the networks, and what they say, or don't say, or how they say it, so on so forth that is the person who controls the minds of the people. So therefore you don't want people to be getting too much information; you don't want them to be getting too much time to think about it; Right? You want them to be in a situation where they could survive, but they have to work all day in order to survive; to pay their bills; and when they go home they have to go to sleep and rest for the next day. They can watch a half hour of news; they can't take much more than that. They can only take just a little bit, a little piece of the truth (if there is any in the mainstream media that is). Of course there are the Hollywood entertainments, the sports, the legal and illegal drugs to weaken their minds and their bodies. After that you can convince them that you're handling it and you've got in under control. God forbid that too many of them should not be able to pay their bills then there would be a revolution, a riot and God forbid that you should not affect their lifestyle because that is going to make them up in arms. As long as you keep people in that general level you can control them, and that's what we have in this society. You can have all the laws you want, but if you don't have the money to implement it your law is worthless. So now they say there is a budget crisis. So now we can't have money to teach our course or have our department in the university. So what's the point? So you need to go back and fix it, you need to go back and demand it, force the issue. And if the demands are not met then don't pay your taxes. If you think that you would go to jail by not paying taxes, perhaps if enough of you do that you would get results. You are not going to have to deal with any jail time. It is the law. You're using the law for what it is. The law has to be pursued diligently and as a group if you want to affect a society. If you are a loner, or care only for yourself and your family, or busy having so many kids, having so many mortgages, having so many different things to worry about that you cannot be an effective revolutionary and the efforts of the revolutionaries will have less chance of success. Today's Kybalion class is talking to people who do not realize they are deluding themselves. It is speaking to those who think they are practicing the teaching correctly, that they are wonderful aspirants, wonderful revolutionaries; but in reality they are not doing what it takes. They are vibrating at a comfortable level that allows them to feel comfortable while doing some spiritual practices but not advancing to the more difficult higher levels. So I'm throwing the gauntlet down as they say on this issue.

Chapter 4: The Principle of Polarity Pt. 1

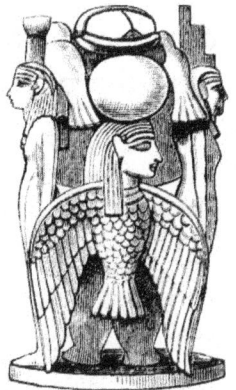

the goddess Bast

We continue now with the discourses dealing with the Kybalion teachings. This is about the fourth lecture in the series. There are seven main principles of the Kybalion and we are dealing with the fourth one today. All of these are continuous meaning that they are not really distinct principles they are all aspects of the one same principle. So last nights principle runs into todays and today's runs into tomorrows. When we get to the end of them they run back to the first.

Last time we talked about the principle of vibration and apparently there were several things that intrigued many people from last week's lecture so we're going to go over some of those things and then we're going to lead into today's lecture which will hopefully captivate you some more and lead into the next one, next week's. Remember that we talked about last week in the principle of vibration how everything vibrates; how nothing is static even though it appears to be and everything emanates from a single source in the universe according to the philosophy. That source is the highest vibrating essence and the farther that thing vibrates from that essence the slower those things appear to vibrate and the grosser therefore, they appear to be. A human being has all of these aspects also within themselves they contain the higher vibrating aspect which is spirit and they also contain the lower vibrating aspect which is the physical body. They have everything in between in that whole range. In that whole range you have different aspects of yourself that are vibrating at different levels. So the grossest meaning the physical and the just above that you have your mind and senses which is actually pretty gross, when you consider compared to your soul which is vibrating at a higher level. There are, as you should now know, different aspects of yourself, there is your body of light, in Kemet it is called your Akhu and beyond the Akhu is pure Self, Asar or Amun or whichever name that you choose. The problem with most human beings is that they are only aware of that part of themselves that is obvious, which is the mind, senses and the body. Therefore their whole frame of reference is based on that which is gross, the gross aspect of themselves. The project of spirituality is to discover those vibrations which are higher, which transcend the physical plane and so on and so forth. How can that be discovered? That is the project of the spiritual teaching.

So all these aspects of creation are vibrating; everything vibrates. So the teaching says: Nothing is static. Even the things that appear to be very solid and remember we discussed that they're actually moving. If you were to examine the floor you are sitting on it seems so solid and yet it is moving. It is changing constantly. It is deteriorating, going back to its original form. The form that it is in is held together artificially. Everything must go back to its initial state as we discussed. The Kybalion is a late text, a Hermetic text that is based on the teachings of Djehuty and the texts themselves say this. The city is Djehuty is Khemenu, the City of the Eight. Djehuty is the God that the Greeks called Hermes, as you all know. He is the one who holds the Caduceus and you recall at the end of last week's lecture it said that whoever masters the teaching of vibration gets control of the Staff of Power and that is Djehuty's staff, which is the Caduceus Staff. What that means is that you control your life force energies. They no longer control you. That led us into a whole discussion into the disciplines for achieving that kind of control as you recall, the discipline of concentrating on different levels of vibration.

That leads us to today's lecture which gives us another indication of the aspects of nature brought forth through the Kybalion text. The Kybalion is a collection of seven principles, seven teachings and if these teachings are known they lead to the supreme wisdom of understanding the nature of self, that is what the Kybalion means. The teaching of Polarity is what we are dealing with today. The teaching of vibration leads us into this.

The teaching says: "Everything is dual; everything has poles; everything has its pair of opposites; like and unlike are the same; opposites are identical in nature but different in degree. Extremes meet; all truths are but half-truths; all paradoxes may be reconciled."

Now we understand that everything is vibrating at different levels, and the reason that things appear to be different is because they are operating, they're vibrating at different levels. Remember we also talked about matter itself. First of all, I didn't tell you last time, do you know that the theory of atoms, the theory of the composition of matter is actually just that, it is just a theory. No one has ever seen an atom, do you know that? Do you realize that? No one has ever seen an atom, or a neutron, a proton. It is theoretical. I'm not saying it isn't true but we're saying that it has been arrived at through deduction of how matter seems to operate. This is how scientists have arrived at the theory of the composition of atoms. Now of course in quantum physics we have expansion on that theory because now they have quarks and different parts of those very same particles. In this theory of the atom there is a nucleus with a proton and a neutron and the electron goes around the nucleus like a planet goes around the sun. However. It is also now known that the electron does not exist in every part of that orbit; it disappears and reappears in a different orbit. Where does it go when it disappears? Also, there is a vast space between the electrons and the nucleus and the nucleus is composed of mostly empty space. Remember, this is supposed to be solid matter we are talking about! Through particle accelerator experiments they have crashed atoms together and they've come up with the theories that there are smaller aspects of those pieces of those atoms. When those pieces get too small they turn into energy, they turn back into energy. Then it comes out of its energy form, it goes back, it coalesces back into the particles that compose atoms. So ultimately everything is composed of these atoms and particles and ultimately those particles dissolve into energy. That energy is what the ancients called the Primeval Ocean, the Nun, which is a kind of subtler undifferentiated matter. When it is acted upon by divine consciousness with will intent it coagulates into what the senses perceive as "physical matter."

If one was to realize as we said just a few minutes ago all of you have those same parts within yourself. You have the gross vibrating aspect, and go all the way up to the Nun. But you don't experience your Nun. If you were to do certain disciplines that allow you to discover that Nun, what would happen to you? What would happen to your notion of yourself? Since Nun is the ocean, you would discover that the world is like the bubbles on top of the waves and Nun is the ocean. All waves are rooted in the ocean. You would discover that you are rooted, like everyone else, in the ocean of Self. Not a little bubble bobbing up and down, ready to burst and blow up into nothing and to non-existence. As discussed previously to that, we discussed the principle of correspondence of as above so below. Everything has its reference, just correspondent. This teaching of polarity brings us even closer to an understanding. What it is leading us to understand is that all of the opposites are but two sides of the same coin as it were. Heads and tails and they are both part of each other. The polarity on the battery, positive and negative - from one end of the positive to the negative, where does the negative end and where does the positive begin? When you are watching the news and you see one person fighting against another who is the good one and who is the bad one? Ask one or the other and they will say they are the good one. If you examine and you will see both of them are doing certain things that are bad and certain things that are good. So in the world you want to say, "Well if that's the case then we should try to be as good as possible or side with the better good." That's a logical theory for the world, you try to side with the most good. For a spiritual aspirant, that is not good enough. That is not going to work. If you maintain yourself like that that is called impurity. Impurity is imperfection. Impurity will lead you to ignorance. It will cloud your intellect. "Oh I'm being mostly good so I can afford to eat a little hot dog here; it's not going to hurt me that much. I've been vegetarian for a few months, so you know it's not going to hurt." "Oh, I haven't lied very much so I can tell a little lie here just to get out of this thing; it's not a big deal." Or you might say, "I'm only human and doing the best I can." and some people use that as a legitimate way to let of the pressure of trying to be good while their ego is compelling them to do negative things. However, there are others who use this as an excuse not to change, to remain as they are and excuse their unrighteous behavior. What we're getting at is that every aspirant must learn how to completely focus themselves on becoming a particular way, particular form of personality and this is what the teaching calls Polarity. So you have the opposites within you and you must learn how to focus completely on one aspect and leaving the other one behind.

Due to your ignorance of how you've lived in this life and previous lifetimes, you have acquired many layers of Karmic entanglements, of aryu. In another lifetime you may have been a very hateful person. You have those layers on you like peels of an onion, those layers that are staying with you. Sometimes you may find it very easy to love certain people because you like them. You like what they do or because something resonates with you. At other times you may find it easy to hate them because they do something you don't like or that kind of thing. Think about that in your own families or in your past. Let's say you're a good person now, think about your past, how you were friends with someone and they did something and all of a sudden you started hating them and yelling at them, etc. So where did the love stop and where did the hate begin? When you hate somebody, do you really hate them, or is there love still there? Can you make up? This is being mixed, this is called impurity.

What you must learn how to do is to polarize yourself. Polarize yourself to whatever vibration that you want to have in your personality. If you learn how to polarize yourself, you become the supreme master as we were discussing last time. You become the complete controller of your life. Only those people who can do that are in control of their lives and everyone else is controlled by nature. Nature dictates your polarity. It dictates where you are vibrating at a particular time, or when or how or why. Therefore you are not a true human being in accordance with the teachings. You are like an animal. Animals are driven by their instincts and by nature.

So understanding this idea of the coins is crucial to understanding the concept of polarity, it's the first aspect. Everything is two sides of the same coin. First we talked about men and women; they are two sides of the same coin. Men appear to come from Mars and women appear to come from Venus but they are not really from Venus and not from Mars, they're really two sides of the same coin. They are two poles, two tendencies. Women tend to be more emotional, men tend to be more intellectual but men have emotions, women have intellect. They are tendencies. Men and women have all the same organs; they have a tendency to be arranged in a certain different way. Therefore this means that, "As above, so below" really means that right here on the physical Earth, is the Divine just like as it is in Heaven. So everybody is looking to get out of the world to find God or to find Heaven and God is in Heaven and God is here too. This is the physical aspect of the Divine; the subtle aspect of the Divine is in Heaven.

How does one discover this truth of this teaching? You enjoin certain disciplines that allow you to polarize yourself. Guess what? That's what you've been getting taught all along! The teachings of Maat, they polarize you towards virtue as opposed to vice. The teachings of vegetarianism they polarize you towards purity in your diet as opposed to impurity and lower vibrations in your diet. Doesn't it? So you've been apparently doing this teaching of the Kybalion all along! Only now it is being intellectually explained to you, why? Because you must understand that you are doing it for a purpose, for a reason. Yes just because plutonium is made of the same atoms, neutrons and electrons that you are made of doesn't mean that you should go eat a bowlful of plutonium. Remember the first teaching? The aspirant should accept the information from the intellect with respect even though understanding that it is illusory. Philosophically you must have that understanding because that leads your mind to stability and sanity and ultimately to freedom; freedom from the opposites.

East and West, they appear to be so different but if you travel long enough going East you come back to where you were from the West, don't you? The teaching of calculus, advanced geometry, what does it tell us? It tells us that two straight parallel lines meet in infinity. This is the teaching of polarity. The ultimate problem that affects a human being was discussed in one of our previous lectures; you who remember last year when we were doing the Pert m Heru lecture series, I believe it was Chapter Nine, it talked about the opposites and the particular opposites that dog human beings and makes human beings life miserable are likes and dislikes. It was in the Pert m Heru text. This is a form of polarity, the swinging of the pendulum as it were, that human beings emotions go through and you like something so you run after it. If you hate something else, you run away from that; this is polarity in the personality, determined by how you have allowed your mind to vibrate in the past and the things you have allowed your mind to gravitate to and hold on to or repudiate in the past. All the while you are embedding more Aryu, or impressions, in your unconscious mind. As long as the error of life that you are leading, that causes you to polarize your mind based on its desires and fears, etc., remains, those impressions are going to forever dog you; they are going to forever lead you into strife, into confusion. Love and hate relationships and running after happiness in the world; running away from unhappiness. Running after the things that you think will make you happy; running away from things that you think are causing you misery. Never understanding that both of these things are illusory and that if you were to try to transcend them with purity and understanding you would have peace immediately. You could have peace today, right now if you realize this teaching. If your mind was pure, if it was not fraught with impurities as we discussed, all you need to do is to hear this teaching once and you would be good to go. Yet you must hear it several times because there is so much impurity there that it has to work through to get to your understanding.

So everything has poles, everything has its pair of opposites. Like and unlike are the same. Opposites are identical in nature but different in degree. This is the key that we've been discussing and that we discussed last time. Extremes meet. All truths are but half-truths. Paradoxes may be reconciled. So for instance you have a problem with fear. You are afraid of things, what should you do? You should concentrate your mind on courage. Read about people who are courageous; about courageous deeds. Then you go and act those out. If you were to do that you would begin to realize and say, "Hey I have courage within me, I can do this, I can." Even if you are internally fearful, if you go ahead and you move forward with your courageous act, your courageous thought, eventually that courage overcomes that fear. Just like in your studies, if you were to understand the teaching that is being given, if you persevere, remember the lecture we did on how to be a successful student, you persevere even if you don't understand in the beginning. Eventually your mind will grasp it. You can have those other negative thoughts, see the positive and negative, you have to have the positive, polarize onto the positive. People are telling you that you can't understand because you are stupid, or you are dumb or you're dull, or you yourself have the negative thoughts. "Oh, I don't have to do this, let me just go do some easier discipline that I don't have to study so much, or that is not so challenging" all of this kind of thing is negative thoughts. You allow those thoughts to come in and you will be unsuccessful. Why? Because you have the power. Since you are the Self essentially you have the power to do anything that you want to do. Do you recall that lecture? Therefore it is up to you what you can accomplish. Only you can control that, only you have the power. If you say somebody is controlling you or on top of you, you have allowed them to take that power over you. In a higher sense nobody can control you. They may control your body, they can't control your feelings and thoughts unless you have allowed yourself to become dull and weak as a personality and as a spiritual being.

What I gave you just a few minutes ago, these are the preliminary disciplines of polarity; acting with virtue and with righteousness, bringing order to your life. Vegetarianism, these are aspects. Purity in your thoughts and vegetarianism as the diet has three aspects: Purity of physical body which is vegetarianism, Purity of the mind which is the Wisdom teaching, Purity of the Soul which is the practice of meditation and this of course leads us to a discussion about meditation again. This is what interested so many people from the lecture last time.

I was talking about a special meditation that is done to develop the higher vibrations in your consciousness. This is part of the Serpent Power discipline; it will be discussed in your new Serpent Power book. The teaching of the Serpent Power basically relates to understanding the seven life force energy centers that are spheres that are swirling around in your astral body. They connect you to the higher aspects of yourself if you were to understand that teaching, that theory. Then you are to work on each of these centers; the lowest vibrating at the lowest level and the highest vibrating at the highest level. You would be able to gradually lead yourself through raising your vibrations. This is a great teaching of vibrations that will be elaborated upon as we move forward.

The Principle of Polarity Pt. 2

In this practice of the Kybalion you are changing your vibrations from the lower vibrations from the lower to the higher, you are changing your polarity, from the negative polarity to a positive polarity, and you are moving from below to above. All of the teachings are all aspects, part of the same teaching. Each sphere or psycho-spiritual consciousness center also relates to some aspect of psychology in your mind. Each of these aspects have vibrational dynamics also. For instance, the vibration at the lowest energy center, at the base of the spine relates to the psychology of fear and of fight or flight or food issues, and these are the lowest vibrating aspects of mental activity; it relates to instinctual food and survival issues.

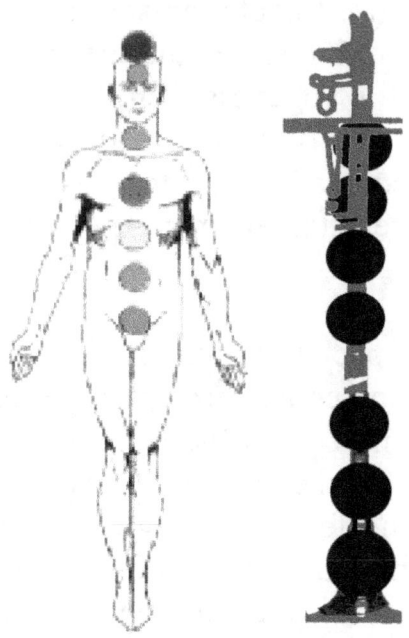

Moving up from there the next spot is sexuality, creation. It is a lower vibration because you are creating on the physical plane. The next one is narcissism, desire. Now beyond those first three which are of the lower polarity. We have one that is in the middle which is love. Moving up from there we have the higher polarity aspects of consciousness. We have will; we have inner-vision and transcendence. We have to concentrate on the three upper psychological dynamics that would begin to polarize the mind, polarize the personality on the higher level. This is the work that is to be done in the special meditation teaching that I was talking about. If you recall I talked about how it should be practiced. You should be building up your practice, starting with 5 minutes, building up to two hours and no more than three hours of practice.

How do you begin? First of all you begin by what we discussed before, which is practicing concentrating the mind on the teaching and on becoming virtuous, even before you start doing this meditative practice, because this is a special meditation, a special discipline. You should have a vegetarian diet; A complete vegetarian diet for at least one to two years before engaging in the more advanced aspects of the serpent power techniques. Of course if you have an organic and or raw diet that's so much the better but that also takes time to adapt to. Doing this because the teachings of Maat, the virtuous teachings, they begin to cleanse your mind from negative vibrating thoughts and the vegetarianism cleanses your physical body and in the Serpent Power teachings you know that there are subtle life force channels, energy centers, the life force channels that go throughout your mental body and your physical body and those need to be cleansed. As you vibrate on higher levels those mettus or those conduits need to be able handle greater energy. As the energy moves up, as it vibrates at a higher level, there is actually more powerful energy than the lower vibrating energy. So a practitioner is to work on each of these aspects of psychology and vibrational energy. You are to do that in the following way, and this is a simplified Serpent Power meditation that I'm giving you now, a simplified teaching related to the Kybalion. The Serpent Power discipline is a little more involved than what I'm giving you right now. As I have said you have to go through the book *The Serpent Power*[10] for that. This is a meditation in relation to the Kybalion teaching.

The Serpent Power teaching has its own nomenclature it has different aspects and specifics. You would meditate on each energy center and its corresponding psychology and then cleanse it out. For example, if you have fear about something at the first energy center you work on

---

[10] *The Serpent Power* by Muata Ashby

dissolving that fear. You get into the energy center, you concentrate on it maintaining and repeating the word of power, "Om", to place that vibration into the energy center; to break up that negative thought/feeling/vibration. Also, by working through it, you begin to realize you were looking into yourself, into your aryu; where did I get this fear thought from? Something that happened to me when I was young, or something that I imagined but never resolved?.... Then you begin to allow yourself to understand, to come to clarity, purity, and balance. You might come to the conclusion: "Oh, now I see this happened to me or why I did that, because I was foolish back then, I didn't understand the teaching back then." You apply the teaching on that situation, you realize the illusoriness of that situation and then you release it. You go through all of the centers re-polarizing them towards their higher vibration. Each lower energy center corresponds to a higher center. The lowest center corresponds to the highest. The second corresponds to the sixth. The third corresponds to the fifth. If you polarize the lower and you cleanse the lower it transmutes the energy into the higher, it's also called mental alchemy. You are turning lead into gold in other words. This is like a cooking process that goes on. You need life force energy, the Serpent Power to cook you, to transform you.

This discipline is not to go on forever; it is an initial phase. This is what you would do in your initial practice. This is before you actually go to the formal meditation. Now you see we're not even to the formal meditation yet. We are just doing a mental concentration discipline for polarizing the mind. Once you have gone through all of the energy centers, once you've been cleansed, you've had a vegetarian diet for a while and you are leading a virtuous life for a while, then you can now go into practicing the formal Serpent Power meditation, the outline of which is as follows:

Assume a comfortable posture, either sitting or lying down on your back, in a comfortable way. The key to the meditation is to not move! This is why the mummy posture is the preferred posture for this kind of meditation, even though if your mind is very dull or you are not rested you can easily fall asleep. You avoid that by getting enough sleep before the practice and practicing control of the breath. Breath is the link between the conscious and the unconscious. It is why you can breathe and you are not even aware that you are breathing, because you are concentrating on other things, it is called autonomic. Or you can take control of your breath and breathe consciously. When you breathe consciously this is why it controls your mind and your emotions. It brings you out of the trance level or the automatic consciousness as most people are living. Remember we talked about this a few times ago, how a person can be walking down the street and the mind will start imagining something or flying off somewhere and all of a sudden they've walked a block and they didn't realize they've walked a block, and then later they came back to their senses. It is a kind of a trance. Most people live in that trance state. Most people are like zombies, there I've said it! This is what it means to be caught as a human being and in ignorance. Only sages are fully awake to what they're doing. Therefore, in spiritual texts like this one and others such as the Bhagavad Gita, it says sages are awake to things that ordinary people are asleep to. When ordinary people are asleep the sages are awake. Here we have in the Kybalion, the teaching says, "All paradoxes are reconcilable." This is reconciliation of that paradox that we're giving right now. So you assume the posture. The key to it is to not move even an inch, concentrating on your breath, beginning to awaken the lower energy center by tapping it. You've seen the snake charmers, how they hit/tap the head of a cobra so they can start making it dance with their flute playing and all of that kind of thing? You are tapping it with life force energy and this is all done by mental will. You are bringing life force energy from the environment through to your lungs and you direct it to hit your lowest energy center. You hit that several times to awaken it; Ten, twenty times with each breath. Breathe in, bring in energy and then direct it to hit the energy center. However long it takes for you to begin to feel it, to be aware of it. This could take several minutes, it can take the first part of your practice, it can take a whole half hour, or an hour and it may still not happen for a few days or weeks, depending on your level of development, cleansing, etc.

Then when you begin its awakening then you begin to raise it to the other energy centers. You breathe in, you direct it down towards your lower energy center and then you bring it up, be still as you've now inhaled, now you are holding your breath, you're sucking in your gut, you are bringing it up towards your point between your eyebrows. Then you let it go, you exhale and let the energy come down. Again you do this continuously and this is what you do for the first hour of your practice; again not moving even a millimeter, in a semi-darkened room. You may burn some incense, you may play some of the music, if you like to begin with but all of this can only go on for the first hour. Remember you build up to this, it just doesn't happen, just like that. The second hour what happens is you stop controlling your breath. You allow it to flow naturally and just remain aware of it. You let the autonomic system take over. Realize that it is very shallow. You become aware of the shallowness; you become aware of your body and without your conscious control. You become aware of your body as being motionless and this practice actually mimics the death process. You want to discover your awareness free from the body.

This is your contemplation, but this contemplation is done from the sixth energy center. You want to place your body in the following position, lying down with your head towards the East or North, with your legs 1 ½ - 2 ft. apart; your arms 1 ft. away from your body with palms facing upwards; eyes closed; concentrating on that sixth energy center. We left out one aspect which is the words of power. Words of power will help to polarize, they will help to bring the lower energy centers into health and to resonate as well as harmonize all of the energy centers and bring the life force energy towards the crown of the head, towards the sixth energy center. Realize that if you were to look at your body from above, it looks like an arrow and it is pointing towards your head, towards the point between your eyebrows. You are doing this for an hour, concentrating on that point for an hour and at the end of that hour you live in that point. You are aware, you may be aware of the physical body so on so forth but you are not in it because after an hour of this practice and not moving your body it has fallen asleep but even though your body has fallen asleep, you, that is to say, your mind, remains awake! If that happens you have reached a great stage in the practice. Afterwards, when you get up, your body feels as if it has been asleep, you feel as if you wake up in the morning after your body has been asleep. But of course you feel that you've been awake the whole time so but now you are revitalized, you are ready to go. It is like having sleep but without the delusion of dreams. Instead you have the conscious experience of visions of your expanded self.

The using of words of power has been especially enjoined for the first part of the practice, the first hour where forceful visualization and manipulation of air and life force energy are manipulated: "Om Maati Maakheru; Om Amun Ra Ptah; Om Asar Aset Heru can be used. As you go through the chant, you are resonating with each energy center beginning with Om at the base of the spine and by the time you get to Heru (in Om Asar Aset Heru) you get to the top, the crown of the head. Or with Om Amun Ra Ptah, by the time you get to Ptah you get to the top. At the beginning stage it is a continuous, repetitious process. Eventually you cannot think of anything but the chant and the practice, the visualization. All of this is going to lead you out of the physical world, into the astral world and then eventually beyond that also. If you were to do this for that first hour, then you reach a point where now you will be able to just simply sit there and rest in your Amun aspect, your Witnessing Consciousness aspect that is now disengaged from the body and physical world. That is going to awaken you to the subtler vibrating aspects of yourself. In other words you are going to awaken to the Astral body. Actually, in this practice first you go through your astral aspect and then if you continue your practice you discover your Amun aspect. So you're coming from your Ptah aspect which is your physical, then you go to your Ra aspect which is your mind and senses. As the practice progresses you are less involved with your physical body; you may be aware of it, but it's there sleeping. Then you get to your Amun aspect where you are not aware even of your mind and its gross thoughts anymore because you are now vibrating on a higher level, a subtler level. When you are aware of being separate from your physical and astral bodies, that is your Amun aspect. This is what makes a human being different from animals; animals don't have this capacity to discover themselves as being different from their personalities, their bodies, senses and their instinctual desires, but human beings have that potential.

If you continue with this practice and you reach a very high level of the practice, now you start to realize that you exist, that you are beyond time and space; beyond the physical world; beyond your body, you exist outside of that, in the: The I Am. If you continue beyond this practice, that I Am dissolves and you become one with the eternal ocean and that is called Neberdjer. There is nowhere else to go but that, beyond that you dissolve.

I should tell you that each succeeding level of this practice is very difficult, but if you have the will and you have the force, as you succeed it becomes easier but most lf all it becomes the most pleasurable and the most joyous practice, at each succeeding level that you discover. At each increasing level you expand in your consciousness, you are vibrating at higher levels and it is more bliss that you experience, more glory that you experience. At each succeeding level you realize that the lower level is just that a lower level of consciousness, a lower level of existence. When you come out of this practice you reflect back and discover more expansion or you feel transformed in stages each time. The more you practice the more transformed you are and the more of it stays with you when you come back into the physical plane. Eventually, if it stays with you in a perennial way then you are called an "Enlightened Being". You are called Sage.

This practice is difficult in the beginning because of years and lifetimes of outward mental experience that all human beings engage in and that is what makes it difficult to keep the mind from fidgeting; For this purpose, the beginning stages of the practice make use of visualization and polarization and the words of power, using the energy, visualizing the energy etc. All that is done to tame the mind and restless personality, to control it is to cause the gross vibrations and polarities to become sharper and more subtle. It is all done to concentrate the mind. It is difficult to keep the body from fidgeting because you want to scratch or you feel some little insect crawling on you or it is too cold, it's too hot; it's too this it's too that. But as you discover higher practice, you will become stronger and the small things will not bug you; you just say the heck with it, I don't care if I'm a little cold or there is a little noise or something is crawling on you!. Your body has to obey; it has no choice but to stay quiet and motionless for the time that you have set. Just make sure that you are covered properly and that you have a proper surface that will not have lumps that will become uncomfortable over a 2-3 hour period. You may wear loose clothing. Also enjoined in this practice is you should have the room at a comfortable ambient temperature, not hot or cold and use loose clothing or go naked all together; just be sure that all body parts including hair are in alignment with the arrow positioning of the body that we discussed earlier. It depends on your environment that you have to work with. You try to avoid noises, street noises, of course the best you can do is the best to promote the practice but whether or not you are able to find a "perfect" environment you must forge ahead anyway.

Up to this point what has been described in this meditation practice leads up to the second hour of the meditation practice. If your body has fallen asleep and you have been abiding in your astral body, in the astral plane, you've lost track of time and space at this point. Then what you do is to have a clock set up so it will give a gentle alarm for whatever time you have set so that you will come out of the meditation at a prescribed time. This is a highly advanced practice I don't recommend you enter into it until you've been practicing the teachings of Maat and studying the philosophy and have adopted a vegetarian diet for some time. You need to become virtuous of character because what happens is that the energy that you are going to release and develop, if you are not of virtuous character and you do not have purity in your conduits, will cause you physical, psychological and or psychic problems. What is negative, within your personality, will be augmented, in your character and physical constitution. When that energy tries to flow through your energy centers and is blocked, by the impurities, it is going to produce a negative outcome; the energy has to go somewhere, so it has to go to some other conduit that perhaps you might not want it to. It is going to cause you sensations that you should not have, that you do not want prematurely also, things that you are not ready for. Also, it's going to lead to psychological problems, compulsive behaviors, uncontrolled desires, psychotic breaks and so on so forth. Therefore, your practice should be measured, progressive and directed by an experienced teacher. This is highest way of healthy polarization. This is the outline of the whole program. It is the earliest program that was enjoined in Kemet, the Arat Sekhem or Serpent Power teaching.

There are some questions about some things that we said about psychic powers. During the practice some of you may discover psychic powers; you will become aware of them on the way to spiritual enlightenment. To keep on the successful road you should not engage them; But you are only to become aware of them, but don't be trying to use them, don't be trying to "enjoy" them, because if you get some psychic insight into something, it can be helpful but just as there is wisdom in the physical realm so too there is the possibility of going astray in the astral realm. If it's a good message like don't go out into the street at a particular time because an asteroid is going to fall on that street, don't go on that street. In this practice also sometimes you will be met by higher beings. If you are strong of will, adept in philosophy, cleansed of body, you need not worry about inimical forces as they would be more scared of you. You might meet Anpu or Ptah or Aset or your Tutelary Divinity or a neteru (divinity) you have concentrated on. You may receive their teaching, you acknowledge them, you respect them, and you show your devotion to them, let them do their duty. If they come to do something to your body such as touching the energy centers to adjust them or clear them, etc., let them do their work and move on with your practice. You will know, you will be aware by the vibration level if they are righteous beings or if they are not. Automatically they will be repelled if they are not. If you are a person of un-virtuous character you will not be able to repel them and you will be sorry by your contact with them. This is why you should enjoin the practice as I've outlined it. If you are righteous, virtuous, pure of heart and pure in your mettus (clean arteries, lymphatic system, digestive system, nervous system, etc.) you will attract all manner of virtuous and righteous energy and they will help you on your journey.

As far as the practice of vibrating at such a level, another Question was asked during the week, about if vibrating at such a higher level that you don't need physical food and that kind of thing. Yes, your higher aspect of your personality should not be dependent upon those things. Your physical body will still need physical food but less and with less covetousness and greed as well. Your mind needs higher food and getting that through this higher practice will allow the cravings and desires for things of the body to abate. Your physical aspect of your personality does need that so let it continue; but now that will be at a moderated rate. However the proper food for the body continues to be the subtler food which is vegetarian food, fruits and vegetables and not the grosser physical foods or meat of any kind. So your mental food should be the subtler mental food; it should not be the grosser mental food (like ignorance, anger, hatred, greed, lust, jealousy, envy, sentimental relationships, etc.). So that means going to movies that are righteous if you want to go to a movie. Don't go to movies that are base, that have gratuitous sex and violence and things like that, images and sounds with lower, grosser vibrations without higher meaning, that are presented simply to tantalize and excite the senses, the base emotions and lower aryu. This is how you should lead your life. Don't go off half-cocked with this practice or don't be going wild and reading all kinds of stuff about wild things that you are going to turn into or this or that. This is a natural practice for human beings to become God-like while they are still alive. You continue with your physical body and yet internally you have transcended. You don't want to be like to those people also who go meditating for six or ten hours a day and then they don't tell anybody, they don't talk to anybody, they don't help anybody, but also they do not reach the heights of the practice; that is not enjoined by this teaching. That is not going to help you or anybody in the world as it should. There have been some of the sages who were meditating constantly, so their students had to bathe them, feed them, etc.. Now I don't think any one of you should be hanging around to be bathing me! I'll take care of that myself. If I can't take care of it, I'll see you later! No reason to hang around at that point. You get my meaning, you get my drift? You are supposed to become an enlightened being and dynamic and powerful on the physical plane but also on the astral plane because the physical will come to an end one day but the astral continues; the question is when the physical body ends do you want your astral body to disintegrate and your soul to reincarnate or do you want it to remain integrated and to progress on to higher spiritual realizations if you have not reached them by that time. That is what this is all about. Hetep.

I'm reminded that there is a 2 tape Serpent Power series if you are interested in starting with this practice. The first tape is on cassette and CD it is enjoined for the practice of cleansing which is the first part of the discipline which as I said before may last for months before you get into the higher aspect of the practice. I'm not recommending, in fact I'm telling you not to enter the high form of practice until you go into the lower. Don't be thinking that you've been doing this for a while that you are on some certain level, all of this kind of thing. Follow the instructions that have been given and do not deviate from those. There is also an important breath and visualization component to this practice but that is held back for personal instruction as it can be easily misused. Another point that I'm being reminded about is that other practices that you do, do have an effect on the life force energy centers. Also recommended is that if you're going to get into this particular practice that you should be doing one single practice as far as your meditation practice is concerned. Of course the teachings of the Maat philosophy, the virtuous teaching, cleanses you and makes you virtuous as I've described in the lecture. Talking about specific kinds of meditation practice, you should only be doing the one. Other practices for relaxation and concentration can continue but as far as this high level of practice, that I've described today, that should be your only practice if you want to enjoin that.

HTP

Chapter 5: The Principle of Rhythm Part 1 B

Thoth and Safekh (goddess of history) write the name of Ramses II on fruits

There's a little bit of evil and there's a little bit of good. Nothing is all bad or nothing is all good. Where is the demarcation point between one pole and another? Where is the exact point where light is and darkness is, or darkness ends and light begins? We talked about how everything is a degree of everything else. For conceptual purposes, human beings think that there is actually a black and white and yet there is no such thing as black and white. From the standpoint of rhythmic pattern degrees, there is no such thing because where does white begin and where does black begin? Where does white end and where does black begin? When you feel elated in the morning and something happens and you feel depressed in the afternoon where is the point where it actually changed? Then it comes back, where is the point where it changes back? It's imperceptible and yet for conceptual purposes, for a better understanding of the lower mind, you are made to think that there is an actual demarcation point somewhere up to this hour I was feeling good, then I was feeling bad up to here and nothing is like that. It is all illusory. Everything is but a degree of everything else. All of this, the Kybalion explains, affects a human being at their conscious level of mind. These energies push a human being, impel and compel them, especially those who have not practiced gaining control over their lives through the yogic techniques, through the disciplines, the art that we've been discussing: the wisdom teaching; practice of the devotional rituals; the Maat philosophy and finally meditation. Remember we talked previously about the unconscious level of mind that leads a human being automatically in their lives. Remember I told you a few sessions ago that if you're walking down the street and then you all of sudden start thinking, imagining or fantasizing and you get to the end of the block but you didn't remember that you have walked that distance, that is the automatic mind that has operated the personality while you were away musing in the astral plane of mind. Your personality has been carried away by its thoughts, emotions and its inner-feelings. You have been swept away with the tide, in other words. People can actually have this happen and by the end of the day they've killed somebody and they don't realize what they've done or they regret it later or they do this or that, the mood swings and so on and so forth. Therefore the teaching has enjoined that an aspirant should begin to start to feel as if they have gained all there is to have gained in the world and as if they have lost everything that they have gained. Imagine what that means. Are you going to be either bothered one way or another internally? And in so doing being undisturbed, having your mind placid like a quite lake or like an ocean with waves whipped up by the stormy winds of desires, regrets and misplaced feelings? Are you going to be unduly disturbed whether you gain something or you lose something? If you reach this point we are talking about all the funny little things that happen in the world, that seem so important, so compelling, they are going to seem petty, but also like a glorious show, an expression of the Divine, stuff that happens, and nothing more; nothing to get overly concerned about, unnecessarily involved with; nothing to pine away over; nothing to be longing over.

> "If you wish to be as a master you must love impersonally, caring for all equally; wants must yield to self-control, live as though you have achieved and acquired everything you need and also as if you have lost everything; even the thing or person you might love most; for material things are transitory."
> -Ancient Egyptian Proverb

Therefore through this practice you are going to come into a balance, you are going to come to a particular point and this is what the Kybalion calls Neutralization of Rhythm. You cannot stop the rhythmic pattern of the world. However, you can neutralize it's affects within your personality and this is what every aspirant must learn how to do. Since this rhythmic pattern has its beginnings, it is like, remember that rock I talked about and throwing it into the lake, and then the ripples come afterwards, the rock falls into the lake of your unconscious mind and that is the sprouting of the unconscious Ari, a subtle impression. That reverberates into your sub-conscious or it emerges as a feeling in the subconscious, and then it emerges as a conscious thought and desire in your conscious mind. You think, "Oh, this is mine, this is what I desired, this is me." In reality it is not you; it is nothing but an established pattern from your present and or previous lifetime or your previous existence in this lifetime - which you have agreed with, accepted and hold onto. What happens next is that when you accept the emergent feelings, thoughts and then act on them you are creating and leaving new impressions in your unconscious mind that will be experienced in the future, that will emerge in the future when stimulated at some point. That leads you to another impression in your mind and more mental agitations and more future desires and experiences, keeping you in a cycle of experiences, impressions, mental vibrations and agitations in a seemingly endless rhythmic cycle of ignorant worldly experiences, death, reincarnation, more ignorant experiences, more mental agitations and gross vibrations, that are going to come out later and to push you in another direction, towards another desire and to keep on reincarnating again and again and again and so on. This can go on indefinitely, unless you break the cycle of the rhythmic pattern, the worldly rhythmic pattern.

How do you break the negative cycle and change to a rhythmic movement that leads to enlightenment instead of more lower, worldly entanglements? The key to this change is focusing on Amun. Amun means Witnessing Self. If you were to practice awareness, concentrating on the Witnessing Self, your mind cannot be swayed with the tides of emotion. If you practice the discipline of the Witnessing Self meditation, which means concentrating on that part of your personality, which is the Witnessing Consciousness, you would discover that you can look at your mind and become separate from your thoughts. As soon as you become separate from your thoughts you are detached from them. You are free from them, you do not have to act on them and they do not have a hold on you. Additionally, you will be less susceptible to the automatic mind that takes over when you fly off into a fancy of imaginations or desires. Of course this is when you perfect the practice.

Recall that there are three aspects of experience, Amun, Ra and Ptah, the Triad, the Trinity of human experience. Amun is the Witnessing Self, Ra is the perceiving instrument and Ptah is the object. So we have: subject, object and interaction between the two. If one of the these three components of perception is missing you cannot have experience, so in your meditation practice, when you go beyond your mind and senses then you lose sight of the physical world, the Ptah component. You would still have your mind to perceive with and you would still have your concept of self that is doing the perceiving, but there is nothing to perceive so therefore you cannot have a triad experience and you would more easily be aware of what is there when the triad is not. The triad or tripod of experience, it is like having a table with three legs, but without any one of the legs the table falls down. If you have the physical objects and you have the Witnessing Self and you don't have any perceiving instruments to perceive them with then the table (of perception) breaks down also. If you place your attention on the Witness Self aspect within yourself, and reflect "I Am", I Exist and there are objects out there and I use my mind to perceive them", and if you study the wisdom teaching you come to understand that the world is an illusion because it does not exist unless it is being perceived in and through the mind so then you can take the world out of the equation. You become aware of yourself as independent of objects (the world, i.e. Creation).

If you practice a meditation technique that uses concentrating on a particular object, that means that you are taking your mind and concentrating on it, and also you are taking your perceiving instrument away from the world (everything else). You can't perceive the world anymore so the tripod breaks down. If you were to be able to stop your thoughts, the result is the same as if you concentrate on one object, the tripod, again, breaks down. All of these are different methods and ways but the primary goal of all is breaking down the triad of perception, being mindful and taking oneself out of time and space by breaking down the triad of perception. The Witnessing Self Meditation also allows this process to occur. It is practiced in the following way:

THE WITNESSING CONSIOSNESS MEDITATION TECHNIQUE AS A WAY TO CHANGE THE RHYTHM OF CONSCIOUS PERCEPTION

There are several stages that have been enjoined. The first stage of the practice is to slow down the movements of the body. Remember we are talking about rhythm as being an ebbing and flowing, a rhythmic movement. If you allow yourself to live in the world at the regular pace of the world, you are more easily susceptible to becoming caught up in the world. If you change up on the world you are going to easily fall out of the pattern of the world. So therefore practice slowing down the movements of the body. That means if takes you half a second to move your arm up, then you take ten seconds. You gradually move up, up, and up and you become aware of your action, it is not an automatic action anymore. Being aware of your action, that is happening very slowly, that takes you out of the world of time and space and brings you into awareness of yourself as actor. When you are aware of self as actor instead of being caught up in the play, or the movie of the world then you are becoming more aware of yourself as the Witnessing Consciousness. This exercise is to be practiced until your movements are almost imperceptible and then you actually stop your physical movements and then you work on your mental movements. Your physical body is allowed to rest completely without any movement at all so then you work on your mental movements. Become aware of your mental movements as passing clouds and you are separate and aware of the passing clouds. As soon as you start moving in this direction, the less hold these movements have on you. Actually, you are polarizing your personality, yourself towards the higher vibration as we spoke about last time, a few times ago. You are polarizing yourself to a particular point in the rhythm. Here working with breath is important. If you become aware of your breath, your breath is the ultimate representation of the sympathetic and parasympathetic aspect of the human being. These are rhythms that allow a human being to exist. When your body is in a sympathetic state your breath is very shallow and you are tense and stressed out and you are ready for a fight. When your parasympathetic system kicks in which is the pendulum flow back the other way, you relax, and you can breathe freely. It is like the breath coming in and out.

Where does the breath stop coming in and where does the breath start going out? Again, you become aware of that. As soon as you become aware realize that the key is that as soon as you become aware of something you are free from it. From this yogic standpoint, you are to be aware of yourself as being separate from that thing. If you are aware of your breath and you are watching your breath, you are free from that breath. If you start becoming aware of your emotions, feelings and thoughts coming into your mind, impression sprouting in your mind, you are free from them, you don't have to act on them. You are aware of the mob coming down the street because they are angry and upset, you don't have to become part of it, and you don't have to get caught up in it. But you are not aware of all this if you are an ignorant human being and you are caught up. Somebody will come knocking on your door, an old friend who was with you and jail and they'll say, "Hey I got a good gig going on here, we're going to break into this place," you are right down there with them. Or they come down with some drugs and you fall in with them using the drugs, and the rhythmic pattern of thinking, feeling and acting must be broken. Otherwise it can continue indefinitely as we say.

But going back to the meditation, this is a meditation practice that begins in a very conscious state; a very awake state and you remain so, going into deeper levels of self-awareness until you are just the Eye, the Witnessing Eye. The next step beyond this is Neberdjer, once you've perfected Amun, which means understanding yourself as a witnessing transcendental being, which is beyond even the concept of Eye. The concept of existence and non-existence these are little concepts to the Self, these are just for mental understanding. Whatever God is, it is beyond even these concepts. These concepts cannot even apply, cannot even be used or explained. So the key is to watching the breath, allowing that stressed out pattern of life, this is a problem with many people. They get a stressed out pattern and their rhythm compensates in another form of stress. The sympathetic pattern is when people are cheated by life, you are in the sympathetic state, you are running away, your blood vessels are constricted; your digestive system is shut down because you are running. People are so stressed out that they are acting this way constantly. "Oh I have to get into work. Oh, I have to pick up my kids at school. Oh, I have to pay the bills. Oh, I have to go here; I have to do this I have to do that. Oh, I have to get some rest, Oh, I have to go on vacation, I have to come back from vacation and go back to work." The compensation is more stress. They never go back to compensation in their rhythm that truly compliments. That means you are out of kilter, you are out of harmony. So aspirants must bring their life to a certain harmony. Breathing is a perfect way to do that.

Practice watching the breath that allows the body to come back to a parasympathetic state, a relaxed state. That opens the door to discovering the Witnessing Self. So you practice by being aware that you are breathing. Breathing is as they say the only, the one aspect of the human constitution that human beings can be fully aware of or can be happening automatically without your awareness. As soon as you become aware of your breathing it starts to take you out of the ordinary world and its pattern of time and space and the worldly rhythms of egoistic desiring and experiencing and brings you closer to the present and the present is a doorway to eternity, the realm beyond time and space. You must realize that if you are involved in the world you can't be fully thinking about breathing. So your body takes that over autonomically. The same thing happens with your automatic consciousness as well as your ego consciousness. Your ego takes over its patterns. If your ego takes over your life, you have no control. If you take control then your ego cannot take control, you see. At the beginning, in the middle of your practice, sometimes the ego is in control, sometimes you are in control, sometimes you break down and you give in to the ego. You ought to try to curtail that. You do that by practicing the disciplines of the teaching. Your morning worship; your listening to the lectures; your study of the teachings; your devotion of the exercises and also your practice of the Maat righteousness teachings, your experience of the world will also lead you to see how defunct the world is and you still keep on believing in it. Even though you may listen to the most wonderful lectures, you go out into the world and you still may eat a little meat, you still may use some pesticides, you still desire to see professional sports instead of meditating, and you still may do some things that you know the teaching doesn't enjoin. Then the teaching eventually will show you the error of your ways. So not to worry, it is all good right? So practice discovering the Witnessing Self. This allows you to stop the movements of the unconscious mind and when that happens the ripple effect that occurs in the sub-conscious and unconscious mind will not affect it. This is the way to master the principle of rhythm. You polarize yourself to the Witnessing Self, to the Witnessing Consciousness, the Eye and allow a spiritual rhythmic movement to emerge and follow that more and more each day. If this is done you have achieved mastery of Self and you are not affected by the world. You have transcended time and space. This is the wonder and beauty of the Mindfulness Meditation, anybody can practice it. Just slow down the movements of your body. If it takes you ten seconds to walk across the room, take ten minutes, real slow. Be aware of your movements, be aware of yourself breathing; be aware of yourself then be aware of yourself controlling the movements of your body and directing it. Your body is not a robot, it is not an automaton. You should realize that there is actually a level of existence; there is a level of happening that you are not previously aware of. Even now you are not aware of this level of your own being. You are still swimming in the ocean. You are to be aware of that Witnessing Self. The more you practice it the more awareness stays with you and in your ordinary life that means real awareness when you are moving at the speed of life. You know you can move at the ordinary speed of life but then you can become aware of yourself even within that movement. You can be like anybody else, appear to be dynamic and being very active and still being internally motionless, internally mindful.

We have a separate little book on the Mindfulness, the Slowness Meditation, the Mindfulness technique, also as talked about in some other meditation books the Path of Enlightenment. The Witnessing Self Consciousness, this is what the Buddhists call "Sat Chin Buddhi" This was in Kemet thousands and thousands of years. That is what the Eye, the top of the Pyramid represents. The point, the Ben Ben at the top of the Pyramid, what the Hindus call "Bindu". The four legs, the four sides of the Pyramid, four aspects of the physical world, four aspects of the personality and so on so forth. This is mastery, this is transcendence. You want to achieve that by mindfulness. Hetep.

Commentary by Seba Dja

I just a couple of comments to add to what was said; actually to correlate with it. One was that Sebai Maa talked about the Slowness Meditation and the Witnessing Consciousness if you recall there is a Kemetic Proverb that says: "Every gesture is a world to be mastered." his relates to the performing actions in that automatic way. There are so many gestures that are performed and it is done with any awareness of the true essence. It also relates to the Sema discipline of righteous action. Performing actions with the awareness and the feeling that you are the doer of the action; the practice of Devotion where you practice actions where you are in the world and you see everyone as the Self. You feel that everyone is the Self and you are serving the Self in others and then there's the practice of righteous action and selfless service in the capacity of now focusing on the action part of it, you as the doer. In the Maat book it talks about the action-less actor, the one who does but doesn't do. Becoming perfected in this area, one has to have that awareness of one's true essence as one is performing or feel that one is a conduit for the Divine energy flow into it and when one is involved in this automatic action. These actions of where you are just doing stuff, doing stuff, doing stuff and there's that lack of awareness. You are not in that higher spiritual plane, so all of these actions and creating impressions that are egoistic. So "every gesture is a worldly master." So a way to start gaining control of the gestures is as Sebai Maa said is the Slowness Meditation. One simple recommendation that is given to students, not even necessarily in the Yoga field but one thing to do I'll tell you is brush your teeth with your right hand, go ahead and try brushing your teeth with your left hand. You will just notice the difference. With the right hand you will go and you will brush your teeth and you won't even know what you did. If you are left-handed you would do everything with the right hand. Now you have to concentrate on doing it because your left hand is not used to it. Now everything takes you longer. For example, if you write with your right hand, now you are going to write with your left hand. Everything you took for granted, how does the letter go, does it turn this way, that way, does the "s" face this way, that way? Everything now becomes a conscious moment. Children in that way they have that capacity that when they are doing things they tend to become focused on the little things that they do. As they get older, there are so many things to do that we want to get focused on the big picture and we lose that sense of focusing at the moment. Be in the moment. We talked about how being in the moment that is the only thing that there is, that really exists. So that practice should be done. Specifically like make a habit, even if it is for 5 or 10 minutes where you are. Whatever it is you are doing. Whether you are doing the dishes, you can do it as a separate mediation in and of itself, just as a mediation where you are practicing and becoming aware of every motion, every movement, you can do it as part of your routine chores that you do but for like 5 or 10 minutes you are going to actually try to just make it a meditation being aware of everything you are doing at the moment. Every step you are taking, every muscle that is moving and that will bring you to more awareness of the mind, keeping the mind focused in the moment so that you can start to master that world of gestures and action. So you can be in the moment so you can have more conscious awareness of what it is you are doing. That also, as Sebai Maa mentioned, allows the mind to become calm and peaceful in that moment.

The other comment was on the aspect of the detached Witnessing Consciousness. What I wanted to say about that was the practice of watching the emotions and becoming detached from the emotions, that's very important, especially in the earlier stages of spirituality. It is an important capacity to start to develop and to gain control over. We often emphasize and we talk so much about purification, purifying the mind, purifying the heart, purifying the emotions so you are not passionate, you are not angry, all of these negative emotions don't come out of you. This is a process and it takes time to become perfected in this process. So as you are going through this whole process of purification all of this negative stuff is still going to keep coming out of you. It is like a pustule or a sore that you know some wounds take a very long time before they heal themselves. So too they ooze and ooze in little bits. So two processes of trying to treat that wound is one is trying to keep that wound clean, trying to purify it; the other aspect is if every time a little pus comes out you are going to get all upset and all frustrated about it. You are going to be misbalancing the mind, so part of it is trying to keep it clean but part of it is also becoming detached from the so called pus that is coming out of the wound, the drainage that is coming out of the wound. Keep changing the dressings, changing the dressings but also with detachment from that because as you continue to purify you will still find anger will still keep coming out, the fear, the insecurities, the whatever all of these different emotions. They are still going to be coming out of you. If every time you hear that I'm not getting better, I'm not growing, I'm not growing spiritually, then that is going to continue. What is that going to do to the mind?

The Principle of Rhythm Pt. 2 Q & A

Commentary by Seba Dja continued

What is happening to me? At the same time this does not mean that in this practice of detachment that one becomes insensitive and aspirants do not hold themselves accountable for what is occurring as a result of their emotions. If it is coming out and it is affecting someone, the off balance of emotions, any of the negative qualities of the egoistic personality, if any of those are coming out it doesn't mean that, "Oh well I'm unaffected, detached, I'm not going to be affected by it so I know I'm going to continue on with my practice." So it is not to become insensitive and say this just happened, "Oh I yelled at this person but it's no big deal that's just a part of the ego stuff coming out, I'm unaffected by it. It is not going to bother me." So that not being bothered by it is not the same as being detached from it. At a higher level it can get there but really it's not. While it is there you should be bothered by it. When I say being bothered by it, you should be aware of it, you should be sensitive to it, you should be accountable to it. If you don't have this accountability then if it is there and you are just saying I'm detached from it, because your concept of detachment is incorrect, you are not practicing detachment at the highest level. Really what you are doing is that you are leaving this baggage there and you are saying "It's not affecting me; that is not who I am." But you are not also dealing with it and you're not also working through it to get beyond it. So you have to step back. You do have to realize that those emotions there are not the real you; they're not the real aspect of the personality; that the real you is unaffected by it and at that level of detachment. But at the same time you have to recognize it; you have to be aware of it and you have to put the restraints on the personality to figure out what you need to do to deal with those emotions through some insight into why you reacted that way perhaps. This insight can be part of your reflective meditation, part of your reflection into the aspect of it. If I'm this personality its unaffected how did I react this way and if I'm supposed to be practicing not getting upset at someone why did I get upset at this one? So it needs to be dealt with, it needs to be worked through. Aspects of working through that are through meditation also. It doesn't only have to be the psychological aspect, just constantly pounding your mind with it. But that is one aspect of it that needs to be dealt with. It needs to be dealt with at all levels of the personality. So you need to continue practice of meditation, you need to develop detachment, the pure detachment, not the insensitive detachment or the detachment that is like you know holding yourself unaccountable for these things that occurred. But the pure form of detachment leads to detachment from the person because along with that true detachment comes purification because if you're detached you are not identifying with the ego. Therefore, if you are not identifying with the ego then you are not going to have these negative emotions coming out anyway, because they are not with the ego. So as long as they're coming out and you are practicing detachment, your detachment is going to be impure until you get to the pure detachment. So there still has to be awareness, you are not trying to become insensitive, you still have that awareness, and you still have the sensitivity to it because that is part of the practice at the level where you are. That is how the mind is set up. The mind is set up that you have a conscience. You have awareness; a conscience is not different from your soul. The conscience is the Divine in you, recognizing it. "Hey, you know, hmmm what I did, or I did that." Recognizing how it impacted the people around you. If you need to apologize to other people around you if you need to adjust to that, make changes for whatever came out, if it caused misbalances externally. But at the very end there is still that attachment and you don't go running after it infinitely. "Oh, I apologize; oh I keep apologizing forever." When I say keep apologizing forever beyond the fact of saying, "You know I'm sorry for what happened and I'll try to do better. I'll correct it." Whatever it is you just make an acknowledgement because that is part of having harmonious relationships. If you are working with a group of initiates or enlightened personalities then that is fine, maybe they don't need you to be apologizing; maybe they don't need you to be accountable. They don't care what you do or don't do. But if you are in the world of time and space this is part of having a harmonious relationship. Sometimes, "well, I'm unaffected by it, I'm detached from it," and they leave the baggage with the other person, it's not there problem if they are affected by it, they should be practicing yoga too. While this is true, you are hampering that interaction in that relationship. Even at the level of initiates because again you are operating with other people around you who are initiates even though you are practicing and striving within the teachings. Sometimes, again that same sensitivity or letting the other person know that you are aware of whatever it was the perhaps you did even at this level allows them to know where you are spiritually. It allows them to know that you are sensitive to it and that you didn't think that it was ok to do it and that allows them to be able to bond with you at a higher level of communication. It allows them to have higher expectations of you and of themselves and they know they can rely on you and they can trust you. So even at that level, the being sensitive is still important to be accountable and maybe apologize. In terms of apologizing to spiritual teachers they don't need you to do that, they don't need you to explain why you did this but part of that again allows for that sensitivity to be there to let them know that you were aware of the shortcomings. That is why it is important for you to hold yourself accountable for whatever it is that you need to work on; so I just want to really emphasize the difference between detachment and being insensitive. We always say that if it was about detachment, the ultimate level of detachment you become the most sensitive personality. You become a very highly compassionate personality. You become, because you are not a part of it, it is not about what you can gain as a result of it. It is not about you are benefitting as a result but how you could facilitate and how you can help the world. That is the highest level of detachment otherwise as we said before, rocks and stones would be detached because they're very insensitive and they're very unaccountable. They don't care what they do or they don't care about anything, they don't have any feelings, they don't care about anything. So it's not just a matter of not caring or being insensitive, having a hard heart, being unaffected in that way. When we talk about the concept of being "unaffected" no matter what, in terms of what enlightenment means that's what Nehast means you become unaffected no matter what. You become highly sensitive. You see this sensitivity is what allows you to keep purifying yourself. Every time there is a misdeed or a mishap done and it is brought to you and you have that sensitivity that little bug in you, you want to become detached from it so that you are not caught up in it and that you are not egoistic. You think about it and say, "Oh, I did this, I'm a terrible person, poor me." You don't want to get into the negativity of yourself, watering the tree of ego in yourself. But you want to become aware of it. That little nag fairy, that little think that is pulling you there, you want to become aware of that because that's the Divine Self pointing to you saying, "Hey, this is an area you have to work on. This is something you need to take care of." So you actually need to become more and more sensitive to the thoughts that are coming in also. So negative thoughts come in and when I say negative I don't mean like to go kill somebody, or I need to go murder, or go steal. Those are gross negative thoughts. But even more subtle negative thoughts coming out: "Oh what is this person doing?" Just little things coming out where you are separating yourself from this person or these people, or what are they? You need to become more and more sensitive at subtler and subtler levels of how the mind is always creating dis-unions between things. Part of that, as I said, is an increased sensitivity to what is coming into the mind. So be very cautious with the differentiation between detachment and insensitivity.

End of Seba Djas' Comments.

Om Hetep, Hetep, Hetep, Hetep.

Chapter 6: The Principle of Cause and Effect Pt. 1A

Chants: Hetep; Om Amun Ra Ptah; Om Asar Aset Heru; Om Maati Maakheru; Amma Su en Pa Neter; Drumming, Dua Maat and Om Hetep.

It is fitting that we did the Maat song just now because as we continue today's talk, today's study in the series on the Kybalion, the Seven Hermetic Principles, the teachings of Djehuty, the Lord of Khemenu, the City of the Eight; the Eight Principles the Opposites we deal today with the law of Cause and Effect which is governed by the Ancient Egyptian Goddess and Neteru or cosmic principle known as "MA'AT". If you recall we learned in the mythic story of the creation, the creation saga where Lord Ra had created the universe, had plants, Stars, all the creatures, all the worlds and finally created human beings out of his own tears. The human beings became arrogant, they started running amok; killing each other, creating lustful desires, despoiling the earth and disrespecting its Creator, and so the elements went to Ra to complain about the people. Air element came and said, "Look at these people, they are dumping garbage in me and look how I smell, look how foul I am." The Earth element went in to complain, "Look they're killing each other and blood in going into me, and their carcasses are on top of me and all that. These people are out of control, there must be some control." So Ra sent down Lord Djehuty to establish some laws. Those laws are called Maat. Those laws govern everything in creation and from that time forward human beings are not free since their actions will have consequences that will in turn affect the doer of the actions. Now moving forward Ra decreed that those human beings that act in accordance with the laws, they will lead a prosperous life. Those who do not, they will suffer untold miseries. That is the Law of Maat. The Law of Right Action, which includes the concept of Cause and Effect. It is one of the most ancient African principles. It is inherent in all the African cultures; and religions, including Kamitan religion. As far as the basis of authentic spirituality that is acting in a way that is in harmony with the Cosmic Order, but everyone strays away from this cosmic order, at some point in time during their lives. That is the time when trouble is fomented. Whether it be your personal body or in your environment, you stray away from the laws. For instance if you stray away from eating the proper food, you are going to get a disease; there is no two ways about it. Just like as if you put water in the gas tank of your car instead of gasoline then there is going to be trouble. The problem is that when we look at the world, because of ignorance, we look at the surface causes and we do not see the underlying causes of things. For instance the car, if you put water in the gas tank who caused that to be so? Why should there be a problem with you putting water in the gas tank? Why shouldn't you be able to put anything you want? Why don't you put apple juice in there? Why can't you put maple syrup? Why should that not be? What is the cause of that? Let me say that it is the engineer; it is his fault, the engineer who designed the car engine. He is the one who made it gasoline instead of water. But who created the engineer who designed the car? Was it his father and mother? Was it their father and mother? He has four grandparents or was it his sixteen great-grandparents? So on and so forth with all the millions of ancestors who together came to create this final engineer and the Ford Motor Company created this car that takes gasoline instead of water. Shall we say it is the progenitor of the physical universe, Ra himself who created certain laws saying that gasoline will be combustible and water will not?

The story of Ra, HetHeru and Djehuty[11] gets into this question, about the causes and the effects of life. You've heard the story of when HetHeru was sent to the world to kill unrighteous people; that was an effect, a consequence and the cause was the unrighteousness that those people engaged in. She did follow Ra's orders but in doing so she forgot who she was. The cause was her action, following her duty and the effect was that she indulged too much, agitated her mind too much and forgot herself, her true identity. She forgot who she was and that was the cause of Ra sending Djehuty to help her, the effect. He told her some parables to enlighten her. One of them was the story of the two crows. One crow had the gift of hearing, he could hear very far away. The other crow had the gift of seeing, he could see very far

---

[11] See the book *The Glorious Light Meditation* by Muata Ashby

away. They were sitting on a branch one day talking and one crow asked the other, "Hey you could see very far, can you tell me what's going on down there, I can't see?" He said, "Yes, there is a fly, flying over there and I see a lizard just went and grabbed it and ate it. Look now a snake is grabbing that lizard. Look again; there is a bird that is coming to grab the snake. He is carrying it out to sea over the waters. I can't hear anything can you tell me what is going on?" He asked the other one. He said, "Yes, the snake was too heavy and the bird dropped it and a fish got it. A bigger fish ate that smaller fish. The fish came too close to the edge of the shore and a lion got her. Look now the lion is going away with the fish in his mouth but now, a *sefer*, a griffin, a mythical supremely powerful beast grabbed the lion and plucked him off the ground and took him up to a nest." One crow asked the other, "What is that great beast?" The other said, "That is the beast of Ra that is the supreme power, a mythical beast, it is part hog, part lion it is a totality of all the physical forces, the ultimate power."

Ancient Egyptian *Sefer* (Griffin)

So what is the ultimate cause of what is happening here of all of these chains of events that seem to be linked in a virtually endless connection of actions and reactions? What lead to the lion being plucked off the Earth? Was it that he ate the fish? Was it that the fish ate the littler fish? Or was it that the littler fish ate the snake? Was it that the snake ate the lizard? Or was it that the lizard ate the fly? Which was the cause? The cause of what the story is giving insight into is many things. But one of the things in particular that pertains to today is the chain of events that leads to everything that happens today. Everything that happens today; you all sitting here; everything that has led to your being here today is part of a chain of events; things that have happened throughout your life; things that have happened before your current lifetime, stretching all the way back to the beginning. Who or what is the ultimate cause in the beginning?

Furthermore, the story gives insight into the fact that the violence that was done to that little fly was taken notice of by Ra. Even a little speck of dust falls under the control of the law in other words. Like that story of the Sage and the King, Akhbar 20:21; do you remember that story where the wise minister who advised the King. There were some people in the court who were plotting against him and he was away on an errand for the King. They plotted against him, filling the King with negative thoughts about the minister, telling the King that the King is the master and the lord of the universe and that he is the greatest and that he is the ultimate cause and the ultimate power and all of this kind of thing. Since they knew that the wise minister doesn't believe in that; doesn't agree with that because God is the ultimate cause, the ultimate power in all things, that he would contradict the King and the King would snap his fingers and have his head cut off for contradicting him. In those days a King could have that power in certain countries, not in Ancient Kemet. They could snap their fingers and people would obey their absolute will. But not so in a country where a government has a King and a counselor such as Akbar or such as the Council of Priests and Priestesses of Ancient Egypt. Laws enacted by the King have to be in line with the precepts of righteous ethical conscience. Otherwise it is a path of despotism and barbarism of tyranny. So the minister came back and the King said, "Greetings, how are you and the customary greetings and pleasantries." Then he said: "My other ministers are telling me that I'm the ultimate power; I'm a God essentially. What do you have to say about that?" So the wise minister says, "Well, I do not think that you are a God, that you have that kind of power." The evil plotters against the minister thought their plan was working and that the king would now kill the minister for saying that. Then the wise minister said: "In fact I think that you are greater than God, you've transcended God. God is smaller than you." All the other ministers looked at each other and "Wow, we didn't expect this. This is like way beyond." So the minister explained, "You see, God is the very essence of this entire universe and nothing can escape God. You have this kingdom and all you survey, so all you have to do is snap your fingers and you can kick somebody out of your kingdom. You can snap your fingers and their head will be cut off, they are gone, you won't have to see them again. God can't do that. God can't kick anybody out of his kingdom. So you are greater than God therefore, logically, it is right."

In this parable we learn about the cause of negative thoughts, negative counsel, and the cause of escaping the evil fate of life, wisdom. Also, we learned about the effect of all-encompassing divinity which is caused by all-encompassing divinity. The same ideas are explained in the Kybalion about the Cosmic Laws, the Laws of Cause and Effect. Even the speck of dust is controlled by a law and even the speck of dust is noticed by the Divine. The speck of dust that may fall on your nose today may lead to all kinds of chains of events that may actually end up in the end of the world at some point in the future, a thousand years hence. Think of it this way, in a very gross, simplistic way, the speck of dust may fall on your nose, it may cause you to itch; the itch may cause you to sneeze; if you sneeze maybe something was going to hit your head that didn't hit your head because you bowed down; since you were upset and you were going to kill somebody, but since you survived and thanked goodness for your good fortune, that person did not get killed; and all the chain of events that that person and their ancestors do will have other effects. The ancestors become scientists; those scientists create a super-atomic bomb that blow up the entire universe; I'm just giving you the possibilities....this can happen.

Think of it as if the parents of Albert Einstein didn't come into being, did not come together, did not meet and have him as their child. Think about what would have happened with the theory of relativity. You could say well somebody else would have devised it but who knows? It could have come a thousand years from now and everything that has happened because of Einstein's discoveries would not have happened yet and the world would be a different place. All of this is governed by the Laws of Cause and Effect.

Those of you who saw the show that I told you about last Sunday, the Real Story of Eve, I think they called it, the African Eve. Showing that all human beings who are alive today can trace their ancestry back to one woman who existed in Africa, 150 thousand years ago, can you believe that? She is the cause of all of us being here today, that is what that means. But who caused her to come into being, caused her to exist? There are different kinds of causes in the study of philosophy. We have the effect and that's what we know, we are all here, the whole chain of ancestry, so on and so forth. We are the effect of the cause and the material of that cause coming into being is called the Efficient Cause. In terms of Creation, the cause of the Efficient Cause may be referred to as the Absolute, the Ultimate Cause, the underlying, substratum cause. Think of it as Khnum is our God, he has his Temple in Aswan, the Elephantine Temple and he is known as the potter. He takes clay and he puts it on his spinning wheel and he fashions bodies. So that Ra can send the Ba to come into the body, inhabit the body and enliven the body; your body is clay and your Ba or soul is sent to the earth by Ra. The body is the effect, the efficient cause is the clay and the sub-stratum cause, the underlying cause, and the ultimate cause is Khnum the God, who is an aspect of Ra. He fashions the clay and the clay can take many forms. You can have a flat and wide pot; those are your fat people. You have a thin and tall pot and those are your skinny people, your thin people. The efficient cause has many possibilities. What determines the shape of that effect is governed by Aryu. Aryu is your Karmic basis, created by you based on your previous actions, and your sub-conscious impressions left behind by those actions in this and previous lifetimes. The shape of your personality, the aspects of your personality and contours of the events in your life are shaped by your Aryu, so your personality as it is today is an effect and the efficient cause is the Aryu, your Khnum aspect, the "creative principle" within you, and the Substratum cause is Ra.

The law says, "Every cause has an effect; every effect has its cause. Everything happens according to law. Chance is a name for law unrecognized. There are many planes of causation but nothing escapes the law."

So in God's world there is no possibility, just like the Akhbar story, just like the HetHeru and Djehuty story, there is no possibility for anything to escape this law. However, if that were so, if it were possible, if there were some way to escape this law then it would mean that the universe is random and there is no law. It is a chance for chance to exist. Everything contained within the Self, within the All, as the Kybalion explains, is governed by the laws of cause and effect. Something happening by chance would not be subject to the law of cause and effect and that would throw everything out of kilter. It is like you have machinery going and you throw a wrench into it and it breaks up the gears and everything blows up.

However, if this is absolutely true then even spiritual aspirants and sages are caught up in the matrix of cause and effect and could not get out. However, we do not experience that effect when the teachings are understood and practiced to their logical conclusion. Therefore, there is indeed a way to break the cycle of cause and effect. Otherwise there would be no purpose to even try to escape the law. We will explore this cause that leads to the effect of spiritual liberation, spiritual enlightenment and freedom from the causality that leads to ignorance, mortality, pain and suffering.

The Principle of Cause & Effect Pt. 1B

The story of your life has not been written and yet the plot of your life, the general parameters of your life are controlled by your Karmic basis, your Aryu, your actions of the past; your thoughts of the past; your desires so on so forth. As we saw in the story of Akbar, you can change your fate by changing your Aryu and that means changing the contents of your unconscious mind by changing your actions of today and going forward by following the teachings of this principle of the Kybalion, the teachings of Ma'at; Acting with righteousness which means acting by truth as best you understand it or as your capacity to understand and act based on truth progresses, evolves in your life. Since you are essentially one with Ra you can change the course of the effects in your life by changing the cause in your life. All ignorant people who are not enlightened are controlled by this process, by these causes, their moods, their feelings, their emotions, their desires, etc., in a virtually endless cycle of cause and effect that will continue until broken by maturing spiritual aspiration. Those people who are governed in this way have no free will. Those who understand the law of cause and effect and have developed the will to live by truth instead of the ego driven desires, can change their life. This means leading oneself out of the realm of time and space and spiritual ignorance (absence of the knowledge of self) and thus being out of the jurisdiction controlled by the law of cause and effect causation.

The Kybalion: Ancient Egyptian Mysteries

Somebody dying and resurrecting from the dead and that kind of thing; somebody falling out of a parachute that doesn't know and they fall to the ground and they bounce off the earth. Another person in another country they fall and they splatter all over the place, their body disintegrates. Why is that? Oh it's just something that happens and it's strange we can't explain it. That is what worldly people say about unexplained events. From the perspective of aryu, cause and effect, the answer is evident. If there is no cause to allow an effect the effect cannot occur; so a person cannot die unless the aryu, the cause, dictates that it can occur.

"Death comes when the purpose of living is fulfilled; death shows what the reason for living was." -EP

The vertical grooves on the Horemakhet, the Great Sphinx what caused that? Oh, we don't know we hope to find some answers to that one day, we don't understand what could possibly do that. We know that it happens because of rain and we know that it rained 10-12 thousand years ago in that part of Africa but we must have some different kind of cause that we must search for. It has to be something else because that means that the Great Sphinx is at least 10-12 thousand years old, making Ancient Egyptian (African civilization) older than any civilization in history with wisdom and longevity unparalleled in human history. People who are governed by their moods, desires, ideologies, and their ignorance instead of the search for truth, these are people who are controlled by the laws. The laws control them. They are controlled. The Kybalion explains this as pawns on a chess game. They are moved in other words. There is somebody moving them. They do not move themselves. They may like to think that they are in control of their lives, and yet it is impossible. You may be thinking you are a smart person, you may think that you are a worldly person, you know about the world and all of this kind of thing but the unconscious impressions that are constantly impelling you, you have no idea about them, where they came from, what they are, how to neutralize them. You think that you are living your life and your thoughts are your own. If somebody were to come and tell you contrary-wise you would not be able to act on their statement. You are a chain smoker and somebody tells you and they actually bring you on a dish, a platter, they show you a piece of lung from a smoker of twenty years and you see it is all black and you are told that person died of lung cancer. Yet, you say, wow that is interesting. Smoking is definitely bad for you. I've got to stop one day. They go on; they are not obviously in control. They are far from the cause; they are living in the effect. They are like on the surface of the ocean, waves are the effect and the depth of the ocean are where the movements come to meet the waves on the surface; a bubbling up of the unconscious impressions of the mind comes up to the surface. An aspirant in order to master the law of cause and effect must go to the source of the causes and that is in your unconscious mind. You must purify and eradicate those Aryus, those impressions. By understanding the world through all this wisdom you prevent new Karmic impressions from forming that are going to impel you in the future. The Kybalion explains that this is done by consciously discovering and becoming one with the law itself; this is what the teaching of Maat, Ankhu Maat means. Remember the Maat chant that we're coming back to the beginning of our program today. Maat,

Ankhu Maat - Maat is the source of life. Cha Hena Maat - Rising with Maat, or the day, the beginning of the day with Maat. Ankh Hena Maat - Living with Maat. Maat is everywhere- Maat Neb-bu-ten. Finally Cha Sema Maat - uniting with Maat. You are one with the Law itself. You become one with the cause itself and then you are not controlled by the cause, you become the causer. You have come from the surface to the bottom, the innermost point. Just like we discussed previously when a wheel is turning, the outside of the wheel seems to be turning very fast. If you were to stand in the country of Ecuador where the equator passes through, you would realize that you are actually moving about a thousand miles per hour, which is how fast the Earth is spinning at its equator, on itself. If you go to the polar region, go to the North Pole or the South Pole you are turning but you are turning extremely slow, maybe like a mile per hour, whatever it is. You are turning on yourself, like a top, very slowly. If you go to the very center of that movement you realize that there is no movement theoretically, if you study your geometry, you are at the very point of the center.

You see how all of the laws, the law of rhythm, the law of vibration, all of these are coming together. You come to understand the cause as the Kybalion says consciously, this is the key. If you start to understand the cosmic laws and you consciously work with those and allow yourself to be an instrument of those, become one with those you are no longer affected by them. You become one with the Creator, the ultimate cause who is controlling those cosmic forces and who is affecting the entire universe. You become the affector instead of the affectee. Only then can you have free will. Only then can you say that you are not a pawn, that you are a human being, that you are not an animal who is controlled by the forces, controlled by other people's opinions, controlled by other people's desires. People who are making wars and who are fighting, you can try to get in between them, you can try to reason with them, but they cannot stop. They are controlled by forces that are beyond them. People who are greedy; people who are lustful all these things are forces beyond people's control.

The Kybalion explains that one consciously becomes one with the law by seeking refuge in that law; seeking refuge in that cause. Hence we have the teaching of seeking refuge in Buddha, seeking refuge in Jesus, explaining the New Testament and the teachings of Dhama Padha of Buddha; seeking refuge in the Hands of the ultimate Good Shepherd which is Asar, of Kemet, by acting with Maat; this is the key. If you act with Maat, if your actions are permeated with Maat those actions purify your personality. They neutralize the Aryus, the previous desires, thoughts, moods and feelings. If you act with Maat it tends to eradicate your erroneous egoistic concept of free will. You are consciously aligning yourself with the Cosmic Order. Cosmic Order dictates that you should not kill. If you agree with that and you act in accordance with that law you are free from the desire to kill, the desire to hate anyone. If your philosophy says it's ok, that it is justified to kill, then you are bound by that. That is not a Cosmic law; rather, that is an egoistic, degraded social development, based on an ideology proffered by leaders who seek power and use religion or ethnic conflict to incite and control the ignorant. Non-violence is a higher cosmic law. The cause and effect of the world, is if you kill somebody, somebody is going to come back and try to kill you and you then go and try to kill them, like the Hatfields and the McCoys or the Palestinians and the Israelis. There are many other groups that you could look at through history not just them. Look at your own life and see what you are fighting against, what trying to kill, what you are trying to destroy. Start wondering why you are trying to destroy it. Is it possible for you to destroy it? Does it matter for you to destroy?

The illusions of the world of time and space; do you want to continue to be caught up in those illusions? Or do you want to find out the ultimate cause for the existence of those illusions? The discovery of which immediately and absolutely frees you from them, allows you to transcend them. This is the path of sages; this is the path of aspirants who want to attain mastery. Finally you come to realize that all of these manifestations of time and space, all of these surface manifestations that you see with your senses, are actually part of a chain of events that lead you back to an ultimate cause. The ultimate cause is the one and single desire of the Divine Self, which has manifested into a myriad of forms; Those forms which interact with each other. Like a pinball game or better yet like a game of billiards. You have all of the balls on the table, playing pool, you hit one it hits a bunch of others and all kinds of different bounces and angles occur and again who brought these balls into being? Who was the one who has the stick? Who is pushing on the stick to push the balls into each other? You are there on the table and most people are like the eight ball. They are getting bounced around and they don't know where to go, how to do it and all they see is a bunch of different colors of balls hitting each other and going back and forth. You must be learning about the cause for the existence of these balls. The stick that every once in a while comes around and starts knocking things around. The person who is behind the stick that is pushing balls around the top of the table, if you were to assume that position, you would realize that you transcend the balls, the colors, the table, and the stick. You are not an ethnic group, a gender, caught on a s, genders and cultures, being manipulated by those who control the table and the balls and force them to knock into each other; if you understood what is going on you could put an end to the manipulation because it is allowed by your own ignorance. At that point you become one with the ultimate mover, the ultimate motivator, the pusher. You are not pushed anymore, you are the pusher. While you are still in the body you will see the stick coming and you will actually help yourself to place yourself in the right position to be hit by the stick, so you can go and bounce into somebody else and knock the heck out of them. You know what I'm talking about. Like some of you, you get into some of these teachings and you say, "Yeah, yeah, that's it. I'm going to be a vegetarian now and everybody around me you are going to be a vegetarian too whether you like it or not." You allow the stick to knock you on your behind so you can go and knock somebody else on their behind. But this is for a good cause now, though here there still needs to be tact and patience, with yourself and with others.

That is what it means when coming in line with the law. Don't forget that if you hit somebody too hard that you are going to have a reaction. So you try to be gentle towards them, but forthright and determined, intent and allowing the world to bend you to its will but rather you bending the world to the will of the Divine. Hetep. You discover the law of cause and effect and then you become the cause instead of the effect and you will be spared the spanking of the Divine. Hetep.

Questions and Answers

Question: I guess being reminded the part about Ari, the destroying of it, that suggests that whatever previous karmas or impressions that you bring into this particular lifetime that comes to bear on how you live your life now is going to determine on what your affect is going to be in this lifetime?

Answer: Yes that is exactly what it means. Your Karmic storehouse creates like a sage explained, it is like an inkpot described in the ancient Egyptian Pert M Heru text, or even your pen that has the ink in it all you could possibly write with that ink that is the actual work that you have control over that you can write. The ink itself is the potential. That is allowed by your previous Ari, your previous Karmic basis. Now if you are controlled by ignorance, what will come out of that ink is ignorance, it will continue in ignorance. Meaning that lets say you have grown up on a family of bigots, of racist people, that is your Karmic storehouse. They have filled you with that, and you have filled yourself with previous lifetimes and that is why you ended up in that family because you believed in those things. Or you need to learn about those things. If you have no control of your life you will write those things in your life too. You will act on those things, you will believe in those things. Even if you have those things in your Karmic storehouse, if you turn towards Wisdom those things will be cleansed, they will be eradicated, they will be transformed. That same energy, that same potential for anger and hatred, and irrational delusion will be changed and you will write a different story. Only those people who are on the path to self mastery, only *they* can re-write their story, others are like animals they, like dogs or cats; they are controlled by their Karmic storehouse in their unconscious minds. You call that instinct. You can call it whatever you want but that is what their doomed to be controlled by, their Karmic storehouse. That is why the Wisdom philosophy to an aspirant is so important. The Kybalion explains also that most people are not knowledgeable of these things and therefore, they are ignorant and controlled by the forces that be, the powers that be. They can be easily duped by other people who have stronger will than theirs; and there is a similar capacity for evil or for good actually. That is why it is so dangerous when people are controlling the media who are themselves unrighteous they can control so many unrighteous, ignorant minds. Likewise this is why the leaders of society have adopted policies that lead to an ignorant population and yet you can have enlightened leaders, and you can still have great things occur and those people who seek the wisdom can arise from the degraded situation to become great people.

Question: Going back to before, with as you say people who do not realize the essence of cause and effect, they are fighting wars, Catholics in Ireland, Protestants so on and so forth, it creates a vicious cycle does in order to abate or in order to? Is a full realization the cause necessary of not suffering the effect or do individuals having come to that understanding in order to break the cycle, dealing with the cycle broken or can there be a higher cause that can break any certain cycles, an earthquake comes and kills everyone else people still carry that Karma with them, but maybe the war would not necessarily go on.

Answer: Ok, you answered your own Question I think. The *Ari* stays with them, they come into being again and they will gain peril to the same feelings the same thoughts and live in the state so you could kill everybody on Earth, they will incarnate someplace else and they will do the same thing again. That's why the first part of your Question, is it necessary for everybody to discover the ultimate cause in order to transcend, that is ultimately true in order to eradicate the effect completely. However human beings cannot move from A to Z all in one stroke. There has to be a process, a degree of development. That is, as I was explaining, what occurs when a person turns toward the Laws of Maat. If you, not even believing in it or thinking about it, if you just make the resolution that I want to follow the path of Maat, if you believe in murder and killing but you stop yourself from doing it, that stopping itself is going to start transforming your Ari, your Karmic basis. It's going to start diffusing and neutralizing your desires to kill. Eventually it is going to eradicate them. You are going to see the wisdom of non-violence and when you realize the wisdom that is the ultimate transcendence of that Karmic basis. So people don't have to become fully enlightened in order to abate certain *ari* but what they have to do is act in accordance with the Laws of Maat (Righteousness). When the higher truth is fully realized then there is complete release from the ari. This is why Maat philosophy is so important. If you act with righteousness eventually it will lead you to be righteous, whether you believe it or not, whether you are a student of the philosophy or not, it leads you to a purification that allows you to intuitively discover the higher wisdom of the law.

Question: The Question is in last week's class the Laws of Rhythm if you are basically hanging out with people who are unrighteous, how to oppose that movement, how to change that rhythm to the opposite.

Answer: Essentially it is very simple; the law has been given in order to neutralize one kind of vibration or in the terms of rhythm one kind of movement that you must polarize yourself into the rhythm that you want to manifest. That simply means, putting it in very simple terms, is that if you have negative association, you must have positive association to counteract that.

> "Consume pure foods and pure thoughts with pure hands, adore celestial beings, become associated with wise ones: sages, saints and prophets; make offerings to GOD." -EP

The negative association is hanging out with people who eat meat, people who smoke, people who are lustful, greedy, with agitated minds; the personality type referred to as having "fire in the belly" as

Sage Ani or Sage Ptah Hetep would say. Spending time with Sages, spending time with spiritual aspirants, philosophers this counter movement balances as well as eventually neutralizes the effect of the negative rhythm or negative vibration. Remember the same teachings from the Kybalion:

"To change your mood or mental state, change your vibration."

•

"Mind, as matter, may be transmuted, from state to state, degree to degree, condition to condition, pole to pole, vibration to vibration. True transmutation is a Mental Art."

Your associations are an aspect determining your vibrations, rhythms and ethical conscience. That is why it is important to have that understanding of the good association. Most people are ignorant and they think, "Well, I can hang out with my brother, but my brother is a killer, or my cousin is a robber, or my friend who is a drug addict etc. But I love them and I can hang out with them and they can be doing drugs next to me and I'll just sit there watching TV and it doesn't affect me, it doesn't you bother me." Or they might say: "They could eat meat and I can be a vegetarian, we could still love each other, we could still have relations and it does not affect me." You must understand that while this is true to a certain extent from a worldly perspective, you can be with others who do unrighteous things and resist being exactly like them, from a spiritual standpoint, unless you have fully transcended the ignorance of life you will be affected in some degree; from the standpoint of absolutely transcending these negative Karmic bindings one must be absolutely free and absolutely transcendent and that means detaching from such personalities either physically, psychologically, becoming internally detached and dispassionate, neither agreeing with them nor acquiescing to their perspectives but remaining separate even when in their company; needless to say the process of detachment is more difficult when there is physical proximity and intimate contact with such personalities. For a beginning aspirant physical proximity is a very difficult force to overcome. For instance I'll give you a very gross example; let's say you want to practice celibacy but you are with a partner who constantly likes to have sex every day, 2-3 times a day, they have to be rubbing up against you and all of this kind of thing, it would be very difficult for you to practice celibacy being in this situation. You are constantly being tempted, stimulated, etc. That needs a physical discipline, a physical separation at some point yes, if you practice the discipline, you separate yourself physically you'll actually and you'll discover your separate from your sexuality so on an so forth. You could have fifty people voluptuous people dancing around you, rubbing against you and you'd be free from that force which ultimately comes from within that you control. In the beginning it has to be a physical discipline related to your achievement. So therefore you should shun the company of unrighteous people and you should seek the company of righteous people. Move away from unrighteous and move towards righteous.

Question: using your example of the billiard table, what is the effect and cause again?

Answer: Yes, we do not put it in those exact terms but the cause and effect mean that what you do comes back to you but thinking in the context of the billiard table that I gave you. When one ball hits that has an effect and there will be eventually some rhythm that the ball that does the hitting will receive from that hitting and in those terms yes an example of this is when the ball that started the hitting itself is hit by another ball that was struck by the ball it hit at first, and so on. However when you transcend the law of cause and effect you go beyond the worldly energies, the physical forces, you become the cause behind those physical forces. Consciousness is behind all physicality. When you become one with consciousness you become the ultimate witness of all that occurs. When that happens you become free from the causes and effects going on around you, even if you continue to be part of those events on a practical human level.

Question: are enjoyable sentiments and feelings to be transcended too? And wouldn't the world be harmonious if everyone adopts this teaching?

Answer: Your comment was a very good comment. In order to transcend the Law of Cause and Effect we must learn how to transcend the beautiful sentiments. It would be nice if everyone was holding hands and we all every evening held hands and turned towards the West and we all looked at the sunset and said, "Oh wow." We hugged each other, and I love you and all the white people, all the black people, all the red people and green people and whoever, the Palestinians, Muslims and Israelis, we all got together and we all had so much fun and we love each other etc. That would be so wonderful if we all realized the Cosmic Laws and that is true. I have that sentiment tucked away somewhere, on a shelf somewhere. I'm not actually making fun of it but trying to give real humor because that is the only way you can live in this world because when you are achieving a higher form of consciousness you start realizing people who are caught in the delusion about life cannot, again, cannot act out of full rationality and or full positive feeling since their ego, beset with the delusion, compels them to feel, think and act otherwise. So from a conceptual standpoint the notion of united world and world peace is admirable, commendable and worthy to be pursued since the pursuit purifies the heart if it is accomplished in a detached and dispassionate manner, without expecting it to ever happen, for the world is replete with insane personalities, so spiritual ignorance is the source of all maladies, therefore there will never be complete harmony on earth but it is possible to have a society with relative peace and harmony for most; Ancient Egypt stands as proof of that. Aspirants should not allow themselves to be deluded that it is achievable since this is the realm of constant changes and where there are always personalities of three types, lucid, agitated and dull, residing together and in all societies. So there will always be dull persons who cause trouble, especially if they get into positions of corporate or political power. So do not waste time saying if only everybody could understand and see the truth, because it will not happen like that. Better to be concerned about your own life and changing yourself, becoming righteous, pure and enlightened and let other people's aryu move them along on their journey. "If only" is one of those phrases that is a very tough statement for people to overcome. "If only this person would do this, it would make me happy." "If only I could do this I would be satisfied." "If only this would happen and I could get rich and everything would be wonderful." You must realize that the world is not about "if only". The world is not about people holding hands and everyone walking into the sunset. Theoretically, yes that is the principle that you must live by because intrinsically, beyond egos and ignorance, we are essentially one; however, by understanding that cause, you should not expect that effect to be realized in the world for all because that is not going to happen for all at the same time because most are beset with delusions, be they good or bad ones. People are not going to turn to each other and realize somehow all of a sudden, we should all be vegetarians and we should not be hurting animals and we should all be friends. In fact that would not even be desirable, because if everybody did that there would not be any strife in the world. Strife and suffering is what leads a human being to struggle and to discover greatness and to transcend. Only because that exists is the only reason why you are listening to me today because you've been troubled and the world has given you certain hard knocks. Think about it, if those hard knocks weren't there you wouldn't be listening to Muata Ashby, you'd be out somewhere having fun, you'd be elsewhere, going to a party or watching a movie or sitting on the couch drinking a beer or hanging out at the beach or something else. You wouldn't be checking out this crazy Sage talking this wild cause and effect stuff and how the world is this and how the world is that. So the strife in the world has its purpose and that is to lead ignorant people to Question the world. But for sages and saints they don't lay awake at night praying for world peace in the sense of wishing that people would somehow turn to each other and everything could be wonderful and happy and great and all of that kind of thing. So think about it in those terms.

It is like the teaching of Akhenaton the Atonism and it is called *Sebait* Aton that is what the *Sebai* (preceptor) teaches the Sebait which is the spiritual philosophy, so that is what it would be called. Khemenu means actually the City of the Eight. This should be understood in terms of seven and the eight is really the return to the first of the seven. Like what I mean is in music, it is the octave. Really we're only dealing with seven notes but octave means eight. What that means is that the octave is a full cycle, a full circle. 1,2,3,4,5,6,7 and the 8 is coming back to the 1st. So that is how that should be understood.

Question: Is Khemenu related to khem?

Answer: Well in Kemetic scripture there is a principle of punning which is the strongest and the most manifested that I've ever seen that principle is in Kamitan language. Even though the exact spelling is not the same the phonetics are the same and the Kamitan language is known expressly for enjoining similarities through phonetics and you have Khem and men and u [Khemenu]. So Khem is associated with blackness. Khem is the blackness, men is established and nu of course is the primeval ocean. So you have this underlying kind of association. So it's like having something on the surface and having something below as well. So there is that association. That is a good observation and whenever you see these terms that is the kind association that is to be drawn.

HTP

Commentary by Seba Dja

Hetep; Hetep; Hetep; Hetep.

The comment was related to what Sebai Maa commented about the beautiful sentiment is that even though Sebai Maa said he has this tucked away on the shelf, doesn't mean he doesn't use, and that you should also not use that sentiment. There are teachings that are given to the masses and then you are coming here for a higher level of the teachings. This is not a worldly association; being in the Kemetic philosophy and certainly not being in the Kemetic philosophy at the level teachings are espoused. It's not like going to a church, it's not just like going to a community function; you are coming here because you want a little something, probably a little bit more than the general platitudes of life. Those little platitudes of "oh yes, let's all get together and Sebai Maa says everything would be wonderful it we could only do, (laughter) I'll be the preaching, I'll be the one teaching." So the best sentiment it should be within your arsenal you should understand there is a basis of it. When you use also what should come after it according to the sensitivity. If you listen to the New Age speakers that is what they do. A lot of these wonderful talks, like, Dr. Wayne Dyer and all these people on the New Age channels that's what they do. They lay out these beautiful sentiments and all sages and saints when they speak to the public, the masses, the Popes everybody they speak for world peace and world harmony and you have to get that out there because you have to put ideal, you have to put the highest ideal for people to gravitate to, to work to. They have to want to start to see and understand that they play a part related to this cause and effect; they actually play a part in this role of coming to world peace. So it is a good sentiment and if you use it, to take it one step even further take it a little bit more perhaps yogic and not just a benevolent sentiment that you know will never manifest in this time and space because that's not how it is set up. It is to say and you know if each person took it upon themselves if one person becomes more peaceful, if one person stops doing whatever it is; if one person forgives; if one person puts down the gun, does not shoot or whatever, your whole world automatically just became more peaceful in that moment that is the power of it, that is the power of the individual. Every personality in the world is part of that effect. So if even just one person saying that is not it, the whole world just automatically (sighed) and became just a little bit more peaceful. So it has allowed people to take them to that level to let them know that and that's really what the whole yogic movement is about. It is about attaining peace on an individual basis and making ones life a vehicle for that peace and so they can understand that as an individual if they take those steps it is leading to the bigger picture so they are accomplishing what they want in the bigger picture but then they will start to look at within their own lives to see how they need to navigate and what they need to change and to actually start becoming less violent in their life. That is how it is. So the spiritual path is a path of the peaceful warrior, you are in a fight, definitely in a battle but this is the path of the peaceful warrior and you are leading the world to peace. Hetep.

Chapter 7: THE PRINCIPLE OF GENDER PART 1

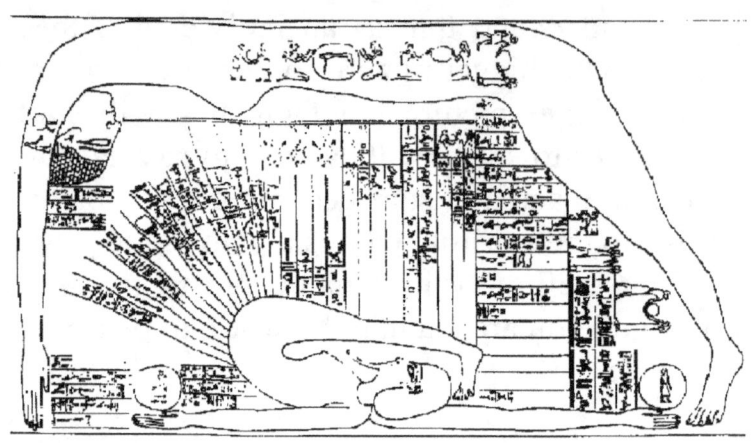

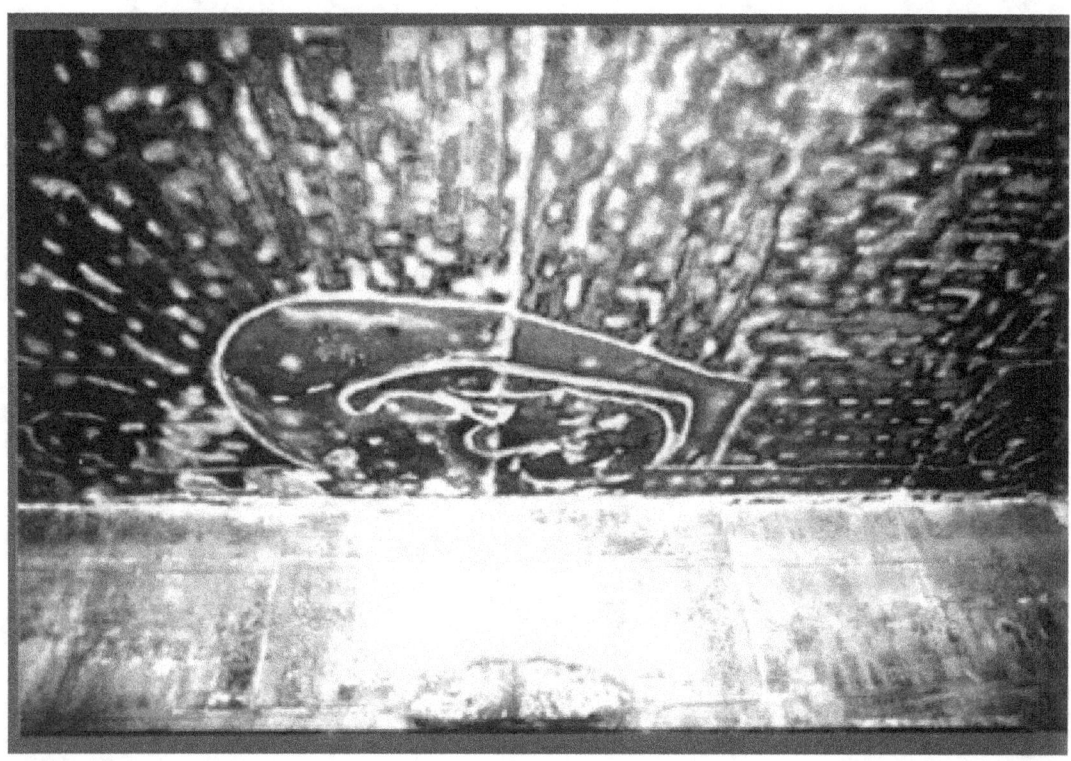

The God and Goddess principles of Ancient Egypt: Geb and Nut

We continue today our current studies of our current series, called the Seven Principles of the Kybalion. In brief, The Kybalion is a collection of seven teachings, Hermetic teachings, and as you know, the Hermetic teachings come from the god Hermes, which is the Greek name for the ancient Egyptian god, Djehuty. So these are an expression of the Ancient Egyptian teachings as they came down through history to the Hermetic period when it had spread to Greece and the Greeks had conquered Egypt but the Ancient Egyptian temples were still in operation.

So these teachings are teachings that were received by the Greeks, from their Kamitan teachers, which is admitted by the ancient Greek writers. This text we are studying is one of those records of those teachings that were received at those times, by people such as Pythagoras, Plato, Socrates, Thales, Plutarch, and others who recorded these teachings. They became known as the Hermetic teachings.

We are finally coming to the end of our brief study of the seven principles. We are currently discussing the seventh Principle, which is called the Principle of Gender. The principle of Gender gives many implications. In an ordinary sense, when we think of gender, we think of male and female, men and women, boy and girl. But in this particular lecture, based on the teaching of the Kybalion, we are going to expand that concept well beyond this gross form of understanding about the Gender principle. Let us begin with the teaching itself, contained in the Kybalion.

Gender is everything; everything has its masculine and feminine principles. Gender manifests on all planes. And mostly people think of gender as sexuality, men and women having sex, or animals having sex and producing offspring. But there are three main planes that are spoken of in the Kybalion and in the rest of the Kamitan teaching, the Shetaut Neter. And one of them is the Ta, or the Physical plane, the Pet or the heavenly plane and the Duat, the Netherworld, the transcendental world.

These correspond to the physical plane, the astral plane, and the causal plane. They correspond to the Divinities; Ptah, Ra and Amun, as well as Khepri, Ra and Tem, or Asar, Aset and Heru, the father, mother and child. This is the great Trinity of consciousness, the seer, seen and sight or object, subject and interaction between the two.

All of these are related to the same conception. Where does this triad of human experience come from? The triad really is a duality in other words as we are going to see. The trinity came out of the duality and the duality came from the one and where did the one come from? When we look at the process in reverse, we see where it all comes from.

We are to understand that before existence came into being there was only The Self, unbounded and formless and nameless Spirit, for lack of better terms. Then from that Self emanated something that we may refer to as not the original Self but something other than Self and this comes into being through the Gender principle, through sex. So God had sex with himself, his shadow, and brought forth generations of things, objects that are "apparently" different from God, at least to the uninitiated mind. Of course, the original Self and its emanations are nothing but itself, therefore nothing has been created that is really, essentially different. In the beginning all was one and after Creation came into being everything is still one, though appearing to be different, a multiplicity of apparently different objects, because of the magic of the trinity effect of refracted consciousness, meaning when each individual spirit [soul], within a person's personality, looks at the world through the prism of the trinity. If that prism were to be transcended through understanding the philosophy and turning away from the illusions of ordinary human life, then the underlying transcendental oneness would be revealed. And the teachings say that gender operates on all planes. So therefore, there must be gender or sex in the astral plane, gender or sex in the causal plane as well; and what is the nature of that gender?

The Kybalion explains that if this principle is known and understood, it would lead a human being to spiritual enlightenment. Sex is the universal principle of creation and it works on the physical plane, where human beings create other human beings, it works as well on the mental plane, in the creation of ideas. On the causal plane, it also operates in the creation of ego, as we are going to see. But first let's explore another issue about this concept of duality and discover its manifestations a little bit further.

First of all we know about the male and female principle, as in men and women. But when we examine a man and a woman, we quickly realize that a woman has male elements in her and men have female elements in them. Half of your chromosomes are male, if you are a woman and the other half is female. And ones' (aryu) tendency makes you appear as if you are a woman. Another slight tendency makes you appear as a man. As we explained before, you have all the same organs; they are just developed in a different way. So what does that mean? It means that you are different only in appearance and tendency. The female architecture, or the way that the nervous system and the organs, hormonal secretions are set up in a woman makes her tend to be more of an emotional personality, as well as makes her tend to be more receptive.

The architecture, nervous, hormonal system of a man, makes him tend to be more emissive, more emotive, putting out, ejecting. This is why a male ejaculates and a woman receives the ejaculation. But this operates on the other planes as well, not just on the physical plane. Women tend to be more listeners; men tend to be more speakers. And these are just tendencies and of course there are men who are receptive and females who are emissive.

However, in the spiritual teaching, the Kybalion and the Shetaut Neter, these tendencies don't actually mean anything for higher initiates, be they male or female. If you are a male, you develop your receptiveness; if you're female you develop your "emissiveness" and in such a way you balance out your personality. And you neutralize the male and femaleness within you. And if your maleness and femaleness is neutralized, then you transcend gender.

The highest manifestation of gender is spirit and matter. Spirit, the underlying cause behind all creation and creation is the effect of the creative process engendered by spirit interacting with itself in such a way as to produce from itself two halves which are interconnected and complementary (spirit and matter). That is why in the Bible it says, that God created man in his own image, presumably, the Bible meant man and woman; but the Shetaut Neter teaching says that, and goes further, teaching that the entire creation itself is created in Gods' image. So Creation is the emanation but as we said earlier, the emanation is no different from the origin and in fact there is no separation between them intrinsically but only apparently, as it appears to the uninitiated senses; for, the emanation is in effect an appearance of the origin or another way to understand it is that Creation is God incarnate, appearing as his/her Creation, what we call matter, animals, plants, planets, human bodies and human souls.

As previously discussed, in the Cause and Effect Principle, everything in creation is, as above, so below, meaning Creation is a reflection of spirit, in time and space, where all the principles of the Kybalion, gender, rhythm, polarity, etc. have their effect. Every human being, every particle of matter, all the animals, vegetation and so on and so forth, are all manifestations of Spirit. Spirit in this context therefore is the male aspect and creation is the female aspect. Unformed matter, Nun, receives the vibration, the will energy of Spirit and therein takes the seed of will energy with vibration and rhythm and transforms itself into the desired forms of Creation, engendered into it by Spirit. And that is why the universe and the world is the way it is. It appears the way it is, because it has been willed so by the design. And you can examine all aspects of nature and you will find the same the same principle of gender operating.

Spirit resides in living beings, as well as in inanimate objects. And science of course, is beginning to support this concept, of an underlying indwelling intelligence which has been in the ancient teachings here for thousands of years but is only now being recognized by others. Even when you go down to the molecular level, you will realize that there is a trinity of existence, there are three basic components of the so-called atom.

You have your protons and electrons, and these are the basic male and female aspects of creations. Protons being the male, positively charged; the electrons being the female, negatively charged. Here positive negative does not mean good or bad, good or evil or strong or weak. This is a concept of gender. In this context, protons don't do any creation, any creative activity. The electrons do that by their movement, by their separation from a particular atom, by their linking themselves to a different atom and thereby making different connections, composing themselves into molecules, compounds, etc. The neutrons are the neutral particle; it is there like an observer, like a witness. And right here you have your Amun, Ra and your Ptah. In this context the Amun, Ra and your Ptah constitute Creation and Om or Neberdjer, the original all-encompassing source, is what they all dissolve back into at the end of time and space, the end of Creation.

Here you have your witnessing consciousness; you have your Ra force or energetic force that wills. Then you have your Ptah aspect that does the work of creation; that turns itself into the elements of being. And since everything is composed of these particles, then it follows that everything is composed of this Gender principle; everything in creation. This is why you have in the Anunian theology the understanding of the creation as arising from sets of male and female gods and goddesses.

In the Anunian Creation teaching Geb is the male principle, who is the earth, static, and does no action; he just lies there on his back. And then you have Nut, who is the heavens, the sky, bouncing around, flying around, and sometimes she sits on top of him, having sex with him and then she gets up and she gives birth to the rest of the gods and goddesses of Creation. Geb just stays there, static, like the earth, his *tekenu,* his penis, the obelisk stays there, erect, journeying out of the earth into creation, into the heavens, into space (Nut). And the goddess is there moving around the tekenu, with all her stars, with all her clouds, all her planets, moving around constantly. This is just like the atoms, where you have the protons and the neutrons in the center and the electrons swirling around in all kinds of different ways.

This concept was well understood in ancient times, so the concept of Geb and Nut, the concept of Asar and Aset, and the other male and female principles in the teaching is a reflection of this principle of gender, from a spiritual point of view. But this principle has nothing to do with sex yoga, with the way some people like to call it or tantric sex and all these kinds of modern day misconceptions about the tantric teachings.

The principle of Gender is the underlying innermost concept of Tantrism and if this concept of tantrism were to be understood correctly, you would realize that, since you have the male and female aspect within you, if you were to discover those and to balance and rejoin those as we discussed, you would have no need for the company of people of the opposite gender; and you would discover the underlying oneness of your innermost self, which is beyond gender. You would be self-satisfied and why is that? Because you would be impregnating yourself and giving birth to yourself which is referred to as *kamutf*. The Kybalion explains that there are two principles in every human being. There is an "I" and a "me". The "I" is your identity, it's like the "I" am; the I is the spirit, the being and the 'am' or the 'me' is the conditioning of that Being, that Supreme Being. In this context your spirit is the Creator and your personality, and its experiences, is the Creation.

If you just say "I", then we are fine, then we are okay, but then you start saying 'I am'; If you do that then you are saying that this "I" is in a particular way, or in a particular form and that conditioning limits, conditions that "I". The "I" should be alone and complete. otherwise we have the situation which most people find themselves in; the "I", the spirit has assumed the identity of the "me" the ego and your soul thinks it is the individual, the mortal, the imperfect, needy personality, searching for love and acceptance and understanding and doomed to ultimate failure, for no one has ever discovered that fulfillment in time and space because it is not possible to find that there. It can only be found in discovering the true identity of self and that is androgynous, or beyond gender qualities and of course also beyond time and space. All these things that "me" does, that "me" desires, that "me" thinks, that "me" wants are tainted by the aryu that that "me" uses to see the world through, the prism of egoism. Therefore, that flawed vision of life will always lead to error, confusion, frustration and failure to discover abiding peace and happiness in time and space. What we are getting at is that, this "I" is your innermost Self and the "me" is the ignorant concept of Self, your ego. This is what the Kybalion, and the wider Ancient Egyptian teaching explains.

How do we change this ignorant perspective to one of wisdom? That ego is susceptible to suggestion, because it is the unenlightened female principle. In this context Spirit is pure untainted consciousness that projects itself into mind so mind is the female principle opposite to spirit or consciousness. Mind is the principle of presided over by the god Djehuty, or Hermes (Thoth) and it is actually the female aspect in this sense; the female aspect of the Supreme Being Ra. So Ra, the spirit, has a mind, Djehuty (Hermes) and likewise, every human being has a soul (spark of Ra) and a Ka or mind, and that mind is their female counterpart to their soul (individual spirit) mind and that female mind if it is beset by ignorance, that "me" then, it is susceptible to impressions (aryu) from the unconscious.

Now if those impressions are enlightened impressions, from a purified intellect that is allowing a message from the innermost "I" to come through, into the field of mind, then that mind will be lucid, leading to enlightenment. Specifically speaking, if the thoughts are coming from the Akh (individual spirit) to the Ka (mind), then that human being is called an enlightened being. If that human being is not Akh, enlightened, if that "me" is beset by ignorance, if the "I" in that person is drowned out by ignorant thoughts, ignorant desires, ignorant feelings and so on and so forth, then that person, specifically, that persons' "me" is going to be susceptible to impressions of ignorance derived from past experiences, feelings and desires that have clouded the vision of the untainted, independent and self-sufficient spirit within (*Aryu*). Karmic (Aryu) impressions of ignorance emerge in a person's mind from it's own past experiences, actions, feelings, and their worldview belief system, etc., that are embedded in the unconscious mind. They are also going to be susceptible to new impressions caused by their experiences in the present day reality.

So that female me, that female mind within you is going to be susceptible to impressions from the world, impressions from ignorant past actions; As opposed to impressions from the Higher Self. That Self is drowned out in all the noise of the mind. That "me" is the creative matrix that every human being has. This is why it is important that that me should be purified. And that occurs when you live a life based on the Principles of Maat (ethical conscience). So here we come again, to virtue, and the importance of virtue in purifying the heart. Allowing you to develop purity of heart, allows you to develop a concept of self that is separated from other; meaning it allows you to have a concept of yourself separate from desires, your ignorant feelings. If you act by righteousness, by the laws of Maat, you will necessarily curtail the willfulness of the ego.

In this practice you will realize that you can exist and you are alright even when your desires are not fulfilled. You realized that there is something within you that is simply a witness to your activities. You come to realize that, there is something within you that transcends your ignorant concept of self and this is when you actually be able to control your personality, otherwise you cannot control your personality. If you are the kind of person who thinks that your "me" is your body, your "me" is the clothes that you where, your me is the things that you like to do. You will first of all lead a very miserable life, because you're the kind of person whose happiness comes from the things that happen to you, the good things, the activities, like going to a movie, to a party, winning a lottery, etc.; and that is where you draw your happiness from. You may have children, you may become rich, and whatever it is, if you are caught in that illusion all of those impressions are constantly coming into your mind and they are embedding themselves in your unconscious and they are going to sprout into new aryu of ignorance and delusion in the future but in the mean time they sustain the present everyday illusions of egoistic life. In time they are going to become the male aspect that sprouts in your conscious female mind and impels you to new desires, new actions, new feelings based on ignorance and this is how most people live their lives in a seemingly endless cycle of egoistic living, dying and being reborn again.

Most people are caught up in this cycle; most people have no awareness whatsoever that there is an underlying "I" or transcendental "self" underlying their individualistic, egoistic, surface understanding of their life, an "I" that is waiting to direct their lives towards greatness, towards spiritual enlightenment, towards glory and they think they have it all figured out; this is the way life is, with ups and downs and that is all there is...

In such personalities when a thought comes into my mind, "I want to go and buy a sports car" or "I want to marry this person" or "I want to go here" or "I want to go there" they accept those thoughts as their thoughts, their reality that belongs to them and as if they are abiding and real and fulfill-able desires, thoughts and feelings. Those un-fulfill-able desires, thoughts and feelings are coming from the unconscious seeds, the aryu of the past, the impressions of the unconscious mind, that were left there from previous actions, thoughts and feelings through varied experiences of the past and previous interactions with other people and the world. Those who live a life like this, as if adrift on a small boat in the vast ocean, bobbing up and down with the waves, become very weak willed, because their will is constantly being pushed around by the their ignorant pursuit of trying to fulfill unfulfillable desires in the world of time and space by seeking objects, fame, fortune, romance, power, etc. in the world. So they are very susceptible to suggestion and susceptible to being emotionally, intellectually and egoistically hurt, disappointed and frustrated as well as manipulated by others or their own egoistic notions.

They are caught in a cycle developed by their very selves. This is because when you fill your mind with enough impressions, a point comes where it develops like a volcano and you cannot stop the eruption. You must act in accordance with those impressions, otherwise you will die. Your mental impressions store up thoughts and energy, if that energy is not channelized properly, it will kill you. You will lead yourself to a drinking binge and go and crash your car into a lamppost. You will commit suicide; you will steal something that will land you in jail. You will mess up your life in some way, shape or form.

This is why it is important for you to carry on good association, so that the impressions of your mind may become purified; so that those things that influence you and that you allow yourself to be influenced by, will lead you to a righteous end. This is why in the Shetaut Neter (Egyptian Mysteries), the student, the disciple is known as *sebat* and the teacher is known as *seba*. The teacher is the male principle, who speaks with words that are like sperm.

The sperm goes into your ear, into the hole, just like the penis goes into the vagina. The wise words of the teacher, if allowed, go into the ears of the student and then impregnate the purified mind; there it gives birth to aspiration, will and understanding (Heru) which is an aspirant emerging as enlightened soul. If you do follow the law of Maat which says, "Do not close your ear to the voice of truth" then you are opening yourself up to Tantric spiritual sex with the teaching which is essential spirit in word. This is why a neophyte aspirant is asked to practice Maat before being initiated into the higher mysteries, because Maat comes first and then the listening comes later, the purity of heart (ethical conscience) comes first and then purity of mind (lucidity) develops and the understanding of the teaching comes occurs. This process occurs when you allow yourself to become female, as an aspirant, regardless of if you are in a male or female body. When you allow yourself to be open, when you allow the teaching to come in and to impregnate your field of mind, you allow that spiritual impression to be lodged and thus you develop spiritual aryu which displaces and dissipates the worldly aryu of the past. Your unconscious mind is like the fertile uterus wherein the word takes root and it will eventually impel and then compel you to righteousness and truth, until you yourself are fully purified and then you can take that same righteous word that is coming from the teacher and you can also realize it coming from your innermost self directly.

PRINCIPLE OF GENDER PART 2

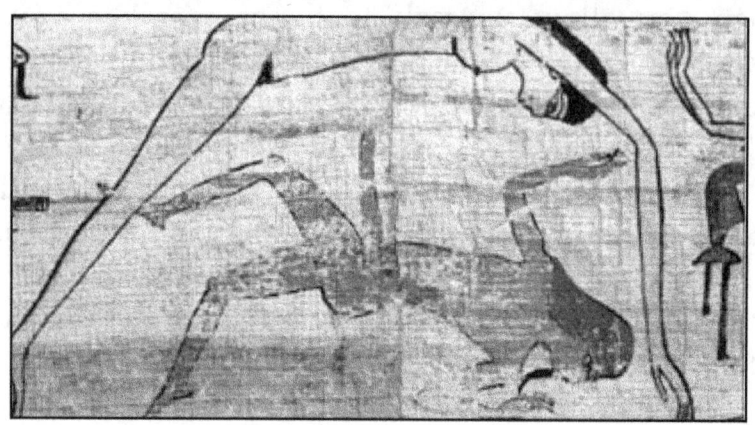

When your mind is cleansed from impressions of ignorance and unrighteousness (actions based on untruth - lack of Maat) you actually can realize that there is an I within you, that has been there all along and that has been actually trying to speak to you and that you can converse with and this is the Asar meeting the Asar. Your personality is meeting its reflective aspect of your higher truth, your higher reality. Therefore you can converse with God directly at this point. You can shake hands with God as it were.

Once you have been satisfied with this, then you can become comfortable and relaxed sufficiently to let go of that lower "I am", that "me" conditioned concept and you realize that it is merely an illusory reflection of self, manifesting in time and space. When this happens, identification of Self shifts from the "me" to the "I" and this is called Nehast. The Awakening, the Resurrection, the Akhu, Enlightenment.

This is actually also referred to in the later Christian teachings of Kemet, Egypt, the Ancient Egyptian Gnostic Christianity. This is known as the Divine Marriage. You would have noticed that there is an aisle up the center of all the Christian churches. This tradition follows the Ancient Egyptian Temple model. Have you ever wondered why that aisle is there? In the Kamitan temples, there is a procession path way that goes directly from the outside, through the center of the Kamitan temples to the innermost reaches of the temple, the sanctuary. The Christians adopted this format with an isle leading from outside directly through the center of the Church leading to the main altar at the back. Actually some of the first Christian churches were converted sections of Ancient Egyptian Temples One major difference is that in the Christian temple everything is more open, you don't have a special room for the Holy of Holies, the mystery is there around the altar and open to the public. That factor tends to bring the mystery to a mundane level and reduces its symbolic importance.

But leaving that aside for now; When a person goes up to receive the host in the Christian temple, the Eucharist, you go up the aisle and actually, what is supposed to be happening is a uniting of yourself with the Christ. This is exactly the same thing that was done in the Kamitan temple, The Ancient Egyptian temple had a Eucharist ritual and this is where the Christians got the ritual from. However, in the Ancient Egyptian temple you go up the central isle and through different gates that demarcate between sections of the temple and then into the innermost shrine room and there you become one with God, after a process of initiation that prepares you for that union, unlike the Christian church which does not prepare you and essentially leaves you to receive the symbolic Eucharist without changing yourself to vibrate at a divine level; thus, in Christianity most people receive the Eucharist every week but are never transformed, improved, and elevated in consciousness, but rather remain with their egos virtually intact.

Taking the *arit* or the Eucharist and is symbolic of the ultimate marriage, the Divine Marriage, that is supposed to take effect in the life of every human being. Your ability to have this kind of higher marriage is enhanced when you have good marriages on the lower planes and your life on the lower plane is dedicated to allowing you to learn how to have the marriage on the higher plane which means righteous relationships, learning how to care for the relationships you have in a non-sentimental and childish or romanticized way but rather mature and patient as well as forgiving way along with following the path of Maat and the regular practice of the shedy disciplines of Kemetic Yoga, the study of wisdom teachings such as the Kybalion, the practice of devotional worship of the Divine, acting in accord with the Precepts of Maat and practicing formal meditation.

In other words your love affair with another person and your relations with others, with family, the community, other countries, with nature, etc. is actually supposed to lead you to actually discover higher forms of love. But if you are an ignorant person and you don't know about that, all you know is about loving one person or only loving your family, community or country and not caring for others and you have the wrong reasons for loving them, your relations are sentimental and egoistic, selfish and possessive, and you don't know that there is supposed to be a higher perspective of your love, then you will constantly impregnate yourself with lower forms of love concepts. This is the gross aspect of the gender principle coupled with mental dullness and spiritual ignorance. The ignorant way of understanding is that love is solely for having sex; love is for having pleasure with another person; relationships are there for the other person to make you happy, for children, for material objects, to bring you pleasure and happiness, your physical love is for you to have children, so you can love them, so you can have somebody to care for and they can love you and give you pleasure through their life and caring for you, and all that kind of thing. All of this is the lower form of thinking, the ignorant and degraded way of life and understanding. If this process operates in the mind, the person will have untold continuous misery throughout lifetimes.

Because impressions that you have taken in, related to this kind of degraded gender understanding, have not been resolved, they will continue to sprout in this and future lifetimes and it will be a cycle of continuous spiritual ignorance. At some point that ignorance hurts you so much, that it turns into deep disdain, disappointment, frustration and suffering and that ***is going to lead*** you to the higher path of life. When suffering batters the personality sufficiently and the aryu in the unconscious has turned from completely deluded to partially deluded but realizing the futility of searching for abiding happiness through degraded ideas of human existence and the egoistic ways of relations, then there dawns in the personality a disposition for desiring and seeking for something better, something true instead of false, stable instead of fleeting and abiding instead of illusory; this is called a mature personality that is ready to seriously follow and authentic and advanced spiritual path of life. When this higher capacity dawns, true aspiration leads to lucid dispassion and that dispassion should lead to strong but un-stressed detachment. In this mental environment not agitated by the winds of worldly illusions, the teachings are able to come in and this allows that detachment and dispassion to turn your attention to higher forms of spiritual love. This is the practice of advanced Tantric Yoga.

Successfully gaining insight into the higher meaning of gender and transcending the Principle of Gender means loving people impersonally, that is, loving the true and higher essence of your partner, your family, community, instead of only their physical and ephemeral sentimental aspects as well as expanding to loving your country, and other people's countries and expanding loving to your world, loving nature and all Creation. If your love expands in that way, that is the Divine Marriage that allows you to transcend physicality and unite with the matrix of existence, the Higher Self. You can imagine that kind of mind, how it is being impregnated by spirit and how it gives birth to goodness for humanity and spiritual enlightenment for oneself –the initiate.

That kind of mind wants nothing but to bring forth beautiful children, children that will bring glory and peace to the world. Sometimes this may take the form of giving birth to ideas, or the children may be in the form of books, in the form of goodwill, in the forms of radiations of energy that actually affect people of lower mind and lift them up. So the words of sages are willed vibrations and they go into the mind, and mate with the maturely disposed mind and give rise to an avid aspirant.

Recently there was a funeral this week of a prominent hip-hop/rap artist; everybody was crying and sorrowful and remarking about how their lives were affected by this person. Think about how a singer of hip-hop/rap or an entertainer person in Hollywood can affect peoples' lives. Just consider that what these people do, they entertain you and sustain your delusions of life and bring you more illusions on the screen or on the radio and that is what affects people? Are people's lives really improving because of those entertainments or are their sentimental and illusory values being supported and sustained but only temporarily relieved, which leaves them empty, agitated and weak to handle the struggle of life? Is it a virtue to entertain people and relieve their miseries for a few hours through entertaining music or is it truly virtuous to help them stop the cycle altogether and rid themselves of the delusions of life so as to end the virtually endless ups and downs of life and the inevitable reincarnations that will follow to repeat the process over and over again?

An avid aspirant is one who has decided to face the truth, a person that realizes temporary entertainments are ultimately useless and injurious because they delay facing the true problem of life; this is recognizing the error of sentimental values, ignorant notions about sex and gender and is seeking for a way to elevate the mind, to be a person of higher mind who is not affected by these things and therefore these things are recognized as illusory. The person of higher mind is affected by higher things, higher thought forms, higher ideas, and higher glories that relate not just to mortal life but to that which comes next and even now exists in an adjacent dimension, as it were.

The pleasures and joys experienced on the lower planes, is a little bit of that ecstasy that can be experienced on a higher plane but most people think that that pleasure from sex or eating or physical comfort is the purpose of life and that is the objective and ultimate purpose of a human being. A person who lives in this way, who evolves in this way will evolve very slowly, in fact they may take millions and millions of years to develop, through many lifetimes.

If this dispassion and detachment are not developed, a human being remains a slave to their negative aryu and also a slave to the desires and generations of gender; they are forced to become involved with relationships they later regret and producing ideas, actions and progeny they later realize they were not ready for or that led to situations (entanglements) of suffering that go on for years and perhaps lifetimes. This is also the cause of addictions, aberrant behaviors and insanity.

That degraded personality is like a dog. Those of you who have pets, you know dogs sometimes they eat stuff that is bad for them and then they get sick because of it and vomit it up but then, after all that suffering, they go back and eat it again and sometimes they eat the vomit itself. It is a gross image, but it is true, people are like that with their feelings, desires and thoughts; even though they know it is bad for them they still pursue it anyway. Another illustration of this is the parable of the robbers who in olden times went investigating old or abandoned buildings looking for riches left behind in the walls. The head robber goes and sticks his hand in the wall, because before banks, people use to put their money and valuables in the walls of the house.

Once they found an abandoned church, they thought something valuable might be in there, so they went in, and the head robber put this hand in one of the walls to search for valuables. He got stung by a scorpion, but he didn't tell anybody, because he didn't want to look weak, he didn't want to lose his status, but he had to go on and act as if nothing was wrong... so he says "wow, that is an interesting feeling, keep on checking the wall everybody". Another person stuck his hand in and got stung and he didn't want to look bad, he didn't want to say anything or buck against the system or seem strange or out of place and so on and so on and so on.

This is how people are with their lives, families, friends and strangers. People go along and do not say their true opinion about life so everyone believes the illusion of life because hardly anyone in leadership positions talk about this. So people do not learn and are doomed to experience more of the same. Your parents go on with the world, because we have to have mortgages and have to have children, a car, to look good, to satisfy the egoistic desires of life. We have to do what they say on television, because that is what everybody else is doing. We have to eat meat, because that is what everybody does; if you stop eating meat you are considered crazy. If you say there must be something more to life than this rat race they think you are depressed and want to put you on medication since doesn't everyone think this is a great way to run society, with narcissism and corruption in politics and popular culture, with unrestricted greed of corporations, with racial, gender and economic disparities? If you are doing yoga, you are one of those crazy people right? As long as we can be entertained with hip-hop, rock and roll, or jazz, watch football on TV, drink and do drugs, go to a movie and escape our problems and delude ourselves that the next politician will fix everything we will be alright. This is the delusion of life that a distorted sense of gender leads to. But it is really the delusion of the culture and does not have to be your delusion.

Those patterns that have been established by the ignorant "me," will continue taking you into a cycle of pain and sorrow, and untold miseries indefinitely, unless you learn the secret of gender. Unless you learn what is happening to you and how it has happened, how you have allowed it to happen and how to stop it from happening.

The Kybalion says you must learn how to lay aside those thoughts of the 'me'. Study of the teaching and practice of meditation is the ultimate way, when you concentrate your mind, you actually can start to discover yourself as separate from your thoughts, your feelings and your ego. You can start observing your thoughts. If this were to happen, you must realize that this is a high attainment in itself.

If this were to happen it would be an advanced attainment and you are well on your way to attaining enlightenment. This is because, you must realize, the entity who is witnessing your thoughts, witnessing your feelings, etc. is something other than those thoughts and feelings. Why? This realization cannot happen if you are so intertwined with your thoughts and your desires and feelings that you believe they are you. So if you are able to start discerning the difference, the demarcation between your higher self and the ego and its thoughts and feelings then this is an advanced movement towards that. Begin to practice detachment and dispassion, the disciplines of silence. Realize that you don't have to speak all the time. You don't have to say things all the time. You don't have to be moving all the time or entertaining yourself all the time and distracting yourself from what you must face within and get beyond, the ego, so you can discover the higher self beyond.

You need to realize that things went on without you before and will go on without you; what you think is so important is merely like a passing cloud in the sky and there have been many in the past and there will be many in the future so just start observing them instead of running after them and thinking you must change everything around you, that you must fix everything that you perceive as being wrong or against what you desire things to be like; you do not want to be like those who worry constantly and are in a constant state of anxiety thinking: if only you could grab one, grab a partner and get married, grab a beer, grab some tasty food, grab a person and have sex, etc. The "if only" never really satisfies fully and is usually a setup for a disappointment and a frustration instead of what you were running after. Realize that your thoughts are not you so you don't have to act on your thoughts. You are controlling your thoughts; you are controlling your feelings and actions. Start realizing that you are separate from your thoughts, separate from your feelings, separate from your actions, and your physical body.

Through this teaching and this discipline of spiritual practices you are to realize you are the witnessing consciousness, and the dawning of this witnessing consciousness, this is what every aspirant is after. In the disciplines of the teaching, the listening, reflection and meditation, you listen to the teaching as it is given and this is having sex with the teaching; and then you reflect on it and this is the pregnancy period. Reflection is actually a form of auto suggestion, but based on reason and the mature disposition we discussed earlier and you are suggesting the truth as opposed to ignorance, religious dogmas or ideologies or your own egoistic desires; the most concise and powerful concentration of all this is in the chant you use to encapsulate the teaching in idea, sound and feeling. For example, "**Om Amun Ra Ptah, Om Amun Ra Ptah**," if you do that you are embedding energy impressions, wisdom and enlightened spiritual feeling into your unconscious mind and thereby changing your aryu and your fate.

Once you know the teaching, that **Om Amun Ra Ptah**, or any chant related that you choose, becomes a formula, a catalyst that goes into your mind and it does fantastic works that you cannot even imagine. A formula, when it is activated, opens up worlds. So in "auto suggestion", you are suggesting to yourself, as opposed to allowing the world to suggest to you, or the television to suggest to you, or your friends, ignorant family members or the sports fans, etc. This is why peer pressure is such a big problem. In a society like this that is guided by 'the me', by the ego or the greater egos in the media, politics or corporations, those pressures cause the susceptible ego to be degraded. Instead you should be guided by the voice of reason and you should keep company with those who also seek after the meaning of life

Peer pressure is a most serious problem for young people as well as adults. Keeping up with the Jones's, running with your friends, all this is suggestion and it stimulates your negative aryu while at the same time creating new negative aryu for the future. If you do not allow the teaching to suggest to you, your ignorance, or the ignorance of others is going to suggest to you and you are going to become ignorant thereby, because that is your association with the ignorant egos of other people.

Therefore, the wise aspirant must learn how to become female and to listen to the teaching and allow that teaching to be impregnated in his or her subconscious and unconscious mind; And then learn to recognize the sproutings; the Divine children of those higher thoughts that are based on reason and ethical conscience and learn how to act in accordance with those positive sprouts and to suppress the negative sprouts based on the ignorant actions, thoughts and feelings of one's own past or coming from other personalities.

An aspirant, who is growing in wisdom, is to allow those negative sprouts to die, in order for this higher process to happen; if you don't want them to grow you don't allow them to receive the sun, the water and care just like a sprout on land. You do not allow it to receive the sun, meaning that you do not nourish it, encourage it, do not agree with it and if possible do not act on it – in other words, when a negative thought or feeling comes into mind you do not greet it warmly, with agreement but rather, with detached witnessing. For example, a thought comes into your mind, so, okay you are practicing the teaching now and you have learned from the teaching that you should not be running after objects. Before you came into the teaching, you used to fill your mind with impressions, because your friend got a red sports car and all of his friends say "oh this is a wonderful sports car and now I'm so wonderful because I have a sports car"; You may start to think, if you have a nice car like that then you would feel good about yourself too. If you greet that notion warmly, with agreement, you too start thinking more and more about the idea of getting the car and then you start running after the car, so you can gain the perceived benefits that your friend has. You have become deluded and even if you hear in the news that there is a recall on the car or there is a flaw, you will still want it because you are now compelled to do the action; you are now controlled by the aryu, since you put so much energy into the desire to get the car.

But now, as the intelligent aspirant, you are realizing that you don't need that car, at least intellectually. That's 'the ego me', because the car becomes like the appendage and indeed you are seeking to unite with that object, to mate with it as if it is an object of gender that you can acquire, merge with and have relations with to make yourself more happy, more complete; again, this is the distortion of the principle of gender. Gender is in everything and if you see yourself as a gender object, a male or female or whatever, you can imagine you can acquire and unite with many objects in time in space which themselves have also been generated from a higher source into the realm of time and space where everything exists as a gender object. Since all objects are ephemeral and it is not possible to really unite with them and for them to cause true happiness you are able to remain detached. You are to realize that your higher self transcends time and space and that your true self is not a gender object and if you realize these truths you would be free from all gender constrictions.

This form of reasoning is important but it is only operating at an intellectual level, which is not enough but it is a start and helps you to eradicate the impressions if you follow all of the teaching and not just the philosophy; but if you don't work on this the impressions remain and they are going to sprout up again, eventually, because you put them there and have not dealt with them. Now you have learned that intellectually, but now you have these thoughts coming up. Now every time you see a sports car running around, the feelings come into your mind and the ideas pop into your head about the great idea and why not pursue it? You may then rationalize and justify it by thinking: "all these years I've wanted a sports car like that" and "I deserve it". The thought comes into your mind and you believe it is you who are thinking it when in reality it is your ignorant self that is resonating with the vibrations of experiences of the past that you have agreed with and dreamed or imagined about and allowed to lodge in your unconscious mind. You yourself have placed importance on those things and have given them energy of desire but then you are unaware when the cravings and desires come up and you are compelled to follow their dictates, you cannot stop yourself from pursuing the desire - because you have an internal (unconscious) thought process that supports it with feelings and ideas like: "It is my life dream, what I have always wanted. And if I do not achieve it your life would be meaningless and miserable right?" If that process controls the unconscious it will not matter what you think you want to do consciously since your unconscious will direct your overall life. Therefore, the process of purification of mind and the ongoing infusion of positive aryu based on truth must go on until enlightenment ensues.

The thought not only comes into your mind, it comes in with an energetic force, because all your thoughts are associated with little bits of energy [*sekhem*]. Remember what I said, if that energy is not channelized, it will ruin you, it will control, it will impel you and eventually compel you to an action you will likely regret. You will find yourself on your way to the car dealership and signing for that car, whether you want to or not and then when the novelty of the care wares off, when it is a model that has gone out of style, you will be left with the bill and the unfulfilled desire still waiting to push you into something else in the future. So it is important to understand this wisdom, be aware of how aryu works and control the mind.

If you are gaining control of your mind what happens? What happens there is that you start to understand the teaching intellectually, you start becoming consciously aware of and consciously recognizing that thought that comes in, "oh here is a thought in my mind, I'm recognizing I have aryu related to the sports car desire and that has triggered this impression in my unconscious mind and now it is sprouting up as a thought, may I get this sports car and I'm witnessing this thought, hmm very interesting." Your feelings about it are there but yet you are aware of them and why they are there and they start losing power over you. If you do what ordinary people do, which is to agree with that thought, saying "yes, yes, I want that sports car," then what happens is that impression goes into your mind, that you've auto suggested and that impression adds to the storehouse of previous impressions related to this feeling. It starts to get stronger and more powerful because you're feeding it with more energy. The next time it comes up, you reinforce it more and that's what ordinary people do, what ignorant people do, until they are forced to take action on the desires they have worked hard to build up since their weak will cannot resist the discomfort their mind puts them through if they do not take the action.

If you practice this mental discipline you become a witness to the feelings and thoughts and you allow them to appear and you watch that thought and or feeling that has emerged in the mind and the urges in the body. You say to yourself: "Hmm, that's the thought I had, that's the thought I put in there, that's interesting. A red car, yea right. Desire it, get it and feel good. How ignorant is that? Even though I feel the desire I learned it is an illusion" In this way you start applying the wisdom to that thought and or feeling that has emerged in your mind and body. You apply the eye of Hetheru that is going to first weaken and then diffuse the negative aryu and eventually burn up that thought, so it dissolves it, destroys it, and resolves that ignorant aryu of the past. You do not feed it; you do not give it the sunlight energy. That same energy that the aryu uses to compel you comes from the same place as the energy you can accumulate in your will power, but you are going to nourish the ethical conscience and will within you with that light, that solar power. Or you are going to feed it to the ego and allow it to destroy your life with that power.

Understanding intellectually allows you to realize the problem and know what the correct path is. Then, with experiences and practice, you gradually turn the negative aryu to positive and the energy that was seeking to pursue unrighteous activities is changed to now pursue righteous activities based on a correct understanding of gender in life. Understanding coupled with righteous action (actions based on and in accord with the truth of the teaching) lead to spiritual enlightenment and freedom from the consequences of the erroneous actions based on ignorance of the deeper meaning of the Principle of Gender. In this exercise you are to practice being a witness to your thoughts and feelings by allowing them to emerge in your mind and not suppressing them and then by shining the light of wisdom on them (reflecting on how the teaching applies to them) and in this way you allow them to dissipate, to diffuse like a bomb, and be dismantled and discarded.

In order to counter the negative thought process of mind the teaching is to engage an opposite thought process, the opposite vibration and thus neutralize and eventually overwhelm the negative with the positive in your conscious and unconscious. So if a thought comes in to the conscious level of mind, such as "I have to run and get that sports car, look at how red it is and look at how it looks so nice, etc. Apply the counter narrative, look how ridiculous that idea is, that I will look good because of a car? That I become a better person? That I will be happy with a red sports car? Training the mind in this way allows one to see the truth of the desire that the desire clouds from view. "Look at my friend who bought a sports car; he has the same issues as before and now he has an expensive car bill on top of that! He has to pay the bill for the sports car, the sports car broke and he had to repair it and the girlfriend that he picked up with the sports car, is no longer with him and she was mad at him one day, so she scratched the sports car with her key and he was so upset he punched the wall and broke his hand and is in pain all the time!" Think about it, all those negative aspects of the choices in life are there for all to see but a person's mind becomes clouded and even refuses to notice them because of the ignorant and negative aryu in the unconscious mind and the emerging thought process from those negative aryus that builds up so much energy that it compels the person to do what the desires dictate to them must be done, all because of this pattern, which is a form of negative reflection and concentration that soils the mind instead of the positive reflections and concentrations that render the mind pure and lucid as well as strong in will power.

If you break that cycle of ignorance and negative thought process you become a full fledged initiate, a real initiate, and you are on your way to mental purity, clarity, and spiritual enlightenment. This is the depth of the teaching of the Principle of Gender. For those who have ears let them hear... Om hetep, hetep, hetep.

Questions and Answers

Question: This is about people who are crazy, talking to themselves, is similar to what we were talking about, the me talking to the I and schizophrenia, which you are really talking about, is actually a degeneration of mind. It is like if there are many mirrors or centers of identity of mind. And those centers of identity which are all illusory, are conversing with each other, or interacting with each other. You follow?

ANSWER: It's as if different aspects of your '*inner*' personality are being multiplied, in whatever numbers and these ignorant identities (based on different feelings, convictions, desires, etc.) are conversing with each other, vying for attention to achieve their goal. Now of course if you have more than one, you are going to have a problem interacting with yourself, let alone, the rest of the world, so you can imagine what the world would be like if you have multiple personalities.

In this talk, here we are talking about 'the me' talking to the 'I'; this is actually the healthy conception of the human being. The ego, though illusory, is where you start from and from here you direct yourself to the "I", the higher self and essential being. There is a parable about this concept that illustrates the issue. There was once a person going on a train, a son-in-law who was going to visit his father-in-law. He reached this village where the father-in-law was and he got off the train and then this other gentleman walks up to him and he says "I will carry your bags for you." The son-in-law thought, "Oh my father sent this guy to carry my bags, how wonderful." So they walked down the platform to where the father-in-law was and the father-in-law saw the son-in-law and thinks, "oh he's doing well, he has got a servant to carry his bags." So they all go home to the house of the father-in-law and after a couple of days, they start conversing with each other, and the father-in-law said, "Oh that's a nice guy that you brought with you". The son-in-law said "what do you mean? I thought you sent him to the train station for me?" The stranger overheard their conversation and left through the back door when he realized his deception was discovered.

The son-in-law is the soul and the father-in-law is the spirit in this story. When they get together and converse, that is the soul and the spirit, the lower self and higher self, they realize there is this shadowy character between them who does not belong there and neither one called him, he just appeared out of thin air. When the soul and the spirit come together directly the ego that was between them dissolves and its illusoriness is revealed. The shadowy character is born of ignorance, it is the ego, the illusory idea you have about yourself as to who and what you are, based on your aryu of the past which is the basis of your self-concept causing you to know yourself as a limited, mortal individual ego personality. So, it is this ignorant ego that is getting in the way of the "me" and the "I". This is what is causing the mental problems from the mild ones like anger, hatred, greed and other maladies regarded as "normal" by society to the more deviant ones like bipolar, and depression to sociopathy and psychopathology to the more degraded psychotic breaks. This illusory notion is what must be eradicated because that is what leads to the ignorance and the consequent mental deviations, degradations from sanity, clarity and truth. If that illusion gets to be powerful enough, it can cause serious mental disturbance since it is a deviation from truth and any deviation from truth (Maat) leads to egoism, unrighteousness and disease and the severity depends on the degree of deviation. Remember I said that those thought forms contain energy, and that would destroy the mind, that will destroy you, that would lead you to schizophrenia, to mental dis-ease, to mental illness and these disturbances are the underlying cause of social diseases and aberrations that lead to conflict, crime, the inhumanity of some human beings towards others and even war. If the deviation into egoism is severe enough, your mind becomes unhinged, as it were, unstuck in time and space and not in a positive way, it becomes dull, degraded and disintegrated. Your mind should be integrated, clear and powerful. The deviation, like other behaviors and thought forms, causes changes in the DNA of the cells and the nervous system as well. However, insanity is not just an issue of the brain but it is an issue of the astral mind and the astral mind affects the physical physiology and physical constitution. On the other hand, just as the body can be physically damaged, the DNA, and the mind can be damaged; however, it potentially can also be repaired as well as enhanced. This is accomplished through a process that leads to truth and integrally cleanses and enlightens the actions, will, intellect, feelings and self-concept of the personality.

All the aspects of your personality, your will, your intellect, your emotions, your actions should all be integrated; they should be under the direction of truth (reason) so as to be healthy and balanced which when successfully accomplished renders the personality with a well-adjusted ego structure with sanity and health as well as enlightenment; otherwise you have insanity in varying degrees. The movement towards a well-adjusted ego structure is positive and necessary even if it is within the realm of spiritual ignorance. Even though it is illusory, the well-adjusted ego is a kind of stable window through which the self looks at the world. In a troubled or ignorant personality, the window has dirt (egoism) and colors and other distortions caused by the *aryu* so it sees but not clearly and tends to want to see things in accordance with its own desires, just as a person wearing yellow sunglasses will see a yellow colored world. The person seeing the world through the tainted mind is accustomed to seeing the world through their egoistic norms so that if anything differs from that the ego develops stress, fear, frustration, etc.

This line of thought recalls another concept that I didn't mention before, called *baka*. The Ba is the specific aspect of the personality known as "soul." In the scriptures of Shetaut Neter we are told that a person can converse with his/her Ba, meaning that your ka (mind/ego) can communicate with your Ba and this is why a pregnant woman is referred to as *ba-ka* or pregnant. Pregnancy is called ba-ka.

When your soul (Ba) impregnates your min (Ka) you have spirit coming into mind and spiritualizing it. If you have ka-ba, the ego is impregnating the soul with ignorance, sentimentality, childish notions, insecurities, fears and diffidence; now you have a terrible condition and this is what everyone in the world who is living life based on ignorance and under the control of egoistic aryu is facing. Their egoism impregnating their concept of self and their soul is miserable because of that. That misery is expressed in the deviations into unrighteousness, unrest and conflict. The ignorance and degraded, deluded worldly tending ego is constantly being impregnated with ignorance and that leads you to lifetimes and lifetimes of pain and sorrow.

HTP

Commentary by Seba Dja

Hetep, hetep, hetep, hetep

Just to add to what Sebai MAA just said. The psychotic state, the schizophrenic state, is actually the state where there is too many thoughts, where the impressions were never cleared out and this identification with the ego concept was never purified. So it is actually, if you want to take the three states of mind, the dull state, you have the agitated state, you have the lucid state.

You have the constriction of mind. The mind becomes more and more constricted down, as you go to the dull state. From lucid to agitated to dull, you get constricted, when you go from dull to agitated to lucid you are getting more of an expansion of consciousness. So the psychotic state of mind is just really intensive states of egoistic, constricted consciousness.

We talked about it on a previous tape, I don't know which series, but we think these are very harmless things, when people act in ordinary egoistic ways…, you see people and they are reinforcing the egoism, they may say things like: "oh this it's my birthday today and this is happening to me"; and those types of ego self-concepts. When people are greedy, believing in ways such as: this belongs to me, this is my stuff and you can't have any of it, etc., the possessiveness, then they even go further from there, where everything is about me, the ego, it is what I want, what I have to get for my life. And you can't allow yourself to think of anyone else, you can't go beyond yourself to serve anyone else, to do selfless service, to do any of the positive movements, to allow the mind to become freer.

These things that lead to freedom really are the principles developed in the Sema Tawi disciplines. Selfless service, devotional practices and devotional service not just in serving the Divine, but *serving/seeing* humanity as the very essence of the Divine; therefore if you are serving humanity, serving nature, you are serving the Divine.

Really what it gets down to and it's very hard for people and very hard for the world, is letting go of self, the egoistic 'me self'. This idea is expressed in the notion of the river and the ocean. The river flows to the ocean; here the little river goes, "what's happening to me, what's happening to me, what is going to happen to me" and that is all the little river worries about, everything is about me. And even the idea that it is going to absorbed into the ocean and it's going to disappear, even that idea is very scary and it's very threatening, for most people. They don't see it as, "oh I'm becoming everything, I'm becoming one," rather, there is a sense of losing me, and fear about what's going to happen after that.

So this degraded condition of the personality, of the psychotic mind, is the mind that is very, very intensely egoistic. The mind that is very, very intensely holding on to its identification as the body and holding on to that as who I am, the mind is who I am. So all of these different people we see in society, all of these different type of psychosis, when the mind becomes affected; it misbalances the energy of the body. The energy becomes affected, the breath becomes affected and the physiology and mind become disrupted.

End of Seba Djas' Comments.

SEMA INSTITUTE

Cruzian Mystic P.O.Box 570459, Miami, Florida. 33257 (305) 378-6253, Fax. (305) 378-6253
www.Egyptianyoga.com

Other Books From C M Books
P.O.Box 570459
Miami, Florida, 33257
(305) 378-6253 Fax: (305) 378-6253

Prices subject to change.

1. *EGYPTIAN YOGA THE PHILOSOPHY OF ENLIGHTENMENT* An original, fully illustrated work, including hieroglyphs, detailing the meaning of the Egyptian mysteries, tantric yoga, psycho-spiritual and physical exercises. Egyptian Yoga is a guide to the practice of the highest spiritual philosophy which leads to absolute freedom from human misery and to immortality. It is well known by scholars that Egyptian philosophy is the basis of Western and Middle Eastern religious philosophies such as *Christianity, Islam, Judaism,* the *Kabala,* and Greek philosophy, but what about Indian philosophy, Yoga and Taoism? What were the original teachings? How can they be practiced today? What is the source of pain and suffering in the world and what is the solution? Discover the deepest mysteries of the mind and universe within and outside of your self. 8.5" X 11" ISBN: 1-884564-01-1 Soft $19.95

2. *EGYPTIAN YOGA African Religion Volume 2-* Theban Theology U.S. In this long awaited sequel to *Egyptian Yoga: The Philosophy of Enlightenment* you will take a fascinating and enlightening journey back in time and discover the teachings which constituted the epitome of Ancient Egyptian spiritual wisdom. What are the disciplines which lead to the fulfillment of all desires? Delve into the three states of consciousness (waking, dream and deep sleep) and the fourth state which transcends them all, Neberdjer, "The Absolute." These teachings of the city of Waset (Thebes) were the crowning achievement of the Sages of Ancient Egypt. They establish the standard mystical keys for understanding the profound mystical symbolism of the Triad of human consciousness. ISBN 1-884564-39-9 $23.95

3. **THE KEMETIC DIET: GUIDE TO HEALTH, DIET AND FASTING** Health issues have always been important to human beings since the beginning of time. The earliest records of history show that the art of healing was held in high esteem since the time of Ancient Egypt. In the early 20th century, medical doctors had almost attained the status of sainthood by the promotion of the idea that they alone were "scientists" while other healing modalities and traditional healers who did not follow the "scientific method' were nothing but superstitious, ignorant charlatans who at best would take the money of their clients and at worst kill them with the unscientific "snake oils" and "irrational theories". In the late 20th century, the failure of the modern medical establishment's ability to lead the general public to good health, promoted the move by many in society towards "alternative medicine". Alternative medicine disciplines are those healing modalities which do not adhere to the philosophy of allopathic medicine. Allopathic medicine is what medical doctors practice by an large. It is the theory that disease is caused by agencies outside the body such as bacteria, viruses or physical means which affect the body. These can therefore be treated by medicines and therapies The natural healing method began in the absence of extensive technologies with the idea that all the answers for health may be found in nature or rather, the deviation from nature. Therefore, the health of the body can be restored by correcting the aberration and thereby restoring balance. This is the area that will be covered in this volume. Allopathic techniques have their place in the art of healing. However, we should not forget that the body is a grand achievement of the spirit and built into it is the capacity to maintain itself and heal itself. Ashby, Muata ISBN: 1-884564-49-6 $28.95

4. **INITIATION INTO EGYPTIAN YOGA** Shedy: Spiritual discipline or program, to go deeply into the mysteries, to study the mystery teachings and literature profoundly, to penetrate the mysteries. You will learn about the mysteries of initiation into the teachings and practice of Yoga and how to become an Initiate of the mystical sciences. This insightful manual is the first in a series which introduces you to the goals of daily spiritual and yoga practices: Meditation, Diet, Words of Power and the ancient wisdom teachings. 8.5" X 11" ISBN 1-884564-02-X Soft Cover $24.95 U.S.

5. **THE AFRICAN ORIGINS OF CIVILIZATION, RELIGION AND YOGA SPIRITUALITY AND ETHICS PHILOSOPHY** HARD COVER EDITION Part 1, Part 2, Part 3 in one volume 683 Pages Hard Cover First Edition Three volumes in one. Over the past several years I have been asked to put together in one volume the most important evidences showing the correlations and common teachings between Kamitan (Ancient Egyptian) culture and religion and that of India. The Questions of the history of Ancient Egypt, and the latest archeological evidences showing civilization and culture in Ancient Egypt and its spread to other countries, has intrigued many scholars as well as mystics over the years. Also, the possibility that Ancient Egyptian Priests and Priestesses migrated to Greece, India and other countries to carry on the traditions of the Ancient Egyptian Mysteries, has been speculated over the years as well. In chapter 1 of the book *Egyptian Yoga The Philosophy of Enlightenment*, 1995, I first introduced the deepest comparison

between Ancient Egypt and India that had been brought forth up to that time. Now, in the year 2001 this new book, *THE AFRICAN ORIGINS OF CIVILIZATION, MYSTICAL RELIGION AND YOGA PHILOSOPHY,* more fully explores the motifs, symbols and philosophical correlations between Ancient Egyptian and Indian mysticism and clearly shows not only that Ancient Egypt and India were connected culturally but also spiritually. How does this knowledge help the spiritual aspirant? This discovery has great importance for the Yogis and mystics who follow the philosophy of Ancient Egypt and the mysticism of India. It means that India has a longer history and heritage than was previously understood. It shows that the mysteries of Ancient Egypt were essentially a yoga tradition which did not die but rather developed into the modern day systems of Yoga technology of India. It further shows that African culture developed Yoga Mysticism earlier than any other civilization in history. All of this expands our understanding of the unity of culture and the deep legacy of Yoga, which stretches into the distant past, beyond the Indus Valley civilization, the earliest known high culture in India as well as the Vedic tradition of Aryan culture. Therefore, Yoga culture and mysticism is the oldest known tradition of spiritual development and Indian mysticism is an extension of the Ancient Egyptian mysticism. By understanding the legacy which Ancient Egypt gave to India the mysticism of India is better understood and by comprehending the heritage of Indian Yoga, which is rooted in Ancient Egypt the Mysticism of Ancient Egypt is also better understood. This expanded understanding allows us to prove the underlying kinship of humanity, through the common symbols, motifs and philosophies which are not disparate and confusing teachings but in reality expressions of the same study of truth through metaphysics and mystical realization of Self. (HARD COVER) ISBN: 1-884564-50-X $45.00 U.S.   81/2" X 11"

6. *AFRICAN ORIGINS BOOK 1 PART 1* African Origins of African Civilization, Religion, Yoga Mysticism and Ethics Philosophy-Soft Cover $24.95 ISBN: 1-884564-55-0

7. *AFRICAN ORIGINS BOOK 2 PART 2* African Origins of Western Civilization, Religion and Philosophy (Soft) -Soft Cover $24.95 ISBN: 1-884564-56-9

8. *EGYPT AND INDIA AFRICAN ORIGINS OF Eastern Civilization, Religion, Yoga Mysticism and Philosophy*-Soft Cover $29.95 (Soft) ISBN: 1-884564-57-7

9. **THE MYSTERIES OF ISIS:** *The Ancient Egyptian Philosophy of Self-Realization* - There are several paths to discover the Divine and the mysteries of the higher Self. This volume details the mystery teachings of the goddess Aset (Isis) from Ancient Egypt- the path of wisdom. It includes the teachings of her temple and the disciplines that are enjoined for the initiates of the temple of Aset as they were given in ancient times. Also, this book includes the teachings of the main myths of Aset that lead a human being to spiritual enlightenment and immortality. Through the study of ancient myth and the illumination of initiatic understanding the idea of God is expanded from the mythological comprehension to the metaphysical. Then this metaphysical understanding is related to you, the student, so as to begin understanding your true divine nature. ISBN 1-884564-24-0 $22.99

10. **EGYPTIAN PROVERBS:** collection of —Ancient Egyptian Proverbs and Wisdom Teachings -How to live according to MAAT Philosophy. Beginning Meditation. All proverbs are indexed for easy searches. For the first time in one volume, —— Ancient Egyptian Proverbs, wisdom teachings and meditations, fully illustrated with hieroglyphic text and symbols. EGYPTIAN PROVERBS is a unique collection of knowledge and wisdom which you can put into practice today and transform your life. $14.95 U.S   ISBN: 1-884564-00-3

11. **GOD OF LOVE: THE PATH OF DIVINE LOVE** *The Process of Mystical Transformation and The Path of Divine Love*   This Volume focuses on the ancient wisdom teachings of "Neter Merri" –the Ancient Egyptian philosophy of Divine Love and how to use them in a scientific process for self-transformation. Love is one of the most powerful human emotions. It is also the source of Divine feeling that unifies God and the individual human being. When love is fragmented and diminished by egoism the Divine connection is lost. The Ancient tradition of Neter Merri leads human beings back to their Divine connection, allowing them to discover their innate glorious self that is actually Divine and immortal. This volume will detail the process of transformation from ordinary consciousness to cosmic consciousness through the integrated practice of the teachings and the path of Devotional Love toward the Divine. 5.5"x 8.5" ISBN 1-884564-11-9 $22.95

12. **INTRODUCTION TO MAAT PHILOSOPHY:** *Spiritual Enlightenment Through the Path of Virtue*   Known commonly as Karma in India, the teachings of MAAT contain an extensive philosophy based on ariu (deeds) and their fructification in the

form of shai and renenet (fortune and destiny, leading to Meskhenet (fate in a future birth) for living virtuously and with orderly wisdom are explained and the student is to begin practicing the precepts of Maat in daily life so as to promote the process of purification of the heart in preparation for the judgment of the soul. This judgment will be understood not as an event that will occur at the time of death but as an event that occurs continuously, at every moment in the life of the individual. The student will learn how to become allied with the forces of the Higher Self and to thereby begin cleansing the mind (heart) of impurities so as to attain a higher vision of reality. ISBN 1-884564-20-8 $22.99

13. *MEDITATION The Ancient Egyptian Path to Enlightenment* Many people do not know about the rich history of meditation practice in Ancient Egypt. This volume outlines the theory of meditation and presents the Ancient Egyptian Hieroglyphic text which give instruction as to the nature of the mind and its three modes of expression. It also presents the texts which give instruction on the practice of meditation for spiritual Enlightenment and unity with the Divine. This volume allows the reader to begin practicing meditation by explaining, in easy to understand terms, the simplest form of meditation and working up to the most advanced form which was practiced in ancient times and which is still practiced by yogis around the world in modern times. ISBN 1-884564-27-7 $22.99

14. *THE GLORIOUS LIGHT MEDITATION* TECHNIQUE OF ANCIENT EGYPT New for the year 2000. This volume is based on the earliest known instruction in history given for the practice of formal meditation. Discovered by Dr. Muata Ashby, it is inscribed on the walls of the Tomb of Seti I in Thebes Egypt. This volume details the

philosophy and practice of this unique system of meditation originated in Ancient Egypt and the earliest practice of meditation known in the world which occurred in the most advanced African Culture. ISBN: 1-884564-15-1 $16.95 (PB)

15. **THE SERPENT POWER:** *The Ancient Egyptian Mystical Wisdom of the Inner Life Force.* This Volume specifically deals with the latent life Force energy of the universe and in the human body, its control and sublimation. How to develop the Life Force energy of the subtle body. This Volume will introduce the esoteric wisdom of the science of how virtuous living acts in a subtle and mysterious way to cleanse the latent psychic energy conduits and vortices of the spiritual body. ISBN 1-884564-19-4 $22.95

16. *EGYPTIAN YOGA The Postures of The Gods and Goddesses* Discover the physical postures and exercises practiced thousands of years ago in Ancient Egypt which are today known as Yoga exercises. Discover the history of the postures and how they were transferred from Ancient Egypt in Africa to India through Buddhist Tantrism. Then practice the postures as you discover the mythic teaching that originally gave birth to the postures and was practiced by the Ancient Egyptian priests and priestesses. This work is based on the pictures and teachings from the Creation story of Ra, The Asarian Resurrection Myth and the carvings and reliefs from various Temples in Ancient Egypt 8.5" X 11" ISBN 1-884564-10-0 Soft Cover $21.95   Exercise video $20

17. *SACRED SEXUALITY: ANCIENT EGYPTIAN TANTRA YOGA: The Art of Sex Sublimation and Universal Consciousness* This Volume will expand on the male and female principles within the human body and in the universe and further detail the sublimation of sexual energy into spiritual energy. The student will study the deities Min and Hathor, Asar and Aset, Geb and Nut and discover the mystical implications for a practical spiritual discipline. This Volume will also focus on the Tantric aspects of Ancient Egyptian and Indian mysticism, the purpose of sex and the mystical teachings of sexual sublimation which lead to self-knowledge and Enlightenment. ISBN 1-884564-03-8 $24.95

18. *AFRICAN RELIGION Volume 4: ASARIAN THEOLOGY: RESURRECTING OSIRIS* The path of Mystical Awakening and the Keys to Immortality NEW REVISED AND EXPANDED EDITION! The Ancient Sages created stories based on human and superhuman beings whose struggles, aspirations, needs and desires ultimately lead them to discover their true Self. The myth of Aset, Asar and Heru is no exception in this area. While there is no one source where the entire story may be found, pieces of it are inscribed in various ancient Temples walls, tombs, steles and papyri. For the first time available, the complete myth of Asar, Aset and Heru has been compiled from original Ancient Egyptian, Greek and Coptic Texts. This epic myth has been richly illustrated with reliefs from the Temple of Heru at Edfu, the Temple of Aset at Philae, the Temple of Asar at Abydos, the Temple of Hathor at Denderah and various papyri, inscriptions and reliefs. Discover the myth which inspired the teachings of the *Shetaut Neter* (Egyptian Mystery System - Egyptian Yoga) and the Egyptian Book of Coming Forth By Day. Also, discover the three

levels of Ancient Egyptian Religion, how to understand the mysteries of the Duat or Astral World and how to discover the abode of the Supreme in the Amenta, *The Other World*   The ancient religion of Asar, Aset and Heru, if properly understood, contains all of the elements necessary to lead the sincere aspirant to attain immortality through inner self-discovery. This volume presents the entire myth and explores the main mystical themes and rituals associated with the myth for understating human existence, creation and the way to achieve spiritual emancipation - *Resurrection*. The Asarian myth is so powerful that it influenced and is still having an effect on the major world religions. Discover the origins and mystical meaning of the Christian Trinity, the Eucharist ritual and the ancient origin of the birthday of Jesus Christ. Soft Cover ISBN: 1-884564-27-5 $24.95

19.   *THE EGYPTIAN BOOK OF THE DEAD MYSTICISM OF THE PERT EM HERU "* I Know myself, I know myself, I am One With God!–From the Pert Em Heru "The Ru Pert em Heru" or "Ancient Egyptian Book of The Dead," or "Book of Coming Forth By Day" as it is more popularly known, has fascinated the world since the successful translation of Ancient Egyptian hieroglyphic scripture over 150 years ago. The astonishing writings in it reveal that the Ancient Egyptians believed in life after death and in an ultimate destiny to discover the Divine. The elegance and aesthetic beauty of the hieroglyphic text itself has inspired many see it as an art form in and of itself. But is there more to it than that? Did the Ancient Egyptian wisdom contain more than just aphorisms and hopes of eternal life beyond death? In this volume Dr. Muata Ashby, the author of over 25 books on Ancient Egyptian Yoga Philosophy has produced a new translation of the original texts which uncovers a mystical teaching underlying the sayings and rituals instituted by the Ancient Egyptian Sages and Saints. "Once the philosophy of Ancient Egypt is understood as a mystical tradition instead of as a religion or primitive mythology, it reveals its secrets which if practiced today will lead anyone to discover the glory of spiritual self-discovery. The Pert em Heru is in every way comparable to the Indian Upanishads or the Tibetan Book of the Dead." ☐ $28.95   ISBN# 1-884564-28-3 Size: 8½" X 11

20. *African Religion VOL. 1- ANUNIAN THEOLOGY THE MYSTERIES OF RA* The Philosophy of Anu and The Mystical Teachings of The Ancient Egyptian Creation Myth Discover the mystical teachings contained in the Creation Myth and the gods and goddesses who brought creation and human beings into existence. The Creation myth of Anu is the source of Anunian Theology but also of the other main theological systems of Ancient Egypt that also influenced other world religions including Christianity, Hinduism and Buddhism. The Creation Myth holds the key to understanding the universe and for attaining spiritual Enlightenment. ISBN: 1-884564-38-0 $19.95

21. *African Religion VOL 3: Memphite Theology: MYSTERIES OF MIND* Mystical Psychology & Mental Health for Enlightenment and Immortality based on the Ancient Egyptian Philosophy of Menefer -Mysticism of Ptah, Egyptian Physics and Yoga Metaphysics and the Hidden properties of Matter. This volume uncovers the mystical psychology of the Ancient Egyptian wisdom teachings centering on the philosophy of the Ancient Egyptian city of Menefer (Memphite Theology). How to understand the mind and how to control the senses and lead the mind to health, clarity and mystical self-discovery. This Volume will also go deeper into the philosophy of God as creation and will explore the concepts of modern science and how they correlate with ancient teachings. This Volume will lay the ground work for the understanding of the philosophy of universal consciousness and the initiatic/yogic insight into who or what is God? ISBN 1-884564-07-0 $22.95

22. *AFRICAN RELIGION VOLUME 5: THE GODDESS AND THE EGYPTIAN MYSTERIESTHE PATH OF THE GODDESS THE GODDESS PATH* The Secret Forms of the Goddess and the Rituals of Resurrection The Supreme Being may be worshipped as father or as mother. *Ushet Rekhat* or *Mother Worship*, is the spiritual process of worshipping the Divine in the form of the Divine Goddess. It celebrates the most important forms of the Goddess including *Nathor, Maat, Aset, Arat, Amentet and Hathor* and explores their mystical meaning as well as the rising of *Sirius,* the star of Aset (Aset) and the new birth of Hor (Heru). The end of the year is a time of reckoning, reflection and engendering a new or renewed positive movement toward attaining spiritual Enlightenment. The Mother Worship devotional meditation ritual, performed on five days during the month of December and on New Year's Eve, is based on the Ushet Rekhit. During the ceremony, the cosmic forces, symbolized by Sirius - and the constellation of Orion ---, are harnessed through the understanding and devotional attitude of the participant. This propitiation draws the light of wisdom and health to all those who share in the ritual, leading to prosperity and wisdom. $14.95 ISBN 1-884564-18-6

23. *THE MYSTICAL JOURNEY FROM JESUS TO CHRIST* Discover the ancient Egyptian origins of Christianity before the Catholic Church and learn the mystical teachings given by Jesus to assist all humanity in becoming Christlike. Discover the secret meaning of the Gospels that were discovered in Egypt. Also discover how and why so many Christian churches came into being. Discover that the Bible still holds

the keys to mystical realization even though its original writings were changed by the church. Discover how to practice the original teachings of Christianity which leads to the Kingdom of Heaven. $24.95   ISBN# 1-884564-05-4 size: 8½" X 11"

24.   *THE STORY OF ASAR, ASET AND HERU:* An Ancient Egyptian Legend (For Children)   Now for the first time, the most ancient myth of Ancient Egypt comes alive for children. Inspired by the books *The Asarian Resurrection: The Ancient Egyptian Bible* and *The Mystical Teachings of The Asarian Resurrection, The Story of Asar, Aset and Heru* is an easy to understand and thrilling tale which inspired the children of Ancient Egypt to aspire to greatness and righteousness. If you and your child have enjoyed stories like *The Lion King* and *Star Wars you will love The Story of Asar, Aset and Heru.* Also, if you know the story of Jesus and Krishna you will discover than Ancient Egypt had a similar myth and that this myth carries important spiritual teachings for living a fruitful and fulfilling life. This book may be used along with *The Parents Guide To The Asarian Resurrection Myth: How to Teach Yourself and Your Child the Principles of Universal Mystical Religion.* The guide provides some background to the Asarian Resurrection myth and it also gives insight into the mystical teachings contained in it which you may introduce to your child. It is designed for parents who wish to grow spiritually with their children and it serves as an introduction for those who would like to study the Asarian Resurrection Myth in depth and to practice its teachings. 8.5" X 11"   ISBN: 1-884564-31-3 $12.95

25. ***THE PARENTS GUIDE TO THE AUSARIAN RESURRECTION MYTH:*** **How to Teach Yourself and Your Child the Principles of Universal Mystical Religion.** This insightful manual brings for the timeless wisdom of the ancient through the Ancient Egyptian myth of Asar, Aset and Heru and the mystical teachings contained in it for parents who want to guide their children to understand and practice the teachings of mystical spirituality. This manual may be used with the children's storybook *The Story of Asar, Aset and Heru* by Dr. Muata Abhaya Ashby. ISBN: 1-884564-30-5 $16.95

26. ***HEALING THE CRIMINAL HEART.*** **Introduction to Maat Philosophy, Yoga and Spiritual Redemption Through the Path of Virtue**   Who is a criminal? Is there such a thing as a criminal heart? What is the source of evil and sinfulness and is there any way to rise above it? Is there redemption for those who have committed sins, even the worst crimes?   Ancient Egyptian mystical psychology holds important answers to these Questions. Over ten thousand years ago mystical psychologists, the Sages of Ancient Egypt, studied and charted the human mind and spirit and laid out a path which will lead to spiritual redemption, prosperity and Enlightenment.   This introductory volume brings forth the teachings of the Asarian Resurrection, the most important myth of Ancient Egypt, with relation to the faults of human existence: anger, hatred, greed, lust, animosity, discontent, ignorance, egoism jealousy, bitterness, and a myriad of psycho-spiritual ailments which keep a human being in a state of negativity and adversity   ISBN: 1-884564-17-8 $15.95

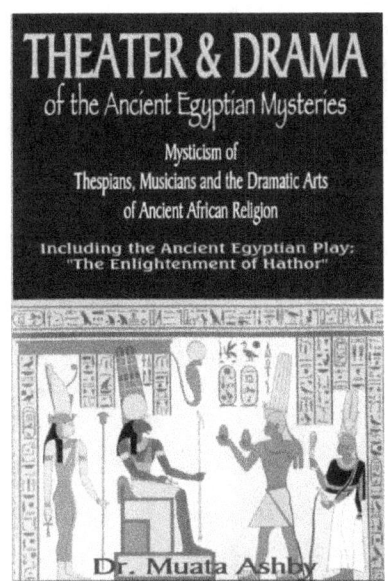

27. **TEMPLE RITUAL OF THE ANCIENT EGYPTIAN MYSTERIES--THEATER & DRAMA OF THE ANCIENT EGYPTIAN MYSTERIES**: Details the practice of the mysteries and ritual program of the temple and the philosophy an practice of the ritual of the mysteries, its purpose and execution. Featuring the Ancient Egyptian stage play-"The Enlightenment of Hathor' Based on an Ancient Egyptian Drama, The original Theater -Mysticism of the Temple of Hetheru 1-884564-14-3 $19.95 By Dr. Muata Ashby

28. *GUIDE TO PRINT ON DEMAND: SELF-PUBLISH FOR PROFIT, SPIRITUAL FULFILLMENT AND SERVICE TO HUMANITY* Everyone asks us how we produced so

many books in such a short time. Here are the secrets to writing and producing books that uplift humanity and how to get them printed for a fraction of the regular cost. Anyone can become an author even if they have limited funds. All that is necessary is the willingness to learn how the printing and book business work and the desire to follow the special instructions given here for preparing your manuscript format. Then you take your work directly to the non-traditional companies who can produce your books for less than the traditional book printer can. ISBN: 1-884564-40-2 $16.95 U. S.

29.   *Egyptian Mysteries: Vol. 1,* Shetaut Neter What are the Mysteries? For thousands of years the spiritual tradition of Ancient Egypt, S*hetaut Neter,* "The Egyptian Mysteries," "The Secret Teachings," have fascinated, tantalized and amazed the world. At one time exalted and recognized as the highest culture of the world, by Africans, Europeans, Asiatics, Hindus, Buddhists and other cultures of the ancient world, in time it was shunned by the emerging orthodox world religions. Its temples desecrated, its philosophy maligned, its tradition spurned, its philosophy dormant in the mystical *Medu Neter,* the mysterious hieroglyphic texts which hold the secret symbolic meaning that has scarcely been discerned up to now. What are the secrets of *Nehast* {spiritual awakening and emancipation, resurrection}. More than just a literal translation, this volume is for awakening to the secret code *Shetitu* of the teaching which was not deciphered by Egyptologists, nor could be understood by ordinary spiritualists. This book is a reinstatement of the original science made available for our times, to the reincarnated followers of Ancient Egyptian culture and the prospect of spiritual freedom to break the bonds of *Khemn,* "ignorance," and slavery to evil forces: *Såaa* . ISBN: 1-884564-41-0 $19.99

30.   **EGYPTIAN MYSTERIES VOL 2:** Dictionary of Gods and Goddesses This book is about the mystery of neteru, the gods and goddesses of Ancient Egypt (Kamit,

Kemet). Neteru means "Gods and Goddesses." But the Neterian teaching of Neteru represents more than the usual limited modern day concept of "divinities" or "spirits." The Neteru of Kamit are also metaphors, cosmic principles and vehicles for the enlightening teachings of Shetaut Neter (Ancient Egyptian-African Religion). Actually they are the elements for one of the most advanced systems of spirituality ever conceived in human history. Understanding the concept of neteru provides a firm basis for spiritual evolution and the pathway for viable culture, peace on earth and a healthy human society. Why is it important to have gods and goddesses in our lives? In order for spiritual evolution to be possible, once a human being has accepted that there is existence after death and there is a transcendental being who exists beyond time and space knowledge, human beings need a connection to that which transcends the ordinary experience of human life in time and space and a means to understand the transcendental reality beyond the mundane reality. ISBN: 1-884564-23-2 $21.95

31. *EGYPTIAN MYSTERIES VOL. 3* The Priests and Priestesses of Ancient Egypt This volume details the path of Neterian priesthood, the joys, challenges and rewards of advanced Neterian life, the teachings that allowed the priests and priestesses to manage the most long lived civilization in human history and how that path can be adopted today; for those who want to tread the path of the Clergy of Shetaut Neter. ISBN: 1-884564-53-4 $24.95

32. *The War of Heru and Set:* The Struggle of Good and Evil for Control of the World and The Human Soul This volume contains a novelized version of the Asarian Resurrection myth that is based on the actual scriptures presented in the Book Asarian Religion (old name –Resurrecting Osiris). This volume is prepared in the form of a screenplay and can be easily adapted to be used as a stage play. Spiritual seeking is a mythic journey that has many emotional highs and lows, ecstasies and depressions, victories and frustrations.

This is the War of Life that is played out in the myth as the struggle of Heru and Set and those are mythic characters that represent the human Higher and Lower self. How to understand the war and emerge victorious in the journey o life? The ultimate victory and fulfillment can be experienced, which is not changeable or lost in time. The purpose of myth is to convey the wisdom of life through the story of divinities who show the way to overcome the challenges and foibles of life. In this volume the feelings and emotions of the characters of the myth have been highlighted to show the deeply rich texture of the Ancient Egyptian myth. This myth contains deep spiritual teachings and insights into the nature of self, of God and the mysteries of life and the means to discover the true meaning of life and thereby achieve the true purpose of life. To become victorious in the battle of life means to become the King (or Queen) of Egypt.Have you seen movies like The Lion King, Hamlet, The Odyssey, or The Little Buddha? These have been some of the most popular movies in modern times. The Sema Institute of Yoga is dedicated to researching and presenting the wisdom and culture of ancient Africa. The Script is designed to be produced as a motion picture but may be addapted for the theater as well. $21.95 copyright 1998 By Dr. Muata Ashby ISBN 1-8840564-44-5

33. *AFRICAN DIONYSUS: FROM EGYPT TO GREECE:* The Kamitan Origins of Greek Culture and Religion ISBN: 1-884564-47-X FROM EGYPT TO GREECE This insightful manual is a reference to Ancient Egyptian mythology and philosophy and its correlation to what later became known as Greek and Rome mythology and philosophy. It outlines the basic tenets of the mythologies and shoes the ancient origins of Greek culture in Ancient Egypt. This volume also documents the origins of the Greek alphabet in Egypt as well as Greek religion, myth and philosophy of the gods and goddesses from Egypt from the myth of Atlantis and archaic period with the Minoans to the Classical period. This volume also acts as a resource for Colleges students who would like to set up fraternities and sororities based on the original Ancient Egyptian principles of Sheti and Maat philosophy. ISBN: 1-884564-47-X $22.95 U.S.

The Kybalion: Ancient Egyptian Mysteries

34. *THE FORTY TWO PRECEPTS OF MAAT, THE PHILOSOPHY OF RIGHTEOUS ACTION AND THE ANCIENT EGYPTIAN WISDOM TEXTS* <u>ADVANCED STUDIES</u> This manual is designed for use with the 1998 Maat Philosophy Class conducted by Dr. Muata Ashby. This is a detailed study of Maat Philosophy. It contains a compilation of the 42 laws or precepts of Maat and the corresponding principles which they represent along with the teachings of the ancient Egyptian Sages relating to each. Maat philosophy was the basis of Ancient Egyptian society and government as well as the heart of Ancient Egyptian myth and spirituality. Maat is at once a goddess, a cosmic force and a living social doctrine, which promotes social harmony and thereby paves the way for spiritual evolution in all levels of society. ISBN: 1-884564-48-8 $16.95 U.S.

35.   THE SECRET LOTUS: Poetry of Enlightenment
Discover the mystical sentiment of the Kemetic teaching as expressed through the poetry of Sebai Muata Ashby. The teaching of spiritual awakening is uniquely experienced when the poetic sensibility is present. This first volume contains the poems written between 1996 and 2003. **1-884564--16 -X $16.99**

36. The Ancient Egyptian Buddha: The Ancient Egyptian Origins of Buddhism

This book is a compilation of several sections of a larger work, a book by the name of African Origins of Civilization, Religion, Yoga Mysticism and Ethics Philosophy. It also contains some additional evidences not contained in the larger work that demonstrate the correlation between Ancient Egyptian Religion and Buddhism. This book is one of several compiled short volumes that has been compiled so as to facilitate access to specific subjects contained in the larger work which is over 680 pages long. These short and small volumes have been specifically designed to cover one subject in a brief and low cost format. This present volume, The Ancient Egyptian Buddha: The Ancient Egyptian Origins of Buddhism, formed one subject in the larger work; actually it was one chapter of the larger work. However, this volume has some new additional evidences and comparisons of Buddhist and Neterian (Ancient Egyptian) philosophies not previously discussed. It was felt that this subject needed to be discussed because even in the early 21st century, the idea persists that Buddhism originated only in India independently. Yet there is ample evidence from ancient writings and perhaps more importantly, iconographical evidences from the Ancient Egyptians and early Buddhists themselves that prove otherwise. This handy volume has been designed to be accessible to young adults and all others who would like to have an easy reference with documentation on this important subject. This is an important subject because the frame of reference with which we look at a culture depends strongly on our conceptions about its origins. in this case, if we look at the Buddhism as an Asiatic religion we would treat it and it's culture in one way. If we id as African [Ancient Egyptian] we not only would see it in a different light but we also must ascribe Africa with a glorious legacy that matches any other culture in human history and gave rise to one of the present day most important religious philosophies. We would also look at the culture and philosophies of the Ancient Egyptians as having African insights that offer us greater depth into the Buddhist philosophies. Those insights inform our knowledge about other African traditions and we can also begin to understand in a deeper way the effect of Ancient Egyptian culture on African culture and also on the Asiatic as well. We would also be able to discover the glorious and wondrous teaching of mystical philosophy that Ancient Egyptian Shetaut Neter religion offers, that is as powerful as any other mystic system of spiritual philosophy in the world today. ISBN: 1-884564-61-5 $28.95

37. The Death of American Empire: Neo-conservatism, Theocracy, Economic Imperialism, Environmental Disaster and the Collapse of Civilization

This work is a collection of essays relating to social and economic, leadership, and ethics, ecological and religious issues that are facing the world today in order to understand the course of history that has led humanity to its present condition and then arrive at positive solutions that will lead to better outcomes for all humanity. It surveys the development and decline of major empires throughout history and focuses on the creation of American Empire along with the social, political and economic policies that led to the prominence of the United States of America as a Superpower including the rise of the political control of the neo-con political philosophy including militarism and the military industrial complex in American politics and the rise of the religious right into and American Theocracy movement. This volume details, through historical and current events, the psychology behind the dominance of western culture in world politics through the "Superpower Syndrome Mandatory Conflict Complex" that drives the Superpower culture to establish itself above all others and then act hubristically to dominate world culture through legitimate influences as well as coercion, media censorship and misinformation leading to international hegemony and world conflict. This volume also details the financial policies that gave rise to American prominence in the global economy, especially after World War II, and promoted American preeminence over the world economy through Globalization as well as the environmental policies, including the oil economy, that are promoting degradation of the world ecology and contribute to the decline of America as an Empire culture. This volume finally explores the factors pointing to the decline of the American Empire economy and imperial power and what to expect in the aftermath of American prominence and how to survive the decline while at the same time promoting policies and social-economic-religious-political changes that are needed in order to promote the emergence of a beneficial and sustainable culture. **$25.95soft** 1-884564-25-9, Hard Cover **$29.95soft** 1-884564-45-3

The Kybalion: Ancient Egyptian Mysteries

38. The African Origins of Hatha Yoga: And its Ancient Mystical Teaching

The subject of this present volume, The Ancient Egyptian Origins of Yoga Postures, formed one subject in the larger works, African Origins of Civilization Religion, Yoga Mysticism and Ethics Philosophy and the Book Egypt and India is the section of the book African Origins of Civilization. Those works contain the collection of all correlations between Ancient Egypt and India. This volume also contains some additional information not contained in the previous work. It was felt that this subject needed to be discussed more directly, being treated in one volume, as opposed to being contained in the larger work along with other subjects, because even in the early 21st century, the idea persists that the Yoga and specifically, Yoga Postures, were invented and developed only in India. The Ancient Egyptians were peoples originally from Africa who were, in ancient times, colonists in India. Therefore it is no surprise that many Indian traditions including religious and Yogic, would be found earlier in Ancient Egypt. Yet there is ample evidence from ancient writings and perhaps more importantly, iconographical evidences from the Ancient Egyptians themselves and the Indians themselves that prove the connection between Ancient Egypt and India as well as the existence of a discipline of Yoga Postures in Ancient Egypt long before its practice in India. This handy volume has been designed to be accessible to young adults and all others who would like to have an easy reference with documentation on this important subject. This is an important subject because the frame of reference with which we look at a culture depends strongly on our conceptions about its origins. In this case, if we look at the Ancient Egyptians as Asiatic peoples we would treat them and their culture in one way. If we see them as Africans we not only see them in a different light but we also must ascribe Africa with a glorious legacy that matches any other culture in human history. We would also look at the culture and philosophies of the Ancient Egyptians as having African insights instead of Asiatic ones. Those insights inform our knowledge bout other African traditions and we can also begin to understand in a deeper way the effect of Ancient Egyptian culture on African culture and also on the Asiatic as well. When we discover the deeper and more ancient practice of the postures system in Ancient Egypt that was called "Hatha Yoga" in India, we are able to find a new and expanded understanding of the practice that constitutes a discipline of spiritual practice that informs and revitalizes the Indian practices as well as all spiritual disciplines. $19.99 ISBN 1-884564-60-7

The Kybalion: Ancient Egyptian Mysteries

39. The Black Ancient Egyptians

This present volume, The Black Ancient Egyptians: The Black African Ancestry of the Ancient Egyptians, formed one subject in the larger work: The African Origins of Civilization, Religion, Yoga Mysticism and Ethics Philosophy. It was felt that this subject needed to be discussed because even in the early 21st century, the idea persists that the Ancient Egyptians were peoples originally from Asia Minor who came into North-East Africa. Yet there is ample evidence from ancient writings and perhaps more importantly, iconographical evidences from the Ancient Egyptians themselves that proves otherwise. This handy volume has been designed to be accessible to young adults and all others who would like to have an easy reference with documentation on this important subject. This is an important subject because the frame of reference with which we look at a culture depends strongly on our conceptions about its origins. in this case, if we look at the Ancient Egyptians as Asiatic peoples we would treat them and their culture in one way. If we see them as Africans we not only see them in a different light but we also must ascribe Africa with a glorious legacy that matches any other culture in human history. We would also look at the culture and philosophies of the Ancient Egyptians as having African insights instead of Asiatic ones. Those insights inform our knowledge bout other African traditions and we can also begin to understand in a deeper way the effect of Ancient Egyptian culture on African culture and also on the Asiatic as well. ISBN 1-884564-21-6 $19.99

40. The Limits of Faith: The Failure of Faith-based Religions and the Solution to the Meaning of Life

Is faith belief in something without proof? And if so is there never to be any proof or discovery? If so what is the need of intellect? If faith is trust in something that is real is that reality historical, literal or metaphorical or philosophical? If knowledge is an essential element in faith why should there by so much emphasis on believing and not on understanding in the modern practice of religion? This volume is a compilation of essays related to the nature of religious faith in the context of its inception in human history as well as its meaning for religious practice and relations between religions in modern times. Faith has come to be regarded as a virtuous goal in life. However, many people have asked how can it be that an endeavor that is supposed to be dedicated to spiritual upliftment has led to more conflict in human history than any other social factor? ISBN 1884564631 SOFT COVER - $19.99, ISBN 1884564623 HARD COVER -$28.95

41. Redemption of The Criminal Heart Through Kemetic Spirituality and Maat Philosophy

Special book dedicated to inmates, their families and members of the Law Enforcement community. ISBN: 1-884564-70-4
$5.00

42. COMPARATIVE MYTHOLOGY

What are Myth and Culture and what is their importance for understanding the development of societies, human evolution and the search for meaning? What is the purpose of culture and how do cultures evolve? What are the elements of a culture and how can those elements be broken down and the constituent parts of a culture understood and compared? How do cultures interact? How does enculturation occur and how do people interact with other cultures? How do the processes of acculturation and cooptation occur and what does this mean for the development of a society? How can the study of myths and the elements of culture help in understanding the meaning of life and the means to promote understanding and peace in the world of human activity? This volume is the exposition of a method for studying and comparing cultures, myths and other social aspects of a society. It is an expansion on the Cultural Category Factor Correlation method for studying and comparing myths, cultures, religions and other aspects of human culture. It was originally introduced in the year 2002. This volume contains an expanded treatment as well as several refinements along with examples of the application of the method. the apparent. I hope you enjoy these art renditions as serene reflections of the mysteries of life. ISBN: 1-884564-72-0
Book price $21.95

43. CONVERSATION WITH GOD: Revelations of the Important Questions of Life $24.99 U.S.

This volume contains a grouping of some of the Questions that have been submitted to Sebai Dr. Muata Ashby. They are efforts by many aspirants to better understand and practice the teachings of mystical spirituality. It is said that when sages are asked spiritual Questions they are relaying the wisdom of God, the Goddess, the Higher Self, etc. There is a very special quality about the Q & A process that does not occur during a regular lecture session. Certain points come out that would not come out otherwise due to the nature of the process which ideally occurs after a lecture. Having been to a certain degree enlightened by a lecture certain new Questions arise and the answers to these have the effect of elevating the teaching of the lecture to even higher levels. Therefore, enjoy these exchanges and may they lead you to enlightenment, peace and prosperity. Available Late Summer 2007 ISBN: 1-884564-68-2

44. MYSTIC ART PAINTINGS

(with Full Color images) This book contains a collection of the small number of paintings that I have created over the years. Some were used as early book covers and others were done simply to express certain spiritual feelings; some were created for no purpose except to express the joy of color and the feeling of relaxed freedom. All are to elicit mystical awakening in the viewer. Writing a book on philosophy is like sculpture, the more the work is rewritten the reflections and ideas become honed and take form and become clearer and imbued with intellectual beauty. Mystic music is like meditation, a world of its own that exists about 1 inch above ground wherein the musician does not touch the ground. Mystic Graphic Art is meditation in form, color, image and reflected image which opens the door to the reality behind the apparent. I hope you enjoy these art renditions and my reflections on them as serene reflections of the mysteries of life, as visual renditions of the philosophy I have written about over the years. ISBN 1-884564-69-0 $19.95

45. ANCIENT EGYPTIAN HIEROGLYPHS FOR BEGINNERS
This brief guide was prepared for those inquiring about how to enter into Hieroglyphic studies on their own at home or in study groups. First of all you should know that there are a few institutions around the world which teach how to read the Hieroglyphic text but due to the nature of the study there are perhaps only a handful of people who can read fluently. It is possible for anyone with average intelligence to achieve a high level of proficiency in reading inscriptions on temples and artifacts; however, reading extensive texts is another issue entirely. However, this introduction will give you entry into those texts if assisted by dictionaries and other aids. Most Egyptologists have a basic knowledge and keep dictionaries and notes handy when it comes to dealing with more difficult texts. Medtu Neter or the Ancient Egyptian hieroglyphic language has been considered as a "Dead Language." However, dead languages have always been studied by individuals who for the most part have taught themselves through various means. This book will discuss those means and how to use them most efficiently. ISBN 1884564429 **$28.95**

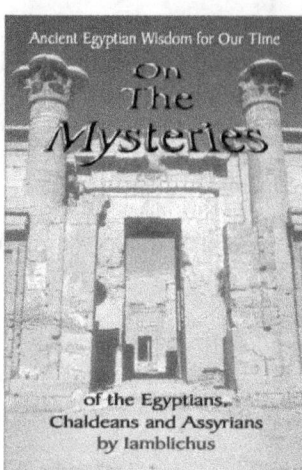

46. ON THE MYSTERIES: Wisdom of An Ancient Egyptian Sage -with Foreword by Muata Ashby

This volume, On the Mysteries, by Iamblichus (Abamun) is a unique form or scripture out of the Ancient Egyptian religious tradition. It is written in a form that is not usual or which is not usually found in the remnants of Ancient Egyptian scriptures. It is in the form of teacher and disciple, much like the Eastern scriptures such as Bhagavad Gita or the Upanishads. This form of writing may not have been necessary in Ancient times, because the format of teaching in Egypt was different prior to the conquest period by the Persians, Assyrians, Greeks and later the Romans. The Question and Answer format can be found but such extensive discourses and corrections of misunderstandings within the context of a teacher - disciple relationship is not usual. It therefore provides extensive insights into the times when it was written and the state of practice of Ancient Egyptian and other mystery religions. This has important implications for our times because we are today, as in the Greco-Roman period, also besieged with varied religions and new age philosophies as well as social strife and war. How can we understand our times and also make sense of the forest of spiritual traditions? How can we cut through the cacophony of religious fanaticism, and ignorance as well as misconceptions about the mysteries on the other in order to discover the true purpose of religion and the secret teachings that open up the mysteries of life and the way to enlightenment and immortality? This book, which comes to us from so long ago, offers us transcendental wisdom that applied to the world two thousand years ago as well as our world today. ISBN 1-884564-64-X $25.95

47. The Ancient Egyptian Wisdom Texts -Compiled by Muata Ashby
The Ancient Egyptian Wisdom Texts are a genre of writings from the ancient culture that have survived to the present and provide a vibrant record of the practice of spiritual evolution otherwise known as religion or yoga philosophy in Ancient Egypt. The principle focus of the Wisdom Texts is the cultivation of understanding, peace, harmony, selfless service, self-control, Inner fulfillment and spiritual realization. When these factors are cultivated in human life, the virtuous qualities in a human being begin to manifest and sinfulness, ignorance and negativity diminish until a person is able to enter into higher consciousness, the coveted goal of all civilizations. It is this virtuous mode of life which opens the door to self-discovery and spiritual enlightenment. Therefore, the Wisdom Texts are important scriptures on the subject of human nature, spiritual psychology and mystical philosophy. The teachings presented in the Wisdom Texts form the foundation of religion as well as the guidelines for conducting the affairs of every area of social interaction including commerce, education, the army, marriage, and especially the legal system. These texts were sources for the famous 42 Precepts of Maat of the Pert M Heru (Book of the Dead), essential regulations of good conduct to develop virtue and purity in order to attain higher consciousness and immortality after death. ISBN1-884564-65-8 $18.95

48. THE KEMETIC TREE OF LIFE

The Kybalion: Ancient Egyptian Mysteries

THE KEMETIC TREE OF LIFE: Newly Revealed Ancient Egyptian Cosmology and Metaphysics for Higher Consciousness The Tree of Life is a roadmap of a journey which explains how Creation came into being and how it will end. It also explains what Creation is composed of and also what human beings are and what they are composed of. It also explains the process of Creation, how Creation develops, as well as who created Creation and where that entity may be found. It also explains how a human being may discover that entity and in so doing also discover the secrets of Creation, the meaning of life and the means to break free from the pathetic condition of human limitation and mortality in order to discover the higher realms of being by discovering the principles, the levels of existence that are beyond the simple physical and material aspects of life. This book contains color plates   ISBN: 1-884564-74-7
$27.95 U.S.

49-MATRIX OF AFRICAN PROVERBS: The Ethical and Spiritual Blueprint
This volume sets forth the fundamental principles of African ethics and their practical applications for use by individuals and organizations seeking to model their ethical policies using the Traditional African values and concepts of ethical human behavior for the proper sustenance and management of society. Furthermore, this book will provide guidance as to how the Traditional African Ethics may be viewed and applied, taking into consideration the technological and social advancements in the present. This volume also presents the principles of ethical culture, and references for each to specific injunctions from Traditional African Proverbial Wisdom Teachings. These teachings are compiled from varied Pre-colonial African societies including Yoruba, Ashanti, Kemet, Malawi, Nigeria, Ethiopia, Galla, Ghana and many more. ISBN 1-884564-77-1

50- **Growing Beyond Hate: Keys to Freedom from Discord, Racism, Sexism, Political Conflict, Class Warfare, Violence, and How to Achieve Peace and Enlightenment**---
INTRODUCTION: WHY DO WE HATE? Hatred is one of the fundamental motivating aspects of human life; the other is desire. Desire can be of a worldly nature or of a spiritual, elevating nature. Worldly desire and hatred are like two sides of the same coin in that human life is usually swaying from one to the other; but the Question is why? And is there a way to satisfy the desiring or hating mind in such a way as to find peace in life? Why do human beings go to war? Why do human beings perpetrate violence against one another? And is there a way not just to understand the phenomena but to resolve the issues that plague humanity and could lead to a more harmonious society? Hatred is perhaps the greatest scourge of humanity in that it leads to misunderstanding, conflict and untold miseries of life and clashes between individuals, societies and nations. Therefore, the riddle of Hatred, that is, understanding the sources of it and how to confront, reduce and even eradicate it so as to bring forth the fulfillment in life and peace for society, should be a top priority for social scientists, spiritualists and philosophers. This book is written from the perspective of spiritual philosophy based on the mystical wisdom and sema or yoga philosophy of the Ancient Egyptians. This philosophy, originated and based in the wisdom of Shetaut Neter, the Egyptian Mysteries, and Maat, ethical way of life in society and in spirit, contains Sema-Yogic wisdom and understanding of life's predicaments that can allow a human being of any ethnic group to understand and overcome the causes of hatred, racism, sexism, violence and disharmony in life, that plague human society. ISBN: 1-884564-81-X

52. Guide to Creating a Kemetic Marriage Contract

This marital contract guide reflects actual Ancient Egyptian Principles for Kemetic Marriage as they are to be applied for our times. The marital contract allows people to have a framework with which to face the challenges of marital relations instead of relying on hopes or romantic dreams that everything will workout somehow; in other words, love is not all you need. The latter is not an evolved, mature way of handling one of the most important aspects of human life. Therefore, it behooves anyone who wishes to enter into a marriage to explore the issues, express their needs and seek to avoid costly mistakes, and resolve conflicts in the normal course of life or make sure that their rights and dignity will be protected if any eventuality should occur. Marital relations in Ancient Egypt were not like those in other countries of the time and not like those of present day countries. The extreme longevity of Ancient Egyptian society, founded in Maat philosophy, allowed the social development of marriage to evolve and progress to a high level of order and balance. Maat represents truth, righteous, justice and harmony in life. This meant that the marital partner's rights were to be protected with equal standing before the law. So there was no disparity between rights of men or rights of women. Therefore, anyone who wants to enter into a marriage based on Kemetic principles must first and foremost adhere to this standard…equality in the rights of men and women. This guide demonstrates procedures for following the Ancient Egyptian practice of formalizing marriage with a contract that spells out the important concerns of each partner in the marital relationship, based on Maatian principles [of righteous, truth, harmony and justice] so that the rights and needs of each partner may be protected within the marriage. It also allows the partners to think about issues that arise out of the marital relations so that they may have a foundation to fall back on in the event that those or other unforeseen issues arise and cause conflict in the relationship. By having a document of expressed concerns, needs and steps to be taken to address them, it is less likely that issues which affect the relationship in a negative way will arise, and when they do, they will be better handled, in a more balanced, just and amicable way.

EBOOK ISBN 978-1-937016-59-3, HARDCOPY BOOK ISBN: 1-884564-82-8

53. Guide for Aspirants Seeking Asaru Initiation

This is a primer on initiatic science. Explains the journey of initiation and the levels of initiation, the reason for the need of having a preceptor and the qualities an aspirant needs to display in order to be qualified for Asaru initiation. What specific disciplines are to be practiced The Asaru initiation or Temple initiation is the level of initiation where an aspirant is given certain secret knowledge for activating the subtle body in order to discover higher planes of being and higher essence of Self. ANSWERS THE QUESTIONS: 1. Why Are there Three Main Levels of Initiation? And How do they relate to the levels of initiation and the levels of initiatic teachings that are imparted? 2. HOW TO UNDERSTAND THE RELATION BETWEEN THE LEVELS OF INITIATION, THE ROLE OF THE TEACHER DISCIPLE RELATIONSHIP AND THE GOAL OF INITIATION 3. WHAT IS THE RELATIVE VALUE OF THE SHEMS LEVEL OF INITIATION IN REFERENCE TO THE ASAR LEVEL AND WHY DOES THE TEMPLE USE A HIERARCHICAL STRUCTURE FOR DELIVERING THE TEACHINGS? 4. WHY IS THE DEMARCATION MADE BETWEEN THE SHEMS LEVEL AND ASARU LEVEL OF ASPIRANTS? 5. WHAT IS COMPASSION IN THE INITIATIC SCIENCES AND HOW DO SAGES APPLY IT WHEN HELPING ASPIRANTS ALONG ON THE INITIATIC PATH? 6. WHY IS IT IMPORTANT FOR SPIRITUAL TEACHERS TO NOT HELP PEOPLE BEYOND THEIR CAPACITY TO BE HELPED? 7. WHY ARE SOME SPECIAL "KEYS" TO UNLOCK CERTAIN MEDITATIVE DISCIPLINES AND PHILOSOPHICAL UNDERSTANDINGS REVEALED TO ASARU LEVEL ASPIRANTS AND NOT TO SHEMS LEVEL ASPIRANTS? 8. WHY IS THE ACCESS TO AN AUTHENTIC SPIRITUAL PRECEPTOR, AND A VIABLE INITIATIC PATH, IMPORTANT FOR POSITIVE SPIRITUAL DEVELOPMENT? 9. OBSTACLES TO BECOMING A QUALIFIED APPLICANT FOR ASAR INITIATION AND

DISCIPLINES TO OVERCOME THEM 10. How to Overcome Failure on the Spiritual Path 11. OBSTACLES INCLUDE: 12. DISCIPLINES TO OVERCOME THE OBSTACLES INCLUDE: 13. What criteria are used to evaluate aspirants and how should aspirants conduct themselves in order to develop the qualities necessary for Asaru initiation? [available only as eBOOK] ISBN:978-1-937016-00-5

54. Maat Philosophy Versus Fascism and the Police State: Understanding why Modern Society does not Experience the Peace and Prosperity of Ancient Egypt ... Law and Order, and Spiritual Enlightenment

Understanding why Modern Society does not Experience the Peace and Prosperity of Ancient Egypt and How To Discover the Pathway to Freedom, True Law and Order, and Spiritual Enlightenment. Understanding the Corporate State and How Maatian Philosophy can Leads to Freedom, Prosperity and Enlightenment

Music Based on the Prt M Hru and other Kemetic Texts

Available on Compact Disc $14.99 and Audio Cassette $9.99

Adorations to the Goddess

Music for Worship of the Goddess

**NEW Egyptian Yoga Music CD
by Sehu Maa
Ancient Egyptian Music CD**

Instrumental Music played on reproductions of Ancient Egyptian Instruments– Ideal for meditation and
reflection on the Divine and for the practice of spiritual programs and Yoga exercise sessions.

©1999 By Muata Ashby
CD $14.99 –

MERIT'S INSPIRATION
**NEW Egyptian Yoga Music CD
by Sehu Maa
Ancient Egyptian Music CD**
Instrumental Music played on
reproductions of Ancient Egyptian Instruments– Ideal for meditation and
reflection on the Divine and for the practice of spiritual programs and Yoga exercise sessions.
©1999 By
Muata Ashby

The Kybalion: Ancient Egyptian Mysteries

CD $14.99 –
UPC# 761527100429

ANORATIONS TO RA AND HETHERU
NEW Egyptian Yoga Music CD
By Sehu Maa (Muata Ashby)
Based on the Words of Power of Ra and HetHeru
played on reproductions of Ancient Egyptian Instruments **Ancient Egyptian Instruments used: Voice, Clapping, Nefer Lute, Tar Drum, Sistrums, Cymbals** – The Chants, Devotions, Rhythms and Festive Songs Of the Neteru - Ideal for meditation, and devotional singing and dancing.

©1999 By Muata Ashby
CD $14.99 –
UPC# 761527100221

SONGS TO ASAR ASET AND HERU
NEW
Egyptian Yoga Music CD
By Sehu Maa
played on reproductions of Ancient Egyptian Instruments– The Chants, Devotions, Rhythms and Festive Songs Of the Neteru - Ideal for meditation, and devotional singing and dancing.
Based on the Words of Power of Asar (Asar), Aset (Aset) and Heru (Heru) Om Asar Aset Heru is the third in a series of musical explorations of the Kemetic (Ancient Egyptian) tradition of music. Its ideas are based on the Ancient Egyptian Religion of Asar, Aset and Heru and it is designed for listening, meditation and worship. ©1999 By Muata Ashby
CD $14.99 –
UPC# 761527100122

HAARI OM: ANCIENT EGYPT MEETS INDIA IN MUSIC
NEW Music CD
By Sehu Maa

The Chants, Devotions, Rhythms and Festive Songs Of the Ancient Egypt and India, harmonized and played on reproductions of ancient instruments along with modern instruments and beats. Ideal for meditation, and devotional singing and dancing.

Haari Om is the fourth in a series of musical explorations of the Kemetic (Ancient Egyptian) and Indian traditions of music, chanting and devotional spiritual practice. Its ideas are based on the Ancient Egyptian Yoga spirituality and Indian Yoga spirituality.

©1999 By Muata Ashby
CD $14.99 –
UPC# 761527100528

RA AKHU: THE GLORIOUS LIGHT
NEW
Egyptian Yoga Music CD
By Sehu Maa

The fifth collection of original music compositions based on the Teachings and Words of The Trinity, the God Asar and the Goddess Nebethet, the Divinity Aten, the God Heru, and the Special Meditation Hekau or Words of Power of Ra from the Ancient Egyptian Tomb of Seti I and more...

played on reproductions of Ancient Egyptian Instruments and modern instruments - **Ancient Egyptian Instruments used: Voice, Clapping, Nefer Lute, Tar Drum, Sistrums, Cymbals**

– The Chants, Devotions, Rhythms and Festive Songs Of the Neteru – Ideal for meditation, and devotional singing and dancing.

The Kybalion: Ancient Egyptian Mysteries

©1999 By Muata Ashby
CD $14.99 —
UPC# 761527100825

GLORIES OF THE DIVINE MOTHER
Based on the hieroglyphic text of the worship of Goddess Net.
The Glories of The Great Mother
©2000 Muata Ashby
CD $14.99 UPC# 761527101129`

MAIN VIDEOS

Egyptian Yoga Exercise Class Level 1
Muata Ashby (Writer), Muata Ashby (Producer), Muata Ashby (Director)

List Price: $25.00
80 minutes, NTSC
UPC: 883629024394
Discover the practice of Egyptian Yoga postures based on the posture system practiced by the Ancient Egyptian priests and priestesses of Ancient Egypt. This is a practice for physical health but also for mental mythological and spiritual journey to higher consciousness.

Introduction to Ancient Egyptian Hieroglyphs
Muata Ashby (Writer), Muata Ashby (Producer), Muata Ashby (Director)

The Kybalion: Ancient Egyptian Mysteries

List Price: $25.00
60 minutes, NTSC
UPC: 883629113227
Introduction to Ancient Egyptian Hieroglyphs Class 1

Introduction to Egyptian Yoga
Muata Ashby (Writer), Muata Ashby (Producer), Muata Ashby (Director)

List Price: $25.00
60 minutes, NTSC
UPC: 883629113159
Introduction to Egyptian Yoga philosophy and its influence on other world religions as well as its implications for spiritual evolution as conceived by the Ancient Egyptian sages Lecture by Dr. Muata Ashby

Glorious Light Meditation System of Ancient Egypt
Muata Ashby (Writer), Muata Ashby (Producer), Muata Ashby (Director)

List Price: $25.00
60 minutes, NTSC
UPC: 883629113104
Glorious Light Meditation System of Ancient Egypt is the oldest practice of formal meditation before Buddhism, Hinduism and Taoism. Ra Akhu, the glorious light was commissioned by the

Pharaoh Sety 1 and it was enjoined for men and women to practice. This DVD is an introduction to the system and a practice session.

Asarian Resurrection: Myth of Asar, Aset and Heru (Osiris, Isis and Horus)
Muata Ashby (Writer), Muata Ashby (Producer), Muata Ashby (Director)

List Price: $25.00
60 minutes, NTSC
UPC: 883629111247
Audiovisual lecture by Dr. Muata Ashby on the most important myth of ancient Egypt based on the myth of Osiris, Isis and Horus, and its spiritual implications for attaining spiritual enlightenment

Ancient Egyptian Music Session Live Performances
Muata Ashby (Writer), Muata Ashby (Producer), Muata Ashby (Director)

List Price: $25.00
60 minutes, NTSC
UPC: 883629113241
Ancient Egyptian Music Session Live Performances using Ancient Egyptian musical instrument reproductions and original lyric from ancient Egyptian hymbs and texts

Introduction to Maat Philosophy
Muata Ashby (Writer), Muata Ashby (Producer), Muata Ashby (Director)

The Kybalion: Ancient Egyptian Mysteries

List Price: $25.00
60 minutes, NTSC
UPC: 883629113234
Introduction to Maat Philosophy, the Ancient Egyptan philosophy of social order, justice and truth

Introduction to Shetaut Neter Part 1 -Egyptian Mysteries
Muata Ashby (Writer), Muata Ashby (Producer), Muata Ashby (Director)

List Price: $25.00
60 minutes, NTSC
UPC: 883629113166
Audiovisual with powerpoint presentation on Shetaut Neter philosophy, the Egyptian mysteries, the Ancient Egyptian religious principles of metaphysics and mysticism. Lecture by Dr. Muata Ashby

Pan-Africanism in Light of Maat Philosophy
Muata Ashby (Writer), Muata Ashby (Producer), Muata Ashby (Director)

List Price: $25.00
60 minutes, NTSC
UPC: 883629113173

The Kybalion: Ancient Egyptian Mysteries

Pan-Africanism in Light of Maat Philosophy relates to how the concept of seein African culture in its totality relates to the promotion of African political, economic and social wellbeing under African principles of spiritual ethics Lecture by Dr. Muata Ashby

Mythology of the Ancient Egyptian Yoga Postures
Muata Ashby (Writer), Muata Ashby (Producer), Muata Ashby (Director)

List Price: $25.00
60 minutes, NTSC
UPC: 883629113265
Lecture series by Dr. Muata Ashby-Course traces the African Origins of Civilization, Religion and Philosophy. This video traces the origins and development of the Ancient Egyptian Yoga Postures. Contains slide presentation with actual original photos of the original postures from Ancient Egypt.

www.ingramcontent.com/pod-product-compliance
Lightning Source LLC
Chambersburg PA
CBHW081105080526
44587CB00021B/3459